THE ENDANGERED PROMISES

SOCIETY OF BIBLICAL LITERATURE

DISSERTATION SERIES

Saul M. Olyan, Old Testament Editor
Mark Allan Powell, New Testament Editor

Number 171
THE ENDANGERED PROMISES
Conflict in Mark

by
James S. Hanson

James S. Hanson

THE ENDANGERED PROMISES
Conflict in Mark

Society of Biblical Literature
Atlanta

THE ENDANGERED PROMISES
Conflict in Mark

by
James S. Hanson
Ph.D., Princeton Theological Seminary, 1997
Donald H. Juel, Dissertation Advisor

Library of Congress Cataloging-in-Publication Data

Hanson, James S., 1960–
    The endangered promises : conflict in Mark / James S. Hanson.
        p. cm. — (Dissertation series / Society of Biblical Literature ; no. 171)
    Includes bibliographical references and index.
    ISBN 0-88414-034-2 (alk. paper)
    1. Bible. N.T. Mark—Criticism, Narrative. 2. Bible. N.T. Mark—
Reader-response criticism. I. Title. II. Dissertation series (Society of
Biblical Literature) ; no. 171.

BS2585.2 .H27 2000
226.3'06—dc21   00-046496

08 07 06 05 04 03 02 01 00   5 4 3 2 1

Printed in the United States of America

CONTENTS

ACKNOWLEDGEMENTS

The experience of writing this piece has reflected very closely the pattern of endangered and reaffirmed promises. I could not have completed it without the encouragement and support of family, friends, and advisors. My doctoral committee at Princeton Seminary, Donald Juel, Beverly Gaventa, and Ulrich Mauser, could not have been more helpful and encouraging; likewise Katherine Doob Sakenfeld, director of Ph.D. Studies. I owe a special debt of gratitude to the chair of my committee, Donald Juel, who, since my time at Luther Seminary, has advised and supported me in ways that extend far beyond academic concerns. I could not ask for a better mentor.

I wish to thank my parents, whose love and support have been unconditional and unflagging. My brothers, Tom and George, have been with me through both the trials of endangerment and the joy of reaffirmation. And I want to thank Gia Hanson for her years of support.

I received no small measure of wisdom from my other teachers at Princeton Seminary: J. Christiaan Beker, Patrick D. Miller, Jr., Joel Marcus, and Steven Kraftchick, and profited greatly from conversations with and support of my classmates Steven Bechtler (and his wife Joy), Leanne Van Dyk, Steven Chase, and Thomas Thompson.

I am grateful for the support of my colleagues at Saint Olaf College, especially Edmund Santurri, Charles Wilson, Douglas Schuurman, and Joel Kaminsky (now of Smith College), and for assistance provided by Jody Greenslade. The college also provided helpful resources for the completion of this work.

ABBREVIATIONS

AARAS	American Academy of Religion Academy Series
AusBR	*Australian Biblical Review*
HTR	*Harvard Theological Review*
JBL	*Journal of Biblical Literature*
JR	*Journal of Religion*
JSNT	*Journal for the Study of the New Testament*
JSNTSS	Journal for the Study of the New Testament Supplement Series
NTS	*New Testament Studies*
NovT	*Novum Testamentum*
NovTSup	Novum Testamentum, Supplements
SBLDS	Society of Biblical Literature Dissertation Series
SBLMS	Society of Biblical Literature Monograph Series
SNTSMS	Society for New Testament Studies Monograph Series
ZNW	*Zeitschrift für die Neutestamentliche Wissenschaft*
ZTK	Zeitschrift für Theologie und Kirche

CHAPTER 1

CONFLICT AND CHRISTOLOGY
IN MARKAN STUDIES

INTRODUCTION

The Gospel of Mark presents the story of Jesus as a story of conflict. From the very opening verses of the Gospel, the theme of opposition to the eschatological redemption the narrative promises is sounded, and it remains a dominant motif as the story moves towards its climax in Jerusalem. A close reading of the narrative reveals, in fact, that three principal conflicts define and give shape the story: That between Jesus and the Jewish authorities, the religious leaders who very early on resolve to seek Jesus' destruction; the struggle between Jesus and the demons, manifested most clearly in the exorcisms and healings of the first half of the Gospel; and the conflict which emerges between Jesus and his followers—above all, the disciples, but also his family and the crowds. This study seeks to show, principally by means of literary-rhetorical analysis, that these conflicts interrelate, interpret and illumine one another in Mark's narrative, and have a common rhetorical goal: To address the experience of conflict in Mark's implied audience between God's promises and the reality of the seemingly unredeemed world inhabited by the audience.

The conflicts serve to lay bare the tension between the necessity of being embraced by God's eschatological redemption in Jesus and the difficulty, even the apparent impossibility of doing so in a world that is in the grasp of forces vehemently opposed to God's goals. This rhetorical thrust of the Gospel can best be captured under

1

the rubric of God's endangered and reaffirmed promises,[1] a characterization that closely links Mark's narrative with a central feature of
the larger story of which Mark's Gospel is a part, that is, the story of
God's dealings with Israel. Each line of conflict threatens, in very
real ways, to undermine the very promises that God sent Jesus to
confirm. The Gospel moves its audience to embrace the ultimate
reliability of God's promise in the face of forces which threaten to
undermine it. It does so by compelling the audience to acknowledge
both sides of the conflict: the reliability of God's promises, but also
the reality of the powers and structures of the world which threaten
the ultimate fulfillment of God's promises. In this way, Mark's
Gospel offers a credible and compelling experience of the "good
news of Jesus Christ."

This study distinguishes itself from much previous work on the
Gospel in that it makes an argument for a particular understanding of
the *effect* the narrative exercises on an audience, rather than focusing
on what the text itself means (or might have meant) in its historical
or literary dimensions. Such an argument calls for a methodological
perspective shaped by a concern for the rhetorical dimensions of a
literary work; I will argue that some form of reader-response
criticism is most appropriate for the goals of this study. The study
goes beyond purely literary interests, however; my primary concern
involves the theological and hermeneutical dimensions of Mark's
text. That is, I am interested in exploring the fruitfulness of a form of
literary approach to biblical narrative for the task of theological
interpretation, for reading the text in a way that fosters an efficacious
encounter with the gospel of Jesus Christ.

I set out originally to explore Mark's christology as it emerges
from the "grammar" in which it is expressed—i.e., narrative.[2] I saw
a parallel between the recent shift in biblical studies toward literary-
critical approaches to biblical narrative and the move many theolo-

---

[1]The phrase is Nils Dahl's, borrowed from his essay "The Crucified Messiah
and the Endangered Promises," in Juel, ed., *Jesus the Christ: The Historical Origins
of Christological Doctrine* (Minneapolis: Fortress Press, 1991), 65-80.

[2]See Leander Keck, "Toward the Renewal of New Testament Christology,"
NTS 32 (1986), 362-377.

gians were making toward a narrative theology;[3] while parallel, the two movements seemed to be proceeding without much interaction between them. I hoped to contribute to bringing the two enterprises closer together through exploring the way Mark's christology is expressed through his narrative. My engagement with Mark's text, however, convinced me that the most important aspect of Mark's achievement lies in the way in which his narrative is shaped not merely to propagate certain ideas about who Jesus is, but in the narrative's impact on its readers. I was affected by the Gospel's capacity to envelop an audience in the world of the story—both the Gospel's narrative and the larger story of God's past dealings with and intentions toward creation—in a way that goes well beyond the formulation of christological statements. It seemed to me that both biblical scholars and theologians were still tending to view Mark's text as a container of ideas which could be mined for the purposes of constructive theological propositions. While I recognize the necessity and validity of this enterprise, as I familiarized myself with the goals and practices of audience-oriented criticism, I realized that I was more interested in the task of preparing an audience for a fruitful encounter with the drama and tension created by the text than in formulating the understanding of Jesus presented in the text in other terms. Mark's narrative works not only on the cognitive level, but on the affective as well, just as response to the gospel involves more than assent to certain propositions, but the shaping of one's life around the reality created by God's eschatological entrance into the world in Jesus.

In traditional theological terms, one might say I agree with those who have seen in Mark more concern for soteriology than christology.[4] The tension Mark's narrative creates by presenting with equal force both the necessity and impossibility of responding

---

[3]See, e.g., Ronald Thiemann, *Revelation and Theology: The Gospel as Narrated Promise* (Notre Dame: University of Notre Press, 1985); Gabriel Fackre, *The Christian Story: A Narrative Interpretation of Basic Christian Doctrine* (Grand Rapids, MI: William B. Eerdmans, 1984); Michael Goldberg, *Theology and Narrative: A Critical Introduction* (2nd ed. Philadelphia : Trinity Press International, 1991; George Stroup, *The Promise of Narrative Theology: Recovering the Gospel in the Church* (Atlanta: John Knox, 1981).

[4]The two are closely linked, of course; see Keck, 363.

faithfully to the gospel focuses one's attention on the question expressed by Peter and the other disciples: "Who then can be saved?" (10:26), or the cry of the demoniac boy's father, "I believe; help my unbelief!" (9:24). Mark's Gospel raises this question in existential terms and addresses it, but not in ways that lend themselves easily to discursive language.

In this first chapter, I will review the major studies of conflict and controversy in Mark's Gospel and suggest that further work is warranted for several reasons. First, most studies of conflict and controversy have been undertaken from a more clearly historical perspective, utilizing the text of Mark to reconstruct the history of the tradition, the history of Mark's community, or the genesis of Mark's Gospel. This holds true, second, for much of the more theologically-oriented studies as well. That is, studies in the historical paradigm which seek to illuminate theological aspects of the Gospel have not sufficiently attended to the narrative itself, viewing, for example, the separation of tradition from redaction as a window onto the author's theology. Third, the recent shift to a literary paradigm, while providing many new insights into the Gospel, has in some ways resulted in the neglect of constructive theological concerns. Finally, those studies that have been theologically oriented, both historical and literary, have focused almost exclusively on the Gospel's christology, its presentation of Jesus, neglecting the degree to which Mark's Gospel is oriented toward its audience.

In Chapter 2, I will lay out the foundations for a more audience-centered approach to the Gospel, and will argue for the way in which such an approach can bear significant theological fruit. Chapter 3 will analyze the prologue to the Gospel in an attempt to reveal the way in which it "prepares" the audience for an encounter with the good news of Jesus Christ, an encounter that will be characterized above all by tension and conflict. In the final two chapters, I will explore the two principal conflicts which give shape to the narrative—Jesus and the authorities (Chapter 4) and Jesus and the disciples (Chapter 5)—focusing on the rhetorical effect the conflicts might exercise on the implied audience.

WILLIAM WREDE

Modern research on Mark's Gospel in general, and its christological focus in particular, has received its shape largely from William Wrede's ground-breaking study, *The Messianic Secret in the Gospels*.[5] Wrede contended that the so-called messianic secret allowed the early church to address the problem that nineteenth-century research on the Gospels had come to see as central: the gap between Jesus' non-messianic and indeed failed career and the conviction, borne of his resurrection, that he was in fact the Promised One.[6] While liberal theology had seized on precisely this gap to support a christology based on the preaching and teaching of the historical Jesus freed from later dogmatic accretions,[7] Wrede rejected the notion that Mark's Gospel provided a clear window onto the life and teachings of Jesus; he attempted to show, rather, that even before the writing of Mark's Gospel, the early church had shaped the traditions about Jesus in light of an overarching theological conception, which for Wrede pervaded the whole of Mark,[8] namely that Jesus, though "declared to be Son of God . . . by resurrection from the dead" (Rom. 1:4), was already such in his earthly ministry.

Of weight here are not the details of the Messianic secret in Wrede's conception, which have been revised considerably,[9] but the

---

[5]Trans. J. C. G. Greig (London: James Clarke, 1971); the work originally appeared in German in 1901.

[6]It was the recognition of this gap, of course, which gave rise to the original "Quest for the historical Jesus."

[7]These liberal "lives of Jesus" were chronicled definitively by Albert Schweitzer, *The Quest of the Historical Jesus* (tr. W. Montgomery; New York: Macmillan, 1948).

[8]That is, the messianic secret involved, in Wrede's conception, 1) the injunctions to silence laid upon the confessions of demons, (e.g., 1:23-25) to those healed by Jesus (e.g., 5:43) and to the disciples (e.g., 8:30, but especially 9:9); 2) his teaching in parables (cf. 4:10-12); and 3) the inability of his followers to understand him and his message (e.g., 8:14-21).

[9]Subsequent scholarship, both liberal and conservative, acknowledged that, in order to make the claims which the early church did about Jesus at all intelligible, there must have been at least an implicit claim of Messiahship on the part of Jesus during his ministry (as even Bultmann acknowledged); as Albert Schweitzer put it, "How can the appearances of the risen Jesus have suggested to the disciples the idea

methodological challenges he set forth. These greatly affected the subsequent course of Markan studies, and in fact the understanding of the christology of the New Testament as a whole, and still influence the discussion today. First, his conviction that the literary deposits contained in the Gospels provide data concerning principally the early church and its theology, and only secondarily, if at all, the life of the "historical" Jesus, proved crucial to the development of both form criticism and later redaction criticism. The former was designed precisely to analyze the formation and transmission of the oral tradition which underlay the Gospel texts, and to place it in particular life settings in the early church. For decades following Wrede, form criticism was employed both by those who accepted Wrede's position and who thus attempted to elucidate the early church's preaching *about* Jesus (the so-called radical historical critics, e.g., Bultmann, Dibelius, Bousset), as well as by those who maintained that through its use they could confidently reproduce the preaching and teaching *of* Jesus (e.g., Taylor, Jeremias, Manson).

Closely related to this, and second, Wrede set in motion a quest to explore the tradition history and use of christological *titles*.[10] In the history of the use of these titles, scholars sought the answer to whether the proclamation of Jesus as, e.g., the Christ, the Lord, the Son of God, or the Son of man originated with the early church or could be traced back to Jesus himself.[11]

---

that Jesus, the crucified teacher, was the Messiah?" (343). In addition, the broad scope of the secret motif as Wrede saw it has been challenged, in most detail by Ulrich Luz ("Das Geheiminismotiv und die markinische Christologie," *Zeitschrift für die neutestamentliche Wissenschaft* 56 [1965] 9-30), who contended that the commands to silence given to the demons and disciples function differently from the ones to those healed by Jesus; cf. also Theodore Weeden, *Mark: Traditions in Conflict* (Philadelphia: Fortress Press, 1971); more recently, Jack Dean Kingsbury, *The Christology of Mark's Gospel* (Philadelphia: Fortress Press, 1983), 1-46.

[10]See the important articles by L. Keck, "Jesus in New Testament Christology," *AusBr* 28 (1980), 1-20; and "Toward the Renewal of New Testament Christology."

[11]It was especially to argue for the second possibility that such studies were carried out, e.g., Oscar Cullmann, *The Christology of the New Testament* (tr. Shirley Guthrie and Charles Hall; Philadelphia: Westminster Press, 1963); C. F. D. Moule, *The Origin of Christology* (Cambridge: Cambridge University Press, 1977); Ferdinand Hahn, *The Titles of Jesus in New Testament Christology* (tr. Harold Knight and

It is not too much to say that these two factors, which derived much of their impetus from Wrede's work, have largely determined the kinds of questions asked of the Gospels, the framing of those questions, and the solutions proposed. The history of early christology became the battleground for the theological debate over the locus and warrant of the church's kerygma and of divine revelation.[12] Wrede's conclusions were accepted by the so-called radical historical critics such as K. L. Schmidt, Bultmann, and Bousset, who set themselves to the task of reconstructing the history of Christian tradition. He was vehemently opposed, however, by those who saw no need for such radical scepticism with regard to the Gospel tradition; scholars such as Vincent Taylor, J. Jeremias, and Oscar Cullman sought to prove the essential reliability of the tradition.[13] The result in both cases, as Keck has pointed out, has been a preoccupation with the history of christology to the neglect of the christology contained in the New Testament itself.[14] That is to say, both for those who located the warrant for revelation in the early church's preaching and for those who would see it in Jesus himself, the Gospels became primarily sources for reconstructing the history of christological development. Even the movement toward redaction criticism (discussed below), which has attempted to consider each evangelist's unique theological perspective, belongs to this conception, for it involves, at least initially, only a shift in focus to a later stage of the development of the tradition.

Thus with respect to the conflicts portrayed in Mark's Gospel, the form critics[15] sought to isolate the pre-literary (i.e., oral) form of

---

George Ogg; New York: World Publishing, 1969).

[12]In a larger sense, of course, one could say that it was the basic scepticism regarding the historical reliability of the Gospels, on the rise since the Enlightenment, that forced the christological debate into a strictly historical framework.

[13]Cf. Cullmann's contention that christology developed "on the basis of facts, not myth" (*Christology*, 8).

[14]"New Testament Christology," 365. Cf. also Robert Morgan's statement: "From the 1920s to the 1960s and beyond history remained the dominant intellectual partner for theology" (*Biblical Interpretation* [Oxford: Oxford University Press, 1988], 105).

[15]The classic statements of form criticism are those of Dibelius, *Die Formgeschichte des Evangeliums* (Tübingen: Mohr, 1971), and Bultmann, *Die*

the material in order to gain insight into the life and thought of the early church, or for "conservatives," to show that it could be traced back to Jesus himself; redaction critics have sought a similar window on the evangelist's thought and his community's struggles by examining the evangelist's use of this material. In both cases, each of the Gospel's three principal conflicts has been viewed as an access to a different facet of the community's life, the development of christological ideas, or the particular author's theology, or one has been singled out as the key to the whole. Hence, past studies have tended to focus on one or another of these conflicts without fully accounting for their interrelationship.

Illustrative of this situation are the form critics' examination of the so-called "controversy stories," the principal form in which the conflict between Jesus and the Jewish authorities is played out, and redaction critics' treatment of the conflict between Jesus and his disciples in Mark.

THE CONTROVERSY STORIES IN FORM-CRITICAL RESEARCH

Although classical form criticism has its roots in the broader goals of the History of Religions school and its attempt to relate all religious experience to its expression in various life-settings, the manner in which it dovetails with the theological convictions of its practitioners is my primary concern here.[16] The work of the major form critics on the controversies between Jesus and his opponents, different though it may be in detail, has as its theological impetus the conviction that the revelation contained in the Gospels is to be sought at some stage prior to the final formation of the Gospel text, either in the life of the historical Jesus or in the preaching of the early church; the Gospel writers, to use Martin Dibelius's language, are to be conceived principally as collectors of tradition, rather than authors in any real sense.[17] Thus, alongside the task of categorizing the stories lies the equally, if not more important quest to determine their

---

Geschichte der synoptischen Tradition (Göttingen: Vandenhoeck & Ruprecht, 1979).

[16]This is not to suggest that theological presuppositions bring suspicion to all historical judgments, but that there is some relationship cannot be denied.

[17]Dibelius, *From Tradition to Gospel* (New York: Scribner, 1965), 59.

origin.[18] The quest yielded a variety of classification systems as well as differing hypotheses concerning the origin of the material, its reliability, and its christological significance.

Several important form-critical studies of the New Testament appeared at approximately the same time. Karl Ludwig Schmidt brought forth his *Der Rahmen der Geschichte Jesu*[19] in 1919, in which he showed that the particular settings of the traditions about Jesus as found in the Gospels were provided by the evangelists as a loose framework for material that had already been formed by years of oral transmission. In the same year, Martin Dibelius published his magisterial *Die Formgeschichte des Evangeliums*, the first attempt at a full-scale classification of and accounting for the formation of the Gospel tradition. Bultmann's *Geschichte der synoptischen Tradition*, a work comparable in scope to that of Dibelius, though quite different in detail, appeared in 1921, as did a study of the pre-history of the controversy stories in particular by Martin Albertz (*Die synoptischen Streitgespräche*[20]). A response to the radical conclusions drawn by the German school regarding the authenticity of the Gospel tradition came several years later from Vincent Taylor in his *The Formation of the Gospel Tradition.*[21]

Because of their scope and continuing influence, the works of Dibelius and Bultmann warrant further attention here.[22] Even more to the point, both of these scholars in later works spell out the

---

[18]Cf. Bultmann: "The proper understanding of form-criticism rests upon the judgement that the literature in which the life of a given community . . . has taken shape, springs out of quite definite conditions and wants of life from which grows up a quite definite style and quite specific forms and categories" (*The History of the Synoptic Tradition* [tr. John Marsh; New York: Harper & Row, 1963]), 4.

[19]Berlin: Trowitzsch, 1919.

[20]Berlin: Trowitzsch, 1921.

[21]London: Macmillan, 1935.

[22]No attempt is made here at an exhaustive examination of form-critical approaches to the controversy stories, which would have to include discussion of Martin Albertz and Vincent Taylor; for fuller discussions, see Arland Hultgren, *Jesus and His Adversaries* (Minneapolis: Augsburg, 1979), 1-38; Wolfgang Weiß, *Eine neue Lehre in Vollmacht: die Streit- und Schulgespräche des Markus-Evangeliums* (Berlin: Walter de Gruyter, 1989), 1-32; Stanley Saunders, "No One Dared Ask Any More Questions" (unpublished doctoral dissertation, Princeton Theological Seminary, 1990), 7-33.

significance of their form-critical work for the christology and theology of the New Testament,[23] to which issue we will return.

Martin Dibelius

As noted, Dibelius' *Die Formgeschichte des Evangeliums* was the first attempt to account for the formation of the whole of the Gospel tradition. His form-critical terminology reflects his conviction that "at the beginning of all Christian activity there stands the sermon;" that is, the overriding impetus for the formation of the tradition about Jesus is to be found in the necessities of missionary work, as well as in the instruction, edification, and exhortation of the Christian community[24]—all tasks of the early Christian preacher. The stories in which Jesus is found in controversy with opponents thus are not classified according to that criterion alone, but belong to a larger group of stories which Dibelius termed "paradigms"—short pieces of narrative formed as illustration for early Christian preaching. The weight of these narrative bits falls not on the controversy dialogue itself, but in the particular saying or act of Jesus which forms their conclusion and supports the preacher's point.

The paradigms are characterized, first of all, by their isolation from their immediate context, an "external rounding off" which betrays their previous existence as independent units.[25] The brevity and simplicity of these stories, a second characteristic, again reflects their origin in preaching; the preacher required no more than that needed to make his point.[26] Third, they possess a distinctly religious or edificatory style—Jesus does not simply "say" something, but he

---

[23]Dibelius in *Gospel Criticism and Christology* (London: Ivor, Nicholson & Watson, 1935); Bultmann in various writings, chief among them his *Theology of the New Testament* (tr. Kendrick Grobel; New York: Charles Scribners Sons, 1951); see below.

[24]Cf. Dibelius, 37.

[25]Dibelius, 44; see, e.g., Mark 3:6, which rounds off the story of the healing of the whithered hand.

[26]"The attractive working out of the details for their own sake, the characterization of persons, the sketching of their surroundings out of liking for the description, all these things Paradigms must lack" (48).

"preaches the word to them" (Mk 2:2).[27] Fourth, most of the paradigms reach their point in and conclude with a word of Jesus, which will prove to be relevant for the faith and life of the hearer.[28] Finally, the overall impression of the narratives derives precisely from this final word or action of Jesus, or the reaction of onlookers.[29]

Dibelius locates the formation of most of the Gospel material, including the paradigms, in Hellenistic Christianity, in which previously Hellenized Jewish believers in Christ adapted the material for their Greek-speaking audiences.[30] He finds in popular Hellenistic literature the closest parallels and greatest influence on the formation of the tradition. For the paradigms, Dibelius cites specifically the *chriae*, which he defines as "the reproduction of a short pointed saying of general significance, originating in a definite person and arising out of a definite situation."[31] Though the content of the paradigms naturally differs greatly, Dibelius sees the early Christians molding the stories about Jesus into a form with which their audiences would have been familiar.[32]

Rudolf Bultmann

Bultmann's form-critical work involved a much more detailed examination of the formation of the Gospel traditions than that of Dibelius. Whereas Dibelius more or less presupposed or logically deduced the broad category of preaching as the origin for most of the material, and examined it in that light, Bultmann proceeded analytically, saying by saying, narrative by narrative.[33] He divides the material broadly into the sayings traditions and narrative traditions. The controversy dialogues, part of the sayings traditions, he consid-

---

[27]Dibelius, 56-59.

[28]Dibelius, 56-57.

[29]Dibelius, 58-60.

[30]Dibelius, 29-31.

[31]Dibelius, 152.

[32]See Hultgren, 33-36, for a critique of the *chriae* as analogies for the controversy stories.

[33]Bultmann, 11.

ers under the larger sub-category of *apophthegms*, or sayings of Jesus set in a brief context.[34]

Typically, the starting point of a controversy dialogue lies in an opponent's challenge to some action or attitude of Jesus or his followers, followed by a reply, often in the form of a counter-question or a parable. As does Dibelius, Bultmann sees the weight of the dialogues falling on the dominical saying.[35] In terms of their composition, Bultmann distinguishes those controversy dialogues which are unitary, i. e., whose saying was developed and preserved along with its narrative context, from those whose setting is a secondary construction.[36]

Beyond terminological differences, Bultmann departs from Dibelius in his understanding of both the place and manner in which the dialogues originated. For Dibelius, the controversy stories, which arose in the Hellenistic Church (see above), do not reflect actual strife between parties; such is neither their principal point nor their origin. Bultmann, on the other hand, deduces from both the form and content of the stories that their *Ursprung* had to be in the Palestinian Church. In form, the dialogues find their closest parallel for Bultmann in Rabbinic debates;[37] the issues dealt with relate to the situation of the church in its self-definition over against Palestinian Judaism. And though he does not deny that some of the traditions may have originated in Jesus' lifetime, he attributes to the church's creativity alone (not surprisingly) the present form and setting of the dialogues,[38] citing the "productive power of the controversy dialogue . . . the increasing tendency of the Church to clothe its dominical

---

[34]Bultmann, 11.

[35]Bultmann, 41-42.

[36]Bultmann, 46-47. This distinction forms the basic classification of the controversy stories in Arland Hultgren's work.

[37]He cites several examples, 41-43; cf. 48. Hultgren takes issue with Bultmann as well here (32-33).

[38]Bultmann, 40, 49-50. This belongs, of course, to the nature of the method as Bultmann conceived it: "the first question to be asked, methodically [*sic*] speaking, must be about the literary form of the controversy dialogues, and its origin as a literary device" (40).

sayings, its views and its fundamental beliefs in the form of the controversy dialogue."[39]

Form Criticism and Christology

The aim of this introduction is to exhibit the interrelationship between method and christological conception—i. e., how particular methods arise out of their practitioners' understanding of the nature of christological inquiry in the New Testament, especially the Gospels. Both Dibelius and Bultmann illustrate their understanding of this relationship in later works. Dibelius treats the question explicitly in his lectures contained in *Gospel Criticism and Christology*; for Bultmann, the relationship is strongly implied in his *Theology of the New Testament*. Though quite different in their conceptions, they share a conviction that the function of the New Testament texts in christology is to lead us *behind* the texts, to point to where real christological discourse is thought to lie.

For Dibelius, the New Testament serves to raise the christological problem, whose solution lies in exploring the formation of the tradition in connection with the needs and situations of the early church. The dilemma raised by the New Testament is the seeming incongruity between the Gospels' interest in the life and teachings of Jesus, and the rest of the New Testament's silence concerning the same: Jesus or Christ? Dibelius rejects both the radical Paulinism of dialectical theology as well as the Life of Jesus movement's dismissal of the church's confession about Jesus. Form criticism provides the way out of the dilemma, for it shows that the Gospels are actually the end product, or deposit, of the first Christians' theological reflection on the meaning of Jesus' life, death, and resurrection.[40] Thus it reveals that the material which comprises the narratives about Jesus' life was motivated from the beginning by the preaching of Jesus as the Christ, and is not simply interested in the Jesus of history for his own sake. In this sense, then, the Gospels are

---

[39]Bultmann, 51.
[40]Dibelius, 7-19; 86-90.

14   *The Endangered Promises*

no less "christological" than Paul's letters and the rest of the NT: "Christology played a role in every tradition about Jesus."[41]

The object of "Gospel criticism" (i.e., form criticism), then, is to lay bare the synthesis of historical tradition and theology which took place already in the first generation after the life of Jesus. Though Dibelius does not spell out what a full-blown Christology of the New Testament might look like, it seems clear that its foundation would lie precisely in this process; the Gospels would function primarily as witness to the process.[42]

The situation with Bultmann is a bit more complicated; his monumental *Theology of the New Testament* does not draw explicitly on his form-critical work.[43] Yet it seems clear that his kerygmatic theology dovetails with his work on the Gospel tradition in at least two ways, one historical, the other theological. First, the amount of creativity he attributes to the early church in his form criticism effectively eradicates the possibility of knowing much more than a minimal essence about what Jesus said and did; thus christology cannot be based on historical knowledge of Jesus. In this sense, the relationship between his form-critical work and his theological ideas could be said to be a negative one. Second, and perhaps more important, Bultmann sees the locus of revelation first and foremost in the preached word; the process by which the first Christians appropriated the message of Jesus as God's saving word to humanity continues in the present time in the preaching of Christ.[44]

As is well known, Bultmann radicalized this Reformation emphasis and applied it to his interpretation of the New Testament, utilizing the framework of the existential philosophy of Kierkegaard and Heidegger. He legitimizes this approach both hermeneutically,

---

[41]Dibelius, 17.

[42]Dibelius, unlike Bultmann, was actually quite "conservative" regarding the historicity of much of the material about Jesus; he emphasized the fact that in recasting and embellishing the traditions for apologetic and preaching purposes, the church's creativity is to be understood as an attempt to state the *significance* of Jesus' words and deeds, most of which actually occurred (cf. 66-71).

[43]For an excellent summary and insightful critique of Bultmann's *Theology*, see Nils A. Dahl, "Rudolf Bultmann's *Theology of the New Testament*," in *Jesus the Christ*, 187-216.

[44]See Morgan, *Biblical Interpretation*, 111-12.

i.e., through his conviction that the task of the New Testament interpreter is to present the text as speaking today, as well as biblically, i.e., he argues that in Paul and John the movement toward an existential understanding of the gospel has already begun. His presentation of the rest of the New Testament is basically *sachkritisch*; he uses the existential theology of Paul and John as the criterion for what in the New Testament can be considered relevant for contemporary faith.

Criticisms of Bultmann's approach, which have, of course, been legion, most often point to the rather reductionist picture of the NT which results.[45] The problem is that one cannot simply object to the fact that Bultmann does not, for example, present the synoptic Gospels on their own terms, without engaging the larger question of the nature of a New Testament theology (or christology) and the problem of hermeneutics.[46] Bultmann's fear that the synoptics' (especially Luke-Acts') presentation of the life of Jesus can lead one into a historicization of the kerygma that obscures the scandal at its heart is well-founded; indeed, this concern is borne out in the New Testament theologies of Jeremias, Goppelt, and others.[47] The danger with Bultmann's conception, however, is that the kerygma finally becomes, as Nils Dahl has put it, "a paradox without content,"[48] and in fact avoids the scandal given in the concrete appearance of Jesus of Nazareth, a scandal of which the Gospel writers (especially Mark) are very much aware.

The question to Bultmann thus becomes, with what, and indeed how is one addressed in the kerygma? Underlying this present study of Mark is the conviction that the story of Jesus as presented in the Second Gospel is no less an address or call to "decision" than Paul or

---

[45]Cf. Nils Dahl's objection that, e.g., Luke-Acts should be presented on its own terms, and not simply in relation to Paul and John ("Bultmann's Theology," 97).

[46]The problem of history, of course, is also central to Bultmann's conception of New Testament Theology. On this, see Steven Kraftchick, "A Legacy in Probate: Bultmann's Use of History" (unpublished paper, 1989).

[47]Joachim Jeremias, *New Testament Theology: The Proclamation of Jesus* (tr. John Marsh; New York: Charles Scribner's Sons, 1971); Leonhard Goppelt, *Theology of the New Testament Volume 1: The Ministry of Jesus in its Theological Significance* (tr. John Alsup; Grand Rapids, MI: Eerdmans, 1981).

[48]Dahl, 104.

John's theology, that the story form in which the kerygma is found here can itself be a powerful vehicle for the gospel. What is more, this preaching occurs precisely in, and not in spite of, its mythological conception. What Bultmann seems to have missed (though we should perhaps not fault him for it) is that Mark, as "literature," does not simply seek to relate the content of the kerygma (which may in fact need to be "demythologized"), but attempts as well through its rhetoric and drama to engender the *experience* of passing from death to life through Christ's victory over sin and death, and thus to elicit a response of faith towards the agent of that experience.[49]

Evaluating Form Criticism

Bultmann was not, of course, unaware of the theological and literary character of the Gospels; he devotes a portion of his *History of the Synoptic Tradition* to the final editing of the material by the individual evangelists, and admits that "Mark has been able to give his collection the appearance of a story coherent geographically, chronologically and in part also materially."[50] Bultmann's sense of the overriding purpose of Mark, however, derives from his understanding of the source material the author had before him, so that the Gospel becomes "the union of the Hellenistic kerygma about Christ, whose essential content consists of the Christ myth as we learn of it in Paul, with the tradition of the story of Jesus"[51]—a formulation that would subsequently prove very important to later redaction critics.

What is significant, though, as we have seen, is that Bultmann does not accord the "theology of Mark" a place in his *Theology of the New Testament*; nor, in the end, does he deem Mark "sufficiently master of his material."[52] Likewise, while Dibelius recognizes Mark

---

[49]On the other hand, literary critical approaches to the Gospels, especially those based on the New Criticism (see below) have been criticized—justifiably—for a certain hermeneutical naïvete. See Lynn M. Poland, *Literary Criticism and Biblical Hermeneutics* (Chico, CA: Scholars Press, 1985); this issue will be taken up in the next chapter.

[50]Bultmann, 341.

[51]Bultmann, 347-48.

[52]Bultmann, 350.

as "the book of secret epiphanies,"[53] and K. L. Schmidt recognizes the appearance of creative editing on Mark's part, none of the form critics view the editorial work of the evangelists as any more than something which must be removed to get at what is truly historically and theologically significant.

In terms of the concerns of this study, then, it is clear that form criticism can address neither the function of conflict in the Gospel of Mark as a whole, nor its impact on Mark's theological and rhetorical achievement. It understands the Gospels to be the end product of an evolutionary growth of the tradition about Jesus, from simpler to more complicated, from less christological to more. The goal of the form critics has been the dismantling of this end product and the correlation of the conflicts to specific life situations in the early church.[54] It has sought the theological significance of the Gospels not in the surface expressions of the text itself, but in something below or beyond it.

CONFLICT AND CHRISTOLOGY IN REDACTION CRITICISM

It is not surprising that the next methodological development in Gospel studies involved the examination of the editorial activity of the evangelists which the form critics ignored; the proponents of redaction criticism set their sights on the material that was "left over" from form criticism. The question for us thus becomes whether redaction criticism, in its concern for the leading theological ideas of each evangelist as reflected in his editing of the material, is in a position to address the christological and literary concerns we have before us.

The roots of redaction criticism, as I noted above, lie already in Wrede's work on the Messianic Secret in the Gospels. To illustrate

---

[53]Though, as noted above, he considers Mark a collector rather than an author (*Tradition*, 59).

[54]Even here, though, it can be argued that, with respect to the controversy stories, the stress the form critics placed on the final saying (as opposed to the dialogue itself) misses much of the dynamic, and even the function of the dialogues in their original settings. See Stanley Saunders, "No One Dared," 24-31; also Werner Kelber, *The Oral and the Written Gospel: The Hermeneutics of Speaking and Writing in the Synoptic Tradition, Mark, Paul, and Q* (Philadelphia: Fortress Press, 1983).

that Mark could not be seen as a transparent window onto the life of
the historical Jesus, Wrede successfully revealed how the creative
activity of the early church and the earliest Gospel render Mark more
than suspect as a source for the historical Jesus. It was not until the
advent of redaction criticism in the 1950's, though, that this creative
activity itself became the focus of inquiry;[55] and indeed, redaction
criticism has remained the dominant mode of Gospel interpretation
for the past three decades.

As defined by Norman Perrin, one of its chief American
proponents, the discipline "is concerned with studying the theological
motivation of an author as this is revealed in the collection, arrangement, editing, and modification of traditional material or the creation
of new forms within the traditions of early Christianity."[56] Two
things are especially significant in this definition: First, the conception of the authors of the Gospels as true authors, not mere collectors,
and as possessing a particular theological point of view or "motivation" which is discernible in the composition of the Gospel has
initiated intense debate concerning each evangelist's christology; this
is especially the case with Mark's Gospel. Second, since redaction
criticism arose out of form criticism, it shares with it an evolutionary
understanding of the Gospel text and it more or less inherited the
form critics' ideas about the make-up and origin of the Gospel
material.[57]

Redaction criticism proved especially helpful with respect to
Matthew and Luke, whose arrangement, editing, and modification of
their Markan source is readily observable. For Mark, though,
redaction critics have had to rely more on form criticism first to
separate tradition from redaction. Above all, Bultmann's understand-

---

[55]The first important redaction-critical works on the Gospels were brought
forth by Willi Marxson, *Mark the Evangelist: Studies on the Redaction History of the
Gospel* (Nashville: Abingdon, 1969); Günther Bornkamm, Gerhard Barth, Heinz
Joachim Held, *Tradition and Interpretation in Matthew* (Philadelphia: Westminster,
1963); and Hans Conzelmann, *The Theology of St. Luke* (Philadelphia: Fortress,
1961).

[56]Norman Perrin, *What is Redaction Criticism?* (Philadelphia: Fortress Press,
1969), 4.

[57]Perrin and his students did, however, end up to be key figures in the
transition from redaction criticism to a more intentional literary criticism.

ing of the primary sources for Mark's Gospel has exercised considerable influence.[58] As I noted above, Bultmann saw Mark as "the union of the Hellenistic kerygma about Christ, whose essential content consists of the Christ myth as we learn of it in Paul, with the tradition of the story of Jesus."[59] The result, as even a cursory reading of the Gospel reveals, is a seemingly contradictory portrait of Jesus: On the one hand, the Gospel portrays him as divine wonder-worker (the Hellenistic kerygma), while at the same time he emerges as one who suffers and dies, and calls others to do the same. That is to say, Mark's Gospel seems to contain two competing christologies: one a "theology of glory," the other a "theology of the cross." Though Bultmann the form critic can leave these two portraits in tension (indeed, remarking that Mark was "not sufficiently master of his material"[60]), the redaction critic, by attending to how the author has shaped the tradition he received, attempts to discern where the evangelist himself has placed emphasis. Thus the two aspects of Perrin's definition are illustrated: The redactor, as the final stage of the "evolution" of the Gospel material, reveals his theological motivations in the way he shapes the material.

The redaction-critical approach to Mark has resulted in a massive bibliography, a full review of which would take us far afield from the concerns of the present study.[61] But two central questions emerge as flashpoints in the literature: What essential features of Mark's understanding of Jesus emerge when one separates Mark's redactive work from the tradition he received? Second, what

---

[58]See, e.g., Johannes Schreiber, "Die Christologie des Markusevangeliums," *Zeitschrift für Theologie und Kirche* 58 (1961), 154-83; Philipp Vielhauer, "Erwägungen zur Christologie des Markusevangeliums," in *Aufsätze zum Neuen Testament* (Tübingen: J. C. B. Mohr [Paul Siebeck]), 199-214; Luz, "Das Geheimnismotiv."

[59]*Synoptic Tradition*, 347-48.

[60]*Synoptic Tradition*, 348.

[61]A very helpful overview of the redaction-critical terrain is to be found in Sean Kealy, *Mark's Gospel: A History of its Interpretation* (New York: Paulist Press, 1982), 159-97; more recently, Clifton Black has evaluated the usefulness of redaction criticism as used to interpret Mark's Gospel (*The Disciples According to Mark: Markan Redaction in Current Debate* [JSNTSS 27; Sheffield: JSOT, 1989]).

historical forces in his community compelled him to develop and express these features?

Theodore Weeden

The debate as to how Mark's theology of glory and theology of the cross relate crystallizes in the question of the relation between the two most prominent titles in the Gospel, Son of God and Son of man. An important methodological presupposition for the redaction critic is, as noted above, that the evangelist has shaped the material he received in light of his theological motivations. Building on Bultmann's assumption of a Hellenistic origin for the Son of God kerygma, and specifically in the conception of a *theios aner*, many redaction critics have seen in Mark's treatment of this received tradition a correction to what the evangelist deemed to be an inappropriate expression of the message about Christ—one, that is, devoid of the message about the cross. This "corrective christology" has found one of its most elaborate statements in Theodore Weeden's work on the conflict between Jesus and the disciples.[62] A brief review of Weeden's work will serve to raise the relevant questions for our study.

According to Weeden, Mark's[63] shaping of this conflict provides the clearest access to the Gospel writer's theological (christological) emphases. In response to the introduction into his community of a heretical *theios aner* christology, which stressed the miraculous powers of Jesus, and whose proponents, so Weeden,

---

[62]His ideas find their fullest statement in *Mark: Traditions in Conflict* (Philadelphia: Fortress Press, 1971); see especially 52-100, 159-168. See also his "The Heresy that Necessitated Mark's Gospel," reprinted in, *The Interpretation of Mark* (ed. W. Telford; Philadelphia: Fortress Press, 1985), 64-77.

[63]It is important to note the very concrete way in which redaction critics generally conceive of "authorship." The goal is the illumination of the thought of the actual historical redactor of the Gospel, the discernment of that figure's intention in shaping the story (cf. Quenten Quesnell, *The Mind of Mark: Interpretation and Method through the Exegesis of Mark 6:52* [Analecta Biblical 38; Rome: Sacra Pagina, 1969). As will be seen below, such a conception of authorship differs greatly from that of literary criticism.

probably manifested that power themselves,[64] Mark was compelled to write a story of Jesus' earthly ministry whose principal aim was to discredit this defective point of view. He accomplished this goal largely through his polemic against the disciples,[65] who really function as foils for Mark's presentation of his christology—a *theologia crucis*. As the Gospel unfolds, Mark portrays the disciples in increasingly negative terms; they move from ignorance of Jesus' identity (1:16-8:26) to misconception of his mission (8:27-14:9) to outright rejection of him (14:10-72).[66] According to Weeden,

> This evolution in the disciples' relationship to Jesus . . . is no acciden-tal development, nor is it intended to be an objective presentation of the actual historical relationship which existed between Jesus and his disciples. It is a carefully formulated polemical device created by the evangelist to disgrace and debunk the disciples.[67]

That this is Mark's intention is shown, for example, in his redaction of the scene of Peter's confession at Caesarea Philippi.[68] Peter's statement of Jesus' identity in 8:29 can only be based on a "divine man" conception of Jesus, since this has been the character of Jesus' activity up to this point. At this crucial point in the Gospel, Mark introduces his corrective to a theology of glory by silencing the disciples (v. 30) and introducing his *theologia crucis* in the form of the first prediction of the passion. For Weeden, the rest of the Gospel makes clear that Mark wishes Jesus to be known not in terms of the signs and wonders associated with the titles Christ and Son of God, but as the suffering Son of Man—i.e., solely on the basis of his suffering and death.[69] The disciples' rejection of this conception of

---

[64]See *Traditions*, 73-81.

[65]Mark's anti-disciple polemic is highlighted already by Schreiber, "Christologie." See also his *Theologie des Vertrauens. Eine redaktionsgeschichtliche Untersuchung des Markusevangeliums* (Hamburg: Furche-Verlag, 1967).

[66]Weeden, "The Heresy," 66; *Traditions*, 23-51. We will, of course, have occasion to engage Weeden's reading of the conflict in more detail in subsequent chapters of this study.

[67]"Heresy," 66.

[68]*Traditions*, 64-66.

[69]*Traditions*, 54. See also Norman Perrin, *Redaction Criticism*, 53-56; also Perrin, "The Christology of Mark: A Study in Methodology," in Telford, 95-108.

Messiahship leads them to reject Jesus; Weeden argues that Mark intends in this way to display before his community the gross misunderstanding of God's purposes that the "divine man" christology represents.[70]

Weeden's redaction-critical methodology, broadly conceived, thus involves three steps: First, the separation of tradition and redaction in the Gospel in order to determine Mark's contribution. Second, the attempt to construct a coherent theological/ christological position from the material deemed to be Markan. Finally, the interpreter infers from this material what kind of situation in the evangelist's community might have given rise to such a formulation, often employing corroborating data from outside the text.

Evaluating Redaction Criticism

A full evaluation of Weeden's work need not be undertaken at this point;[71] we will have occasion to take up his specific reading of Mark's story later in this study. My intent in this survey is to explore the focus and methodology of previous inquiries into the conflicts in Mark. In view of this goal, it is important here to note, first of all, that insofar as Weeden purports to have discovered the key to the whole of Mark in the conflict between Jesus and his disciples, and thus to

---

[70]So Weeden:

The reason for Mark's giving central importance to the christological controversy between Jesus and the disciples is obvious. It is the same controversy which rages in his community between himself and his *theios-aner* opponents. Mark's greatest fear is that his community will reject the 'authentic faith' of Jesus and succumb to the heresy of his enemies. (*Traditions*, 98)

[71]A principal objection to Weeden and all "corrective christology" approaches has been the tenuous evidence for the *theios aner* conceptuality's existence; see, e.g., Kingsbury, "The 'Divine Man' as the Key to Mark's Christology—The End of an Era?" *Interpretation* 35 (1981), 243-57. This is not an objection to redaction criticism per se, though. Kingsbury argues that it is illegitimate methodologically to employ data from outside the text as the key to the meaning of the text itself; this can hardly be avoided, though, and to hold this view represents a rather extreme form of literary criticism's anti-historicism. In fact, as Eugene Boring, in his review of Kingsbury's *Christology*, points out, Kingsbury himself utilizes a key outside the text: namely, the Old Testament (in *JBL* 104 [1985], 732-35). The question is more about the appropriateness or viability of the outside data.

account for the Gospel as a whole in a single, overriding purpose,[72] his reading must be judged inadequate. Without question, this conflict is central to the purposes of the Gospel; but it is doubtful that this single factor was responsible for the genesis of the Gospel. And it is certainly the case, as will be shown below, that the other conflicts in the Gospel narrative provide more than a backdrop for the controversy with the disciples.[73] That is to say, Weeden's *focus* is much too narrow.[74]

Most important here, though, is the way in which Weeden's work illustrates the presuppositions, strengths, and weaknesses of redaction criticism. While it remains very close to the heart of Gospel interpretation, the method has come under sharp attack.[75] One common objection is that it reduces the evangelist's thought to the observable *alterations* he performed on the tradition he received—what cannot be shown to have been deliberately shaped by Mark is often dismissed, implicitly or explicitly, as "some unreflective accident of composition."[76] Moreover, it practically necessitates that the author be at odds at some point with the tradition he received; thus Weeden claims that the "divine man" motif in the first part of the Gospel is only something set up to be shot down in the second half.[77] Where there is tension between tradition and redaction, the goal of

---

[72]See, e.g., 8.

[73]Norman Perrin's account of Mark's christology falls short in the same way (see, e.g., "Christology," 101-2). Moreover, as Dan Via has pointed out in his critique of heresy as the impetus for the writing of the Gospel, those who hold this view "do not explain very precisely, if at all, why Mark's particular kind of narrative was necessary or especially appropriate for countering the particular heresy in mind" (*Kerygma and Comedy in the New Testament* [Philadelphia: Fortress, 1975]), 92.

[74]Though there are exceptions, this tendency to reduce the Gospel to one purpose has characterized redaction criticism as a whole.

[75]Indeed, Perrin himself came to recognize its limitations. But see especially Petersen, *Literary Criticism for New Testament Critics* (Philadelphia: Fortress Press, 1978); Stephen Moore, *Literary Criticism and the Gospels: The Theoretical Challenge* (New Haven and London: Yale University Press); Black, *Disciples*.

[76]Weeden, *Christology*, 91-92.

[77]See "The Heresy," 67. Mark, for instance, waves the "red flag of *theios aner* Christology" by "introducing Jesus as the Son of God, saturating the first half of his Gospel with wonder-working activities of Jesus, and interspersing his own summaries on this *theios aner* activity (1:32ff.; 3:7ff.; 6:53ff.)."

the interpreter is to resolve it in some way. I will argue in subsequent chapters that the tension produced by these conflicting images of Jesus is at the heart of the Gospel's purposes and effects.

More fundamentally, the question arises whether making the case for the *genesis* of Mark's Gospel leads to an adequate statement of the Gospel's "meaning," and thus whether such a genetic approach is the most appropriate for getting at the Gospel's purposes. This genetic concern reveals the essentially historical character of redaction criticism in its traditional forms. As already suggested, most redaction criticism must be seen in the same light as other historical-critical methodology in that it directs itself primarily to the genetic enterprise of accounting historically for the presence of the principal features of the text. As Norman Petersen and others have pointed out,[78] redaction critics share with form and source criticism an understanding of the Gospel text as "evolutionary" in nature—i.e., the Gospel material developed over time under the influence of the developing Christian communities.[79] Since interpretive method is oriented to the understanding of the object being interpreted, analysis of the Gospels developed in ways appropriate to this evolutionary understanding: originally, source criticism in the nineteenth century was interested in the earliest stage of the material, that of the historical Jesus himself; form criticism concerned itself with the early church's formulation of the message about Jesus, and understood the Gospels to be the literary remains of this activity. For its part, redaction criticism has focused on the final stage of the evolution, as noted above, in order to determine the evangelist's theological ideas and the situation on which he brings them to bear.[80] Here what is valued theologically is the evangelist's "personality," that is, the way he has brought the tradition he received to bear on the situation he faced.

---

[78]*Literary Criticism*; Edgar McKnight *Meaning in Texts: The Historical Shaping of a Narrative* (Philadelphia: Fortress Press, 1978), 245-51.

[79]*Literary Criticism*, 15. An excellent example is Weeden, *Traditions*, 70.

[80]Petersen notes that redaction criticism deals with the "literary remains" of the form critical work of Wrede and K. L. Schmidt, among others, whose work revealed that the "world" created by Mark's narrative did not correspond to the "world" to which it ostensibly referred; not until redaction criticism, though, did the worlds created by the evangelist become the focus of study (23).

Each of these approaches has in common the basic presupposition that the meaning of a text lies in something *outside* of the text itself—namely, a specific point in its historical evolution; the text provides *access* to that which is deemed to be the most significant level in its development. Thus, for example, in Weeden's study, the reading of the conflict between Jesus and the disciples is but a prelude to the real work of determining the *reason* for such a conflict:

> What meaning could the presentation of such a christological conflict between Jesus and his disciples have for Mark? Why must he discredit the disciples and their christological position? . . . [T]he only way to account for Mark's consuming interest in it is that it has some existential importance for the situation in his own community. . . Does Mark provide us with any descriptive clues of his *Sitz im Leben* that could help us to find such an explanation?[81]

Weeden brings most of his efforts to bear on this question, suggesting that in the Gospel's *Sitz im Leben* lies the key to its christology; here lies the real significance of interpretation. The text itself thus becomes an allegory whose real significance lies in the aspects of Mark's community which correspond to the story.[82]

The irony here, as Petersen shows, is that the very recognition that the evangelist has put together a story with settings, plot, characters, a narrator, and in so doing has reflected his theological interests—that, in other words, the Gospels possess literary qualities—means that the Gospel text is now conceived in terms other than strictly historical; redaction criticism, in other words, "leads to literary problems that it is not designed to deal with."[83] This tension between the aims of redaction criticism and the recognition of the nature of the text is aptly illustrated by Weeden:

---

[81] *Traditions*, 69.

[82] This approach has affinity with J. L. Martyn's "two-level drama;" see his *History and Theology in the Fourth Gospel* (Nashville: Abingdon Press, 1979).

[83] *Literary Criticism*, 23. See also Morgan, *Biblical Interpretation*, who notes that redaction criticism "investigates a literary activity, and even though it concentrates on the 'seams' where the editors' work can be detected and tradition distinguished from redaction, it has to look at each writing as a literary whole. . . Its failure to develop in a properly literary-critical direction is therefore striking" (211-12).

> The difficulty of finding material in the Gospel which provides us with a transparent and clearly defined picture of the community is monumental. *For Mark's subject matter is not himself nor specifically his community but rather a narrative of the activities and teaching of the historical Jesus.*[84]

Like all historical-critical method, redaction criticism seeks to utilize the Gospel as a *window* onto an aspect of the Gospel's history;[85] yet, paradoxically, it realizes that the "subject matter" of the text itself is something else.

It is precisely here, in this "eclipse of biblical narrative," as Hans Frei has put it,[86] that the principal objection to historical methods in general, and redaction criticism in specific, really lies. The issue is not whether the historically-oriented explorations which have dominated Gospel studies are legitimate, helpful, and necessary; they clearly are.[87] The question concerns rather first, the implicit or explicit limitation of a text's meaning to a statement concerning its development or genesis, and, related to this, the appropriateness of

---

[84]*Traditions*, 70 (emphasis added).

[85]See Petersen, 19. The "window" metaphor, as Petersen notes, comes from Murray Krieger, *A Window to Criticism* (Princeton: Princeton University Press, 1964), 3-4. Of course, redaction criticism's positive feature is that it recognizes the timeliness and appropriateness of God's revelatory acts. That is to say, the message about what God has done in Jesus is always directed to a particular situation—always a "word on target," to use J. Christiaan Beker's description of Paul's hermeneutic (see, e.g., *Paul the Apostle: The Triumph of God in Life and Thought* [Philadelphia: Fortress Press, 1980]). Paradoxically, though, in showing how a particular text was God's word to a certain people, the distance between that moment and the present becomes critical, and can inhibit if not preclude the word's speaking to the present.

[86]*The Eclipse of Biblical Narrative: A Study in Eighteenth and Nineteenth-Century Hermeneutics* (New Haven: Yale University Press, 1974).

[87]Robert Morgan has provided one of the more helpful clarifications of the relationship between the historical and literary/theological tasks; history, he says, can really only play a *negative* role, heading off interpretations of the historical data which render the Christian claim impossible—such as that found in Reimarus's reconstruction of the intentions of the disciples. Once such interpretations are sidelined based on historical argument, history's role can really only be secondary. See *Biblical Interpretation*, and also "The Historical Jesus and the Theology of the New Testament," in *The Glory of Christ in the New Testament: Studies in Christology in Memory of George Bradford Caire* (ed. L. D. Hurst and N. T. Wright; Oxford: Clarendon Press, 1987), 187-206.

historical work alone for understanding the theological purposes of a particular text.[88] As Pat Keifert has put it, those who work in the historical paradigm "organize their interpretation of the text and authorize their christological claims either in reference to the events behind the text or to the intention of the author and community who are witnesses to those events."[89] From a hermeneutical standpoint, it must simply be asked in what *sense* a narrative text is understood when it is understood "historically"—when its development and genesis is accounted for, or its ideas "restated" in propositional form.[90] From a christological perspective, the dominance of the historical authorization of christological statements has proved ultimately reductionistic, robbing a text of a significant aspect of its power to persuade.[91] The question, in other words, is not whether the

---

[88]The reason for the dominance of historical approaches, as Keck notes, roots in the way the discipline has been defined since the Enlightenment split between the Jesus of history and the Christ of faith; christology has been coextensive with the *history* and development of christology; see "Jesus in New Testament Christology," 6-10. Hans Frei offers a more basic reason for the preoccupation with meaning as reference to an historical aspect of the text, namely, the "positivity of revelation" (*Eclipse*, 255; cf. Werner Kelber, "Gospel Narrative and Critical Theory," in *Biblical Theology Bulletin* 18 [1988], 130-36).

[89]"Interpretive Paradigms: A Proposal Concerning New Testament Christology" in *Semeia* 32 (1983), 203-216, 204. Regarding James Dunn's work on New Testament Christology in the same issue, he notes that "discovering the author's and community's mind by way of these texts is the goal of his interpretation and presumably a critical moment in the writing of contemporary christology, *though he does not state that explicitly*" (207, emphasis added). This is precisely the point I wish to stress: The hegemony of the historical aspects of the texts has been an unexamined assumption on the part of historical critics.

[90]See William Beardslee, *Literary Criticism of the New Testament* (Philadelphia: Fortress Press, 1969). The problem with the historical paradigm is also hermeneutical. History that intends to have positive theological significance gets caught in Lessing's ugly ditch (see Gordon Michaelson, "Faith and History: The Shape of the Problem," *Modern Theology* 1 [1985] 277-90). No amount of historical spade work—either into the historical Jesus, the early church, or the evangelist's theological ideas—can of itself make what is thereby discovered relevant for the contemporary person. It is not a matter of how much one can discover, but of how what one discovers impinges on present reality.

[91]Cf. Patrick Keifert: "If [the labors of historians] are to be of use [for christology], they must consider the extent and the place of historical claims in a christological proposal" ("Interpretive Paradigms," 212).

biblical text provides a transparent window onto events outside it, but whether these events ought to provide the primary authorization or locus for christological statements.

Thus, both the nature of Mark's Gospel and the nature of theological inquiry itself call for an approach which takes into account Mark's shape as a narrative and theology's task of interpreting and advancing the witness of the New Testament. I would suggest that redaction criticism, and the historical method in general, more properly belong to the history of early Christian life and faith—an enterprise related to, but not coextensive with, the christology of the New Testament.[92]

THE LITERARY TURN

It is clear, then, that the history of research into Mark's Gospel has been dominated by historical concerns of one kind or another; the locus of meaning and theological purpose has been sought in something beyond the text, in the history to which it refers or of which it is a product. Redaction criticism uncovered the essentially literary nature of the text, but failed to provide a means of interpreting it in light of this. Moreover, studies of the major conflicts in Mark have sought to isolate each and determine the external *Sitz im Leben* which gave rise to the stories.[93] I have begun to suggest some reasons why a strictly historical approach may be inadequate to the task of clarifying Mark's theological purposes. In this section I wish to review briefly the major features of the turn to a more literary paradigm for interpreting biblical narrative and to argue that such a

---

[92]As Robert Morgan has put it, "The beginnings of Christian theology are of interest to the historian, and thus indirectly relevant to New Testament theology. But to make these hypothetically reconstructed early experiments normative for Christian faith and life today would be an extraordinary novelty" ("The Historical Jesus," 203).

[93]Another example of the way in which Mark's conflicts have been seen to refer primarily to something outside the text is to be found in Etienne Trocmé's view of the conflict between Jesus and the authorities. This conflict, she contends, represents Mark's polemic against a Jewish-Christian group in Mark's community which seeks reconciliation with Judaism (*The Formation of the Gospel According to Mark* [tr. Pamela Gaughan; Philadelphia: Westminster Press, 1973], 70-95).

move is both in keeping with the nature of the texts, as well as more fruitful and appropriate for theological reflection.

The move to a literary paradigm in biblical studies has already reached the point where it has become impossible to talk about "*the* literary approach."[94] The methodological landscape of biblical studies has been changing with dizzying speed, and will no doubt continue to do so.

It is beyond the scope of this introduction to chart the development and current practice of literary approaches to biblical narrative in detail;[95] it will be helpful, though, to sketch in broad outline the major options, in order, again, to assess their fruitfulness for our task. It is useful to consider the current literary approaches in terms of two broad categories: those centered on the *text* and those centered on the *reader* or the *reading experience*. That is to say, if historical-critical methodologies can be said to be concerned primarily with the world "behind the text," literary approaches exhibit a move from here first to the "text itself," its formal relations, to the world "in front of the text" that is, the interaction between text and reader. Important studies of Mark have appeared in both of these categories.

---

[94]Cf. Meir Sternberg, *The Poetics of Biblical Narrative: Ideological Literature and the Drama of Reading* (Bloomington, IN: Indiana University Press, 1987), 3-7.

[95]Stephen Moore's *Literary Criticism* is by far the most insightful work on the subject to date, providing a "map" of current literary practice, its origins, and suggestions for future development. See also Morgan, *Biblical Interpretation*, especially chapters 1, 6, 7, 8; Donald McKim, ed., *A Guide to Contemporary Hermeneutics : Major Trends in Biblical Interpretation* (Grand Rapids, MI : Eerdmans, 1986; Clarence Walhout and Leland Ryken (eds.), *Contemporary Literary Theory: A Christian Appraisal* (Grand Rapids, MI: Eerdmans, 1991); John Barton, *Reading the Old Testament: Method in Biblical Study* (Philadelphia: Westminster, 1984); Janice Capel Anderson and Stephen D. Moore (eds.), *Mark and Method: New Approaches in Biblical Studies* (Minneapolis: Fortress, 1991); Frank McConnell, ed., *The Bible and the Narrative Tradition* (New York: Oxford University Press, 1986); Werner Kelber, "Gospel Narrative and Critical Theory;" Regina Schwartz, *The Book and the Text: The Bible and Literary Theory* (Cambridge, MA: Basil Blackwell, 1990), especially chapter 1.

Narrative Criticism of the Gospels

Text-centered literary approaches proved to be the initial contact point between biblical studies and "secular" literary criticism, and have led to a relatively stable form of interpretation which has come to be known as narrative criticism.[96] The theoretical supports of this approach to biblical narrative are provided by two pillars: New Criticism, or formalism, a movement which roots in the anti-historical turn of secular literary criticism in the 1920s and 30s,[97] and the contemporary narrative theory of Seymour Chatman.[98] A brief description of each of these pillars will aid in understanding and evaluating the movement.

New Criticism. It is important to keep in mind the original motivations of the New Critical movement in North America, for in many respects they parallel the concerns of biblical critics who have moved away from strictly historical approaches to biblical narrative. First, there was a perceived need to put the study of literature on a footing that was every bit as solid as the natural sciences; the New

---

[96]See Moore, 1-68; Mark Allan Powell, *What is Narrative Criticism?* (Minneapolis: Fortress Press, 1990). The influence of Hans Frei's *Eclipse of Biblical Narrative*, and even earlier, Erich Auerbach's *Mimesis: The Representation of Reality in Western Literature* (tr. W. Trask; Princeton: Princeton University Press, 1953) is often noted. But the actual practice of literary criticism has drawn very little from either (though cf. Donald Juel, *Messiah and Temple: The Trial of Jesus in the Gospel of Mark* [SBLDS 31; Missoula, MT: Scholars Press, 1977], 44-46); Frei's influence has been felt much more with respect to the narrative theology movement, which, strangely enough, has really developed separately from literary criticism of the Bible. This is most likely because the original impulse for "the Bible as literature" movement came from "secular" circles (e.g., Alter, Kermode, Sternberg), from university settings. But perhaps more importantly, it represents as well, I think, the difficulty biblical studies has had with the theological subject matter of the texts. A "literary approach"—especially of the formalist bent—allows an interpreter to avoid these questions. That the guild has not, for the most part, exploited the potential of narrative for the theology of the New Testament (or biblical theology) is one of the principal methodological arguments of this study (cf. Moore, 56-68).

[97]Helpful reviews and critiques of the New Critical movement can be found in Sternberg, Poland, Morgan/Barton, Barton, Walhout/Ryken, Moore.

[98]Especially his *Story and Discourse: Narrative Structure in Fiction and Film* (Ithaca, NY: Cornell University Press, 1978). Stephen Moore has taken the "narrative critical" movement to task for its lack of theoretical reflection (see 41-55).

Critics emphasized that the kind of knowledge imparted by literature was not inferior to, but only different from (complementary to) hard scientific knowledge.[99] Second, the movement was a reaction against the over-historicizing tendencies of previous literary criticism; interpreters had consistently appealed to elements external to the texts themselves—social and historical setting, aspects of the author's life, psychological factors—as the final determinant of the correctness of an interpretation. As with biblical historical criticism, the referential aspect of the literary text was viewed as the most significant. Out of this concern emerged the much-debated question of the role of the literal author's *intention* in interpreting a literary text. Historical models of interpretation have held this to be the most significant criterion for judging interpretations, for arriving at the meaning of a text.[100] Formalists termed this feature of historical method the "intentional fallacy,"[101] and attempted to temper (though not eliminate) its prominent role in interpretation.

It follows from this, then, finally, that the New Critics fought for the notion that a literary text comprised a unity unto itself, an object whose form and content were inextricably intertwined. Form, in fact, *is* meaning, and so the question became not so much *what* a text means, but *how*. The "heresy of paraphrase" was to be avoided at all costs. The technique thus involves close reading of texts to discover the way in which formal aspects of the text reconcile structural tensions and so make meaning.[102]

Seymour Chatman. The second principal pillar supporting the biblical narrative-critical movement is, as noted, the work of the narratologist Seymour Chatman. His analysis of narrative structure in fiction and film has been widely drawn upon as a tool for under-

---

[99]See, e.g., Charles Anderson, "New Criticism," in *Literary Theories in Praxis* (ed. Shirley F. Stanton; Philadelphia: University of Pennsylvania, 1987), 12-61; Walhout and Ryken, 4.

[100]Cf. John Barton: "All historical-critical work in biblical studies, it is not too much to say, depends on this notion" (*Reading the Old Testament*, 148)

[101]This issue has, of course, received much attention in literary circles. See the helpful overview of the debate by Frank Kermode, "The Single Correct Interpretation," in *The Art of Telling: Essays on Fiction* (Cambridge, MA: Harvard University Press, 1983), 201-220.

[102]See Anderson, "New Criticism."

standing and interpreting biblical narrative, especially the Gospels.[103] Fundamental to Chatman's narrative analysis is the distinction between the *story* of the narrative and its *discourse*. The former involves the "what" of the story—principally events, characters, and settings. The latter is the "how" of the narrative, the rhetorical means by which the author communicates the story elements to an audience. These two basic elements provide a way of analyzing the inner workings of a narrative, with emphasis on the narrative as a "communication event"—a means by which an author conveys a message to an audience. Almost every literary text itself can be understood as the interweaving of these two basic elements: a story communicated in a particular manner. Chatman drew on conceptions already present in literary theory to develop his model: implied author, narrator, narratee, implied audience.[104]

Chatman's analysis was not intended to be a method for reading texts; the concern of narratology (a form of structuralism) is to use texts to arrive at a model for understanding how narrative per se works, not any particular narrative. Yet his narrative model has found affinity with New Critical emphases because it seems to affirm the latter's insistence that the text be treated as a unified world, a self-contained artifact; the text's communicative power adheres in the text itself, not in that to which it refers. The distinguishing of the narrative elements provides a convenient vehicle for understanding the way in which the form of a text works integrally with the content to produce meaning.[105] Chatman himself placed much more emphasis on the discourse aspect of stories, for the *how* of the narrative is most directly related to narratological concerns. Biblical narrative critics, though, have put more emphasis on the *story*, which, as I will note below, has limited its usefulness for theological appropriation of Mark's Gospel.

---

[103]See especially the previously cited works by Kingsbury; a very helpful introduction to the application of Chatman's method is Alan Culpepper's work on the Gospel of John, *Anatomy of the Fourth Gospel: A Study in Literary Design* (Philadelphia: Fortress Press, 1983).

[104]See, e.g., Wayne Booth, *The Rhetoric of Fiction* (Chicago: University of Chicago Press, 1983).

[105]See Moore, *Literary Criticism*, 45.

This combination of New Criticism and Chatman's narratology has provided the impetus for most literary analyses of biblical narrative, including the Gospels. Significant works have been produced within the last decade or so which have proven the fruitfulness of this turn away from predominantly historical concerns, especially with respect to developing understanding and appreciation of the literary/aesthetic qualities of the Gospels, which have long been overlooked. But there are also limitations with respect to what this way of reading the Gospels can accomplish, especially hermeneutically and theologically.

Jack Kingsbury. Two works of Jack Kingsbury provide a helpful illustration of the method's prospects and problems; that he has written on Mark's christology from a literary perspective,[106] as well as on conflict in Mark's Gospel[107] makes an assessment of his work important for this study. *The Christology of Mark* does reveal how a reading of Mark's Gospel in terms of its formal aspects can break through certain interpretive impasses reached in the historical paradigm. For example, as already noted above, it becomes very difficult to maintain that Mark corrects what he deemed to be a faulty "divine man," Son of God christology with one centered on the "suffering Son of man" (Weeden et. al.) when one takes seriously the evaluative point of view of the narrator of Mark's Gospel.[108] There can be no question that the point of view of Mark's narrator is that Jesus is the Son of God; the opening verse of the Gospel makes that clear, and even if that textual difficulty is resolved with the removal

---

[106] *The Christology of Mark's Gospel.*

[107] *Conflict in Mark: Jesus, Authorities, Disciples* (Minneapolis: Fortress Press, 1989); see also *Conflict in Luke: Jesus, Authorities, Disciples* (Minneapolis: Fortress Press, 1991).

[108] Kingsbury draws on the very helpful work of Norman Petersen on Mark's point of view, "'Point of View' in Mark's Narrative" (*Semeia* 12 [1978] 97-121); cf. also Booth, 73-9. Kingsbury's critique of "corrective christology" actually is four-fold: 1) The concept of a *theios aner* is not well-established enough in Mark's milieu to make it useful for understanding Mark's thought (33-37); 2) the tenuous circularity of establishing a pre-marcan tradition against which the evangelist would be polemicizing (37-40); 3) to allow a hypothetically-reconstructed tradition history to provide the key to understanding Mark is also methodologically suspect (40-41); 4) the false notion that Son of man "corrects" Son of God in the Gospel narrative (41-42).

of the title from the text, 1:11 reveals that it is the point of view of God's own self (see 9:7). Jesus' implicit acceptance of that designation (in his carrying out the mission his identity entails) means that the narrator, God, and Jesus all line up over against any other point of view on Jesus in setting forth his identity as God's beloved son; it is the "normative" point of view.[109] Kingsbury is also surely correct in deriving the most appropriate understanding of the title in the Old Testament—i.e., as a royal figure.[110] What is more, Kingsbury also shows convincingly that in Mark's story, "Son of Man" does not function primarily as a christological title (there is no secrecy around it; it is never used as a predicate; it never incites opposition).[111]

Kingsbury's *Conflict in Mark* represents a typical narrative-critical treatment of Mark which seeks to elucidate the elements of the Gospel's story in terms of the principal conflicts which give it shape. It complements Kingsbury's *Christology* in that, while the latter focuses on the titles in Mark, the work on Mark's conflict concentrates on the story itself. Indeed, the work focuses almost exclusively on the "story" side of the story/discourse model—settings, characters, events (plot)—with scant attention to the rhetoric or discourse. After setting forth these story elements of Mark's Gospel, he examines each of what he sees as three major "story-lines": That of the main character, Jesus, and the two groups with which he comes into conflict: the religious authorities and the disciples.[112]

Kingsbury's strength is his ability to explicate the formal aspects of the story-world of the Gospel in an exceptionally clear manner, allowing the reader to grasp connections among the story elements that might easily be missed by a less attentive reader. However, his work on Mark's Gospel falls far short of what a literary

---

[109]Kingsbury, 47-50.

[110]See Donald Juel, *Mark* (Minneapolis: Augsburg Press, 1990).

[111]*Christology*, 157-73.

[112]In this, Kingsbury follows Rhoads and Michie (*Mark as Story: An Introduction to the Narrative of a Gospel* [Philadelphia: Fortress Press, 1984]), although the latter include Jesus and the demons as a distinctive story-line; this is preferable, but, as I will show below, the separation of these story lines undermines the essential unity of the conflict in Mark.

approach might accomplish, both for understanding the story and with respect to theological appropriation. This is partly due to the particularities of his interpretation, but also, and more important, to the limits of "narrative criticism" itself.

In terms of his actual reading of the conflicts in Mark, Kingsbury's separation of the three story-lines does not allow the essential unity of the conflicts to emerge. The dissolution of these narrative strands has the ironic result of fragmenting the text in a manner not unlike more genetic methods. Of course, the isolated treatment of a particular line can provide valuable insights into the text as a whole; but wanting in Kingsbury's *Conflict in Mark* is a reintegration of the story to show how the conflicts interweave in the larger story.[113]

Regarding his *Christology* it must be said that, in spite of the significant advance in the discussion the book represents, his focus on the *titles* of Mark's Gospel is far too restrictive.[114] His main conclusion, that Mark presents Jesus as God's royal Son of God,[115] does not significantly advance our understanding of what Mark means by this term. He rightly rejects the "corrective christology" of Weeden et. al.; but in its place he has given us something almost as one-dimensional: Jesus as the Davidic Messiah-King, the Son of God. Of course, he acknowledges that Mark presents this conviction in a story in which its reality and validity are contested by human thinking; indeed, the messianic secret motif—which Kingsbury suggests has really only to do with Jesus as Son of God[116]—functions precisely to show "how 'human thinking' about Jesus is, under God's

---

[113]As Rhoads and Michie note, "it is important to note that in the narrative itself the two major conflicts [religious authorities and disciples] overlap and interweave, each one anticipating and paralleling the other at key point, and each illuminating the other by comparison and contrast" (*Mark as Story*, 100). This is the conclusion of their treatment of the plot in Mark, but it remains only a suggestion, since they, too, treat each story-line separately.

[114]Cf. Tannehill, "Mark's Gospel as Narrative Christology," *Semeia* 16 (1979), 57-95; Kingsbury is not unaware of this danger, and defends his approach (144, n. 2).

[115]See 47-155. Ironically, of course, this is not shown by the narrative alone, but with reference to something "outside" the text—the Old Testament; cf. Boring's review of *Christology*.

[116]*Christology*, 13-23.

direction, brought into alignment with 'divine thinking.'"[117] But there does not emerge in Kingsbury's interpretation any real sense of the cosmic and existential conflict such a movement entails. That is to say, Kingsbury does not allow the narrative to fill out the particular—and scandalous—*manner* in which Jesus fulfills his role, both for the world of the Gospel and for the reader.[118] This difficulty, in fact, emerges as the principal problem with his narrative-critical approach. Kingsbury's description of the theological or hermeneutical function of the Gospel, the only such explicit statement of the theological "pay-off" of his reading of the Gospel, reveals this clearly. The purpose of this movement in the story

> is to invite readers to appropriate for themselves that "thinking" about Jesus which places them "in alignment" with God's "thinking" about Jesus. This occurs when the readers, in "hearing" Mark's story of Jesus, are brought to the realization that Jesus of Nazareth is of decisive importance as far as their relationship to God is concerned. The reason Jesus is of decisive importance is that it is he whom God affirmed to be his only Son and empowered and chose for messianic ministry. . . . Should now the readers of Mark be brought to realize the decisive importance of Jesus Son of God, there opens for them the possibility of entering upon, or being confirmed in, a life that is "in alignment" with the will of God because it is "in alignment" with the life of Jesus himself: "If anyone desires to come after me, let him deny himself and take up his cross, and follow me."[119]

Such a statement raises far more questions for a reader than it answers, and aptly demonstrates the limits of formalism. Indeed, here is where the theoretical bases of narrative criticism prove inadequate to the task of rendering biblical interpretation relevant for contemporary theological inquiry: as noted above, both New Criticism and Chatman's narratology treat the text as an *artifact*; the goal of each

---

[117]*Christology*, 141.

[118]Leander Keck, following Riceour, argues that the titles ought to be considered metaphors; in the "metaphoric process" there is a *two-way* movement of properties between the two elements of the comparison, so to say that "Jesus is the Son of God" is to create a new understanding of Son of God as well as to say something about the identity of Jesus ("The Titles of Jesus in Christology," 14).

[119]*Christology*, 141-42.

is a *descriptive* poetics.[120] There may very well emerge an enhanced appreciation for the formal aspects of the piece, but the lack of substantial hermeneutical reflection, the absence of significant discussion of the way in which such an artifact can actually engage a reader, either ancient or, especially for our concern, contemporary, makes narrative criticism as often practiced unsatisfactory for the task of rendering the text "intelligible and persuasive" to an audience.[121]

Evaluating Narrative Criticism

If the hermeneutical problems suggested here were unique to Kingsbury's work, the significance of this critique would be limited. But as Lynn Poland and, more recently, Stephen Moore have argued, the problem can be seen as inherent in approaches whose principal focus is the *story* of the Gospels.[122] In her study of biblical hermeneutics, Poland undertakes an examination of the hermeneutical problems and prospects of formalist approaches as they have been applied to biblical narratives, using the work of John Dominic Crossan and Dan Via, Jr. on the parables of Jesus and Hans Frei's thesis that the Gospels represent "realistic narrative."[123] She argues compellingly that formalist approaches cannot accomplish what the approach's proponents hope: "The central difficulty . . . is that the centripetal focus of New Critical theory—its stress on the autonomy, self-sufficiency, and objectivity of the literary work of art—tends to prevent literature from exercising those cognitive and thus

---

[120]This is essentially the critique of Lynn Poland (*Literary Criticism*, 142-59).

[121]Pat Keifert, "Interpretive Paradigms," 210. See also David Cunningham, *Faithful Persuasion: In Aid of a Rhetoric of Christian Theology* (Notre Dame: University of Notre Dame Press, 1991), especially 219-238.

[122]Moore goes so far as to suggest that, since redaction criticism pays more attention to the "how" question, it is more "theological" than story-centered Gospel criticism. There are, of course, more satisfying formal analyses of biblical narrative and the Gospels; the works of Robert Tannehill and, especially, Alan Culpepper (cited above) come to mind. Tannehill's work on Mark will be considered in subsequent chapters.

[123]The position he set forth in *The Eclipse of Biblical Narrative*; see, e.g., 13-16. He developed this idea in *The Identity of Jesus Christ* (Philadelphia: Fortress Press, 1975).

transformative powers which this theory also wishes to claim for it."[124] In other words, even those practitioners of "narrative criticism" who explicitly intend to bring alive the Gospel text and make possible an intelligible and fruitful hearing of the story fail, in her view, because by its very nature the method creates *distance* between text and audience. In light of this concern, Poland re-presents Bultmann's hermeneutical program and finds his concern for the existential reinterpretation of the kerygma still valid. She rightly points out, though, that Bultmann is to be faulted for his failure to appreciate the significance of the narrative shape of the texts (see above). Thus she concludes her study with an argument for the wedding of these two concerns, and in a preliminary way, she suggests Paul Riceour's work offers a potential model for this synthesis.[125] I will argue below that a more rhetorically-oriented literary criticism can bring one closer to this goal.

In his *Literary Criticism and the Gospels*, Stephen Moore also points out the limits of narrative criticism, though on slightly different grounds. He argues that narrative critics, in rejecting redaction criticism for its genetic concerns, also replaced redaction criticism's underlying concern for the theology of the evangelist with a concern for the *story* side of the story/discourse model. In opting for the story as the focus of analysis, though, they "diminish the power of the Gospels, reducing them to ordinary works of literature."[126] In effect, story-centered criticism also separates form and content; a "retelling" of the Gospel story a la Kingsbury's *Conflict in Mark* passes over the most salient feature of the narrative: the discourse, the *manner* in which the story is mediated to the reader.[127] Thus narrative critics separate the story from the discourse

---

[124]Poland, 159.

[125]Poland, 162-96. See also the provocative article by James F. Kay, "Theological Table-Talk: Myth or Narrative? Bultmann's 'New Testament and Mythology' Turns Fifty," *Theology Today* 48 (1991), 326-32.

[126]*Literary Criticism*, 58.

[127]See above; this is where Kingsbury's failure to show how the conflicts in Mark interweave and overlap for rhetorical effect becomes important.

that mediates it.[128] The artificiality of the separation of story and discourse becomes clear, so Moore, when one realizes that plot cannot be considered apart from a particular instance of plotting; one cannot analyze the "events" of the story without attention to the voice that mediates those events.[129]

Moore concludes that the two elements, the story and its discourse, can be treated together if one asks not just "What happened?," but "What kind of involvement in the plot does the narrator's discourse elicit at this moment or at that?"[130] Here Moore makes the transition from the text-centered literary approach of narrative criticism to one that centers on the reader and the reading experience; it is a move that, broadly defined, brings us to the center of the most recent concerns of literary theory.

The Reader and the Text

There is no question that a close reading of Mark's narrative in the manner of narrative criticism will shed light on the central conflicts of the Gospel, and much of the analysis I undertake in the subsequent chapters will assume that form and meaning are closely related in the narrative. And there are narrative critics who pay closer attention to the intended effect of a narrative's discourse.[131] On hermeneutical and theological grounds, however, it must be judged

---

[128]Moore notes the irony of the situation: Narrative critics "rely themselves...on a separation of form and content, reenacting in a different register the very thing that many of them are reacting against" (63).

[129]In this regard, N. Petersen's treatment of Mark's plot in his *Literary Criticism* is preferable to those of Kingsbury and Rhoads and Michie, since it represents an argument for Mark as narrative by showing how story time and narrated time are artfully, intentionally related for rhetorical effect.

[130]*Literary Criticism*, 63.

[131]See especially Tannehill's two essays, "The Disciples in Mark: The Function of a Narrative Role," in *The Interpretation of Mark*, 134-57 and "Narrative Christology," in which Tannehill nicely states the potential for attention to compositional, formal aspects of a narrative: "Careful study of the literary composition of the sayings, including their rhetorical and poetic features, enables the interpreter to clarify the kind of impact which particular sayings were designed to have on the hearer" ("Narrative Christology," 59).

less than fully adequate.[132] Hermeneutically, the objective "text as artifact" model creates a distance between text and reader which inhibits the transformative power ascribed to the Gospel narrative, and, in many ways, places us back in the historical paradigm; theologically, the separation of the story from its mediating voice, the "what" from the "how," ignores the rhetorical—and therefore theological—importance of the "how," for it is only through the discourse that a narrative becomes more than a string of unconnected events; it is here that the truth claims about the story are contained and here that the author seeks to persuade the audience to embrace those claims.

In other words, that the move from the world "behind" the text (the historical methodologies) to the world of the "text itself" does not by itself render the text intelligible and persuasive suggests the need for more attention to the world "in front of" the text: that is, to the *interaction* between text and reader. To state, as Kingsbury does, for example, that Mark intends "to invite readers to appropriate for themselves that 'thinking' about Jesus which places them 'in alignment' with God's 'thinking' about Jesus" is only to raise another, more important question: *How* is Mark's "ideal" reader/ hearer invited to take on this evaluative point of view? To what extent and in what way is there likely to be tension between the Son of God presented by Mark's Jesus in the Gospel and this reader's willingness to shape his life around this conviction? And further, how can a contemporary, real reader respond to Mark's narrative world as Mark would wish?

To study conflict in Mark in view of these questions means not only to show how the conflicts interrelate and interpret one another in the narrative, but to ask, on the one hand, in Stephen Moore's

---

[132]Mark Allan Powell, in the final section of *What is Narrative Criticism?*, gets into trouble when he both acknowledges the hermeneutical problem of narrative criticism ("Even when a reader has come to understand what a story 'means,' the significance of that story's meaning for real life remains to be determined" [100]), and touts the "expanded" hermeneutical possibilities of the method ("Narrative criticism attempts to [address the contemporary appropriation of texts] by examining the ways in which texts become meaningful to readers" [99]). The overall effect, in any case, is to underscore the need for further attention to hermeneutical and theological appropriation of biblical narrative.

words, "What kind of involvement in the plot does the narrator's discourse elicit at this moment or at that?"[133] and on the other hand, what in the world of a contemporary, real reader might inhibit such involvement? That Mark's Gospel is so infused with conflict suggests, as we shall see, that Mark anticipates that the encounter between the world of his text and that of the ideal reader will be a violent one.

The next chapter of this study will be devoted to a more detailed discussion of reader-oriented interpretation. Here a few remarks are warranted in order to complete the movement of this chapter. In terms of literary theory,[134] the basis for attention to the world in front of the text is to be found in the broad category of "reader-response criticism," which, in various forms has, in the last decade or so, moved to the fore-front of concern.[135] The movement's basic interest is the reader's—or audience's—role in the creation of meaning from a text. This concern for the reader has many facets, which order themselves around how the reader is conceived—as "ideal" or "real"—as well as what forces—cultural, psychological, ideological, etc.—shape the reader's interaction with the text. That is, in its most theoretical form, reader-response criticism can be seen simply as the mirror-image of narrative criticism, involving the examination of the implied reader, the one who "embodies all those

---

[133]Moore, 63.

[134]This has been a concern of theological and philosophical hermeneutics since at least Schleiermacher; indeed, one "branch" of reader-response theory is often linked with German hermeneutics, or "Rezeptionstheorie" (Dilthey, Bultmann, Gadamer).

[135]The classic study is that of Wolfgang Iser, *The Act of Reading: A Theory of Aesthetic Response* (Baltimore: Johns Hopkins University Press, 1978); see also *The Reader in the Text: Essays on Audience and Interpretation* (ed. Susan R. Suleiman and Inge Crosman; Princeton, NJ: Princeton University Press, 1980), which contains essays by many of the principal reader-response theorists, e.g., Iser, Jonathan Culler, Tzvetan Todorov, Peter Rabinowitz. See also Terry Eagleton, *Literary Theory: An Introduction* (Minneapolis: University of Minnesota Press, 1983, esp. 54-90. Biblical critics have provided some helpful overviews of the approach as well; see Moore, *Literary Criticism,* 71-107; Robert Fowler, *Let the Reader Understand: Reader-Response Criticism and the Gospel of Mark* (Minneapolis: Fortress Press, 1991); also his *Loaves and Fishes* (SBLDS 54; Chico, CA: Scholars Press, 1981), 149-84; Jeffery Lloyd Staley, *The Print's First Kiss: A Rhetorical Investigation of the Implied Reader in the Fourth Gospel* (SBLDS 82; Atlanta: Scholars Press, 1988), 6-48.

predispositions necessary for a literary work to exercise its effect—predispositions laid down, not by an empirical outside reality, but by the text itself. . . . [The implied reader] is a construct and in no way to be identified with any real reader."[136] Its most empirical form actually finds expression in post-structuralist thought, or deconstruction, which denies a text any stable meaning and places responsibility for creating meaning solely with a real, flesh and blood reader under the influence of various cultural forces.[137] Until very recently, however, the influence of reader-response criticism on biblical studies has been almost exclusively from the former, more theoretical side of the spectrum.[138]

Two recent works on Mark's Gospel merit special note, both for their use of reader-oriented categories and, of course, for their particular readings of Mark. Robert Fowler's synthesis of reader-response criticism in *Let the Reader Understand* provides a helpful model for understanding Mark's rhetorical moves, and I will draw on it in my own analysis of conflict in Mark. The recent work of Mary Ann Tolbert also exhibits concern for Mark as a rhetorical piece, though in a somewhat different respect; her *Sowing the Gospel* seeks to set Mark's Gospel in its "literary-historical" context, that is, to read Mark in light of the literary conventions and rhetorical moves as they would have been intended by the author and understood by Mark's first-century audience.

Though they come at Mark from these somewhat different perspectives, both Fowler and Tolbert agree that Mark's Gospel is essentially a *rhetorical* piece: it attempts not just to communicate a message which could be stated in other terms, but to *affect* the audience.[139] As I intend to make clear in subsequent chapters, what

---

[136]Iser, 34.

[137]Stephen Moore is one who has moved more into deconstruction, a move adumbrated in his *Literary Criticism and the Gospels*, and developed in more recent works —*Mark and Luke in Poststructuralist Perspectives: Jesus Begins to Write* (New Haven: Yale University Press, 1992).

[138]This observation is made in the form of a critique in a recent volume of *Semeia* on reader-oriented criticism; see Temma F. Berg, "Reading In/To Mark," *Semeia* 48 (1989), 187-206.

[139]See Fowler: "No longer can the language of the Gospel be regarded as primarily referential or informative; it has become rhetorical, affective, and powerful"

does emerge from Mark is, on the one hand, the clear sense that what God has done in Jesus is crucial for one's relationship with God, and hence for one's ultimate destiny. Equally true, on the other hand, is that human characters in Mark's story fail to embrace this conviction. The effect of these two observations, in my view, would be similar in both ancient and modern contexts: "Who then can be saved?" I hope to show that one of the primary rhetorical effects of Mark's Gospel is to raise this question for the audience to the point of crisis, and that the conflicts on the cosmic and historical level serve this purpose. The more audience-centered approaches to narrative will serve well toward this end.

CONCLUSIONS

I set out to survey the methodological landscape of Markan studies with a particular question in view; my interest in Mark is in theological interpretation which contributes to an intelligible and persuasive experience of the Gospel in the present. My specific focus is the way in which conflict in the Gospel functions in that experience. Historical methodologies, I suggested, which share a concern with the world "behind" the text (an important concern in its own right), do not place the interpreter in a position to view (or experience) the Gospel holistically, and have tended to treat each of the conflicts in Mark separately, as a window onto a particular aspect of the Gospel's development (struggle with the synagogue, "divine man" christology, "heresy" in the community). Moreover, in theological terms, the focus of such studies has been on Mark's christology, often related to the question of how Mark employs christological titles.

The literary turn in biblical exegesis has provided helpful new insights; narrative criticism, with its concern for the unity of the text, furnishes a model on which to read the Gospel's conflicts as discoursed events, as the unfolding of a unified plot. But insofar as narrative criticism treats the text as an artefact, as an aesthetic object to be explored, it keeps the text at a distance, where its formal beauty

---

(3; cf. 4, 11, 23); see Tolbert, 88, 91.

can be admired, but its transformative power diminished. I suggest, finally, that models of reading which focus on the world "in front of the text," on the interaction between text and reader, provide the most fruitful means of reading the text for theological interests. Simply recasting Mark's narrative either with discursive statements about his theology or christology, or even paraphrasing his story, ultimately leave unadressed crucial hermeneutical issues and circumvent the rhetorical effect of an experience of the narrative itself.

In what follows, I will first want to explore more fully the shape and implications of an audience-centered approach to the Gospel of Mark, in preparation for an engagement with the text of Mark, which will follow in the subsequent chapters. I am especially interested in how this conflict is shaped rhetorically to "do something" to the reader; in my view, that something, broadly stated, is to address the crisis or conflict in the audience brought about by the narrative's presentation of the *necessity* of embracing God's act in Jesus on one level, and on another level the *impossibility* of doing so without divine intervention.

We turn, then, to examine how an approach to the text which takes seriously the audience-oriented character of Mark's Gospel addresses these concerns.

CHAPTER 2

READER-RESPONSE CRITICISM
AND CONFLICT IN MARK

I am arguing in this study that when an audience is prepared to experience the various conflicts in Mark's Gospel as a whole—that is, when it is in a position to see the way in which the conflicts overlap and interweave—the conflicts work together to address the experience of conflict in Mark's audience between the promises of God and the reality of the seemingly unredeemed world inhabited by the audience. In methodological terms, the conflicts in Mark's story reach their ultimate aim only when viewed as a means of communication between the author and the audience, and not solely as a window onto aspects of Mark's history, theology, or even storytelling. In this chapter I seek to clarify further the methodological approaches informing this study.

The literary and theological (specifically soteriological) concerns outlined in the previous chapter suggest that an analysis of conflict in a strictly formalist mode will not suffice. My principal interest lies in what involvement in Mark's story accomplishes for the "reader."[1] As Stephen Moore has put the reader-response critic's question, "What kind of involvement in the plot does the narrator's discourse elicit at this moment or at that?"[2] I am, in other words, in essential agreement with Robert Fowler's assertion that Mark's

---

[1]My understanding of the identity and nature of the reader will be addressed in detail below.

[2]Moore, *Literary Criticism and the Gospels: The Theoretical Challenge* (New Haven: Yale University Press, 1989), 63.

45

principal aim is not to convey information (though it certainly is that as well), but to mold and shape in a particular way those who have an encounter with his text. The Gospel, so Fowler,

> is not so much designed to construct its own world as it is designed to construct its own reader; it is not designed so much to say something about its implied world as it is to do something to its implied reader; the narrative does not strive to convey meaning as referential content as much as it strives to achieve communion with its audience by means of a forceful event that takes place through time.[3]

Fowler, following other reader-response critics, works out of a model of reading which construes a text's meaning not as something "in" the text to be culled by the interpreter, but as an "event" which takes place in the interaction between the text and the hearer/reader. Reader-response criticism calls attention to the performative aspect of language, focusing on the rhetorical goals of the text: what does the text actually seek to accomplish in the life of the hearer/reader, and how?[4]

---

[3]Fowler, *Let the Reader Understand: Reader-Response Criticism and the Gospel of Mark* (Minneapolis: Fortress Press, 1991), 57. Fowler relies in part on an article by Paul Hernadi, "Compass for Critics" (*Critical Inquiry* 3 [1976], 369-86), in which the author lays out a communication model which takes as its central structural feature two intersecting axes: one a rhetorical axis of communication and the other a mimetic axis of representation. In biblical studies, the mimetic axis has predominated (see previous chapter).

Though not self-consciously a "reader-response" critic, Robert Alter's groundbreaking work has focused on precisely the rhetorical techniques biblical authors employed to shape the reader's understanding and behavior. As he puts it, the biblical narratives aim "to 'draw me out of myself,' using the medium of narrative to transform my sense of the world, urgently alert me to spiritual realities and moral imperatives I might have misconceived, or not conceived at all" (*The World of Biblical Literature* [New York: Basic Books, 1992], 9).

[4]Cf. Meir Sternberg, who views a narrative text "as a functional structure, a means to a communicative end, a transaction between the narrator and the audience on whom he wishes to produce a certain effect by way of certain strategies." *The Poetics of Biblical Narrative* (Bloomington, IN: Indiana University Press, 1987), 1.

FROM TEXT TO READER

This question is to be distinguished from a more formalist approach, the "narrative criticism" described in the previous chapter studies, which often seeks chiefly to describe the settings, characters, plot, and structure of a narrative;[5] as I pointed out in Chapter 1, this type of analysis can result in the interpreter approaching the text as an object, with "critical distance" (in this case, literary-critical) as important as in more traditionally historical methodologies; here I wish to develop this point further.

Jack Kingsbury's *Conflict in Mark: Jesus, Authorities, Disciples*[6] provides an excellent example of this approach, especially germane because of its focus on conflict in Mark's Gospel. Kingsbury's goal in this study is to trace and interpret the three principal story lines in the Gospel: Jesus, the religious authorities, and the disciples.[7] The focus is thus on character as it relates to and is developed through plot—classic formalist concerns.

Kingsbury delivers an often insightful but ultimately unsatisfying reading of these story lines; in the process, he displays the fundamental weakness of a strictly formalist approach. Careful descriptions of the various characters and character groups emerge from his analysis—the "traits" they possess, and how the author reveals them through their actions.[8] For example, Jesus displays the "root trait" of being "uniquely related" to God; from this flow other traits developed in the story: Jesus is authoritative, whole, possesses integrity, is faithful, compassionate, confrontational, self-giving.[9]

---

[5]See, e.g., Jack Kingsbury, *Conflict in Mark: Jesus, Authorities, Disciples* (Minneapolis: Fortress Press, 1989); David Rhoads and Donald Michie, *Mark as Story: An Introduction to the Narrative of a Gospel* (Philadelphia: Fortress Press, 1982); Mark Allan Powell, *What is Narrative Criticism?* (Minneapolis: Fortress Press, 1990). The latter two works do include a section on "rhetoric," but the predominant concern lies in analyzing events, characters, and settings in the story.

[6]See previous note.

[7]Kingsbury, vii.

[8]Like most biblical narrative, Mark reveals character traits more by "showing" than "telling;" see, for example, Robert Alter, *The Art of Biblical Narrative* (New York: Basic Books, Inc., 1981), 114-25.

[9]Kingsbury, 4-8.

The disciples manifest conflicting traits: they are both "loyal" and "uncomprehending;"[10] the religious authorities are hypocritical, conspiratorial, deceitful, envious, and blasphemous.[11]

While these descriptions certainly hold true, as does much of Kingsbury's interpretation of how Mark's plot reveals them, the end result is unsatisfying. For Kingsbury rarely moves beyond mere description to address the real point of the things he observes in the text: How are these characterizations designed to move the reader to a new level of understanding of and a new mode of being in relation to Jesus and God? The focus on "the world of the story" so characteristic of narrative criticism often treats that world as an entity unto itself. Here Stephen Moore's observation concerning narrative-critical approaches to the Gospel narratives is relevant: they have tended to focus on the story, the "what" of the narrative, and pay less attention to the discourse or rhetoric, the "how."[12] According to Moore, only with attention to the latter does an interpreter have access to the core of a narrative, its poetics. Moreover, the distinction between the "what" and the "how" is misleading as narrative critics apply it, for "[i]f story is to be understood strictly as the 'what' of the narrative, and rhetoric as 'how' that story is told, then everything in the narrative (which is all a 'telling,' after all) is rhetorical."[13] This attempt to "abstract the story (plot, character, etc.) from the narrator's discourse that mediates it"[14] precludes a full accounting of that discourse; and it is precisely in the discourse that the narrative's ideological point of view—for Mark, its "theology" or "christology"—through which he is trying to influence the reader, is to be found. It is a narrative's poetics that reach out from the "story world" and attempt to mold and shape the reader. As Lynn Poland has put it,

---

[10]Kingsbury, 13.

[11]Kingsbury, 18-19.

[12] *Literary Criticism*, 60-62. Powell's *What is Narrative Criticism?* moves toward a recognition of this problem; he observes, for example, that "[s]imply to consider events as the content of a narrative or as definitive of what we have called the story is not enough. One must also consider the 'story-as-discoursed,' the manner in which the events are presented by the implied author" (35).

[13]Moore, 60.

[14]Moore, 63.

The central difficulty [with a formalist approach] is that the centripetal focus of New Critical theory—its stress on the autonomy, self-sufficiency, and objectivity of the literary work of art—tends to prevent literature from exercising those cognitive and thus transformative powers which this theory also wishes to claim for it.[15]

To be sure, narrative criticism sets itself off from source, form, and redaction criticism in its conviction that an interpreter's primary orientation ought to be toward "what is written" rather than "what is written about."[16] The charge so often leveled by literary critics against historical criticism, that it commits a "referential fallacy" by attempting to peer *through* the text into the events or ideas which lie behind it contains much truth.[17] As Hans Frei has pointed out, much is lost if the ultimate goal of interpretation lies in reconstructing historical events or distilling discursive ideas from the story; such concerns eclipse the narrative itself.[18] But this observation is misleading if it results in a reading which gets stuck on the story level, and sees it as merely self-referring, a mirror reflecting back on itself whose image can be examined at some distance. I would argue that Mark's Gospel *is* referential, in at least two ways: its discourse is attempting to shape a real flesh and blood reader, who will always remain "outside of," but addressed by the text; the concern here is for the world "in front of the text," as it is often termed, for what happens to the reader who engages Mark's Gospel.[19] Second, the text's discourse is in service of a reality which is not contained by the world of Mark's text, viz., the reality of God. This latter referent can be more specifically defined as the reality of the God manifested in Israel's scriptures; Mark's story remains incomprehensible apart

---

[15]Lynn Poland, *Literary Criticism and Biblical Hermeneutics*, (AARAS 48; Chico, CA: Scholars Press, 1985), 159.

[16]See Frank Kermode, *The Genesis of Secrecy: On the Interpretation of Narrative* (Cambridge, MA: Harvard University Press, 1979), 18-19.

[17]See, for example, Norman Petersen, *Literary Criticism for New Testament Critics* (Philadelphia: Fortress Press, 1978), 39-40.

[18]See Hans Frei, *The Eclipse of Biblical Narrative: A Study in Eighteenth and Nineteenth Century Hermeneutics* (New Haven: Yale University Press, 1974).

[19]See, e.g., Donald Juel, *A Master of Surprise: Mark Interpreted* (Minneapolis: Augsburg Fortress, 1994), 11-30.

from this referent, and it provides the framework for the underlying unity of the three principal conflicts, as I will argue below.

For these reasons, narrative criticism as practiced has not put itself in a position either to address adequately a Gospel's theology as it emerges from the discourse, or to interpret and evaluate the claims of the narrative on its readers. For literary criticism to be of service to New Testament theology and for proclamation of the gospel, both of these questions must be in the fore. Indeed, as Donald Juel has noted concerning academic biblical interpretation more broadly, "[O]ne of the principal agendas of current interpretive strategies is to keep the reality of God at bay."[20] The problem is how to bring this referent into an interpretive strategy while preserving the narrativity of the text.

At first glance, it may seem that to grant these questions primacy would lead us away from the narrative, back to propositional ideas abstracted from the narrative. However, as Moore rightly points out,

> [o]ne way in which the narrating discourse and the narrated action might be kept to the fore simultaneously is to consistently subordinate one's reading of the gospel to the following type of question: What kind of involvement in the plot does the narrator's discourse elicit at this moment or at that?[21]

The goal of such interpretation should be to prepare an audience for a fruitful encounter with the text, not to reduce the text to a window onto "actual history" or to theological propositions. A fruitful encounter with Mark's Gospel could not take place apart from uncovering the ways in which it seeks to convey the reality of God behind every verse of the text.

READER-RESPONSE CRITICISM AND THE GOSPELS

Thus reader-response criticism, in its attention to the rhetoric or discourse or poetics of a text, will form the principal methodological framework for this study. But some further precision needs to be

---

[20]Juel, 10.
[21]Moore, 63.

given to the terms and concepts utilized by reader-response critics, since there is considerable diversity and disagreement even among those who use this approach, and I will adapt the method for the specific concerns of this study. Two principal questions continue to be debated among critics, and merit further attention here: First, who is the reader or audience in reader-response criticism? Is it the "implied reader" posited by the narrative, the "original" historical audience, present "flesh and blood" readers, or an "ideal reader"? Second, what is the nature of the reading process itself, and of critical interaction with it? These two questions are closely related, and together circumscribe the task of a reader-oriented interpreter.

This theoretical ground has been well mapped out in recent work both outside biblical scholarship and within it; the focus in the following methodological reflections will be on how interpreters of the Gospels, especially Mark, have utilized a reader-oriented approach in interpreting the Gospel. I will highlight the importance of the concept of the "ideal reader" for interpretation, as well as the gap-filling activity characteristic of the reading process.

The Reader in Reader-Response Criticism

It is important for an interpreter to achieve some degree of clarity with respect to the concept of the reader, for how one envisions the reader—whether implied, ideal, or real—will impact greatly the kind of reading that results. As Wolfgang Iser has put it, "It is evident that no theory concerned with literary texts can make much headway without bringing in the reader, who now appears to have been promoted to the new frame of reference whenever the semantic and pragmatic potential of the text comes under scrutiny. The question is, what kind of reader?"[22]

The principal issue involved in any discussion of the nature of the reader is the degree to which he is to be tied to the structures of the text itself. Reader-oriented literary theories range from merely a slight shift in focus within Narrative Criticism (or Formalism in

---

[22]Wolfgang Iser, *The Act of Reading: A Theory of Aesthetic Response* (Baltimore and London: The Johns Hopkins University Press, 1978), 34.

secular literary theory), in which the "reader" is the one implied in the text itself, to radically reader-centered approaches which place a real reader "over" any stability attributed to the text itself. In Gospel scholarship, variations of the former, the reader "in" the text, have proved most influential; more recently, post-structuralist approaches which place the reader over the text have been undertaken appear.[23]

When the discussion is of the reader in the text, interpreters generally refer to the well-known literary adaptation of Roman Jakobson's communication model developed by Seymour Chatman.[24] If a literary text is seen as a communication of a message between a real author (the sender) and a real reader (the receiver), the components of the message can be further broken down, for a literary text does not communicate its message directly, but through the various components that make up the narrative. A real author creates a literary version of himself (the implied author), which he embodies concretely in the narrator of the story; the narrator tells the story to an imaginary hearer (the narratee); the implied reader fits into this model as the mirror image of the implied author: the sum of all those features, values, and competencies which are required to make the cognitive and affective moves along with the text.

Sender ———————>>   **Message** ———————>> **Receiver**
Real —>[*implied author* -> *narrator* -> *narratee* -> *implied reader*]—> **Real**
Author   **Reader**[25]

It is through this complex vehicle that the real author attempts to communicate with a real reader. An author can manipulate the relationship among the various components of the "message" for rhetorical ends. For example, an author can choose to have the narrator be a character in the story whose point of view is at odds

---

[23]Stephen Moore has been perhaps the most ardent proponent of poststructuralist biblical criticism; see *Literary Criticism, 108-70*; *Mark and Luke in Poststructuralist Perspectives: Jesus Begins to Write* (New Haven: Yale University Press, 1992); *Poststructuralism and the New Testament: Derrida and Foucault at the Foot of the Cross* (Minneapolis: Fortress Press, 1994).

[24]*Story and Discourse: Narrative Structure in Fiction and Film* (Ithaca, N.Y.: Cornell University Press, 1978), 151.

[25]Chatman, 151.

with that of the implied author, resulting in tremendous potential for irony. Perhaps the most famous literary example is Twain's *Huckleberry Finn*, in which Huck thinks he is doing something bad in helping the slave Jim go free, and so asks for forgiveness. The implied author's point of view, however, clearly condemns slavery. *Forrest Gump* is another good example; in the book, the author uses the "denseness" of the narrator to induce a wry smile and ironic awareness in the reader at just about every line.[26]

The question for reader-response critics is whether interpretation deals with the implied reader, the one embedded in the text as a part of its rhetorical structure, or with the real reader and her interaction with the text. In recent Gospel scholarship, the former has been the predominant focus. As Stephen Moore points out, reader-response interpretations of the Gospels have involved little more than an extension of narrative criticism's interests in the unfolding plot and in characterization, now, however, viewed from the perspective of a cerebral mirror-image of the implied author.

Several descriptions of the reader in recent works illustrate his point. Richard Edwards, in his introduction to *Matthew's Story of Jesus,* states that "when I speak about the reader I am not attempting to describe a real person . . . but the person posited *by the text* as the reader."[27] Likewise, Rhoads and Michie note that

> the 'reader' we [refer] to is not an actual reader since it is not possible to predict the responses of an actual reader. Rather our reader is a hypothetical 'implied reader,' an imaginary reader with the ideal responses implied or suggested by the narrative. . . . The implied reader is properly an extension of the narrative, a reader that the author creates (by implication) in telling the story.[28]

---

[26]It has become common to note that the distinction between implied author and narrator all but disappears in biblical narrative. But this has its own rhetorical effect: an alignment of point of view among real author, implied author, and narrator lends biblical narrative a sense of omniscience and omnipotence reflective of the ultimate "author" of the story. See Sternberg, *Poetics*, 51-57.

[27]Richard A. Edwards, *Matthew's Story of Jesus* (Philadelphia: Fortress Press, 1985); quoted in Moore, *Literary Criticism*, 99.

[28]Rhoads and Michie, *Mark as Story: An Introduction to the Narrative of a Gospel* (Philadelphia: Fortress Press, 1982), 137.

With such a conception of the reader, the typical reader-response interpretation of a Gospel text casts the critic in the role of "hero," providing a "story of reading" for a text which unfolds how the implied author envisions the implied reader reacting to the various twists and turns in the plot and how he forms judgements about the characters.[29] Moreover, Moore asserts that the reader in most Gospel criticism is a cerebral, "unfeeling" figure—that is, the focus is on the cognitive moves the implied reader must make to "understand" what is happening; ignored is the affective dimension, the reflection of the emotional impact most literary texts seek to exercise on their audience.[30]

Moore attributes this tendency among biblical critics to two factors. First, the strong institutional pull of the critical establishment, which enforces "strict rules of accreditation" in interpretations, limits the full appropriation of secular literary methodology. Despite the new insights offered through literary-critical readings of the Gospels, the individual interpreter is accountable to the guild to such an extent that the interpretive "freedom" granted by attention to real flesh and blood readers as in poststructuralism is severely curtailed. "For biblical studies," he complains, "the moral is plain: criticism is an institution to which real readers need not apply."[31] Reader-oriented approaches to the Gospels are "stunted versions of regular reading that disallow the personal associations that reading invariably sparks [and] that disallow the affective aspects of reading as opposed to its cognitive aspects. . . . Which is simply to say that the reader-

---

[29]Moore, 81-4; 98-106. Moore gives several examples: Robert Tannehill's essay "The Disciples in Mark: The Function of a Narrative Role" (*JR* 57 [1977] 386-405); Resseguie's "Reader-Response Criticism in the Gospels;" Fowler's *Loaves and Fishes: The Function of the Feeding Stories in the Gospel of Mark* (SBLDS 54; Chico, CA: Scholars Press, 1981); J. Bassler's "The Parable of the Loaves" (*JR* 66 [1986] 157-72). He concludes that "By and large, reader-oriented critics of the Gospels have seized on the undifferentiated, prescriptive side of Iser's implied reader—its textually defined, manipulated side—and relegated its individualistic, actual-reader side to the margins" (102).

[30]Moore, *Literary Criticism*, 95-98.

[31]Moore, *Literary Criticism*, 106.

oriented exegete is a *homo institutionis,* just as the more conventional exegete is."[32]

The second factor to which Moore attributes the narrow range of appropriation of reader-oriented approaches is the secular interpretive model on which most of them are based. A particular (and, according to Moore, one-sided) understanding of Wolfgang Iser's concept of the implied reader provides the theoretical background for much reader-oriented exegesis. Iser defines the implied reader as that reader who

> embodies all those predispositions necessary for a literary work to exercise its effect—predispositions laid down, not by an empirical outside reality, but by the text itself. Consequently, the implied reader as a concept has his roots firmly planted in the structure of the text; he is a construct and in no way to be identified with any real reader.[33]

The key aspect of this understanding of the reader, as well as its most potentially confusing point, lies in the second sentence: the implied reader is integrally related to the literary text itself; he is, in effect, the reader projected by the text, with whom a real reader interacts as she would with any of the characters in the story.

In describing the implied reader this way, Iser tries to develop a mediating position between two other conceptions of the reader he finds inadequate: the "real" reader, "known to us by his documented reactions," and the "hypothetical" reader, "upon whom all possible actualizations of the text may be projected."[34] Iser rejects both of these concepts, and specific theories attached to them, because each in its own way attempts to predetermine the character of the reader without regard to the indications in the structure of the text itself.[35]

---

[32]Moore, *Literary Criticism,* 106. Moore makes this argument on the way toward proposing a poststructuralist model for the biblical guild, which, he asserts, is the natural next move for exegetes to make if they can only shed the institutional constraints. He fails to entertain the notion, however, that the hesitancy on the part of biblical interpreters to embrace poststructuralism may be due to its philosophical underpinnings.

[33]*Act of Reading,* 34.

[34]Iser, 27.

[35]Iser, 29-34.

As has been recognized by other critics, both the strength as well as the problem in Iser's theory emerges in his failure to achieve conceptual clarity on the question of the relationship between his implied reader and a real reader engaged with a literary text. Although he acknowledges that, as a phenomenon constructed by the text itself, the implied reader is meant to exercise some constraint in interpretation (as over against a "hypothetical" reader), he also emphasizes that a key component of a text's rhetoric involves leaving gaps in the narrative which a real reader will fill, at least to some degree, in accordance with her "existing stock of experience."[36] Whether one is an atheist or a Christian will color one's reading of a narrative dealing with claims about God, for example. A real reader's real experiences will affect the way a text is encountered.

Moore notes that, while in theory, Iser's concept of the reader allows for the individual appropriation of a text in accord with a reader's location and experience, in practice he—and especially the biblical critics who use him—take it away.[37] But the situation is more complicated than Moore allows; as Jeffrey Staley observes in his study of the implied reader in John, Iser has come under fire both from those who see his conception of the reader as too closely tied to the text, as well as not closely enough:

> Iser's understanding of the implied reader has been seen as ambiguous; a term used to denote both an ostensibly real reader's (but actually an ideal reader's or reader-critic's) moves, the qualities in the text itself which move this reader, and the area "in between" the real reader and the text. Due to this phenomenal fuzziness, Iser has been condemned by sociological critics for positing an "implied reader" who is nothing less than an educated, slightly liberal European; by hermeneuticists like Stanley Fish, for being determined by a false notion of text; and by formalists and rhetorical critics, for being too little tied to the text.[38]

---

[36]Iser, *The Act of Reading*, 284.

[37]Moore,101-102; he makes this point through an examination of James Resseguie's article "Reader-Response Criticism and the Synoptic Gospels" (*JAAR* 52 [1984], 307-324).

[38]Jeffrey Staley, *The Print's First Kiss: A Rhetorical Investigation of the Implied Reader in the Fourth Gospel* SBLDS 82 (Atlanta: Scholars Press, 1988), 32.

While Moore's criticisms of reader-response criticism as appropriated by biblical critics is cogent in many respects, I am not convinced that the only logical alternative remaining is to pursue poststructuralist theory. He may be correct in his assertion that Gospel criticism has remained staunchly author-centered in spite of its move toward reader-oriented approaches; but, perhaps especially in biblical studies, the relationship between text and reader needs to remain in tension. Poststructuralism's rejection of any talk of a text's stability would seem to render interpretation a one-sided affair. It is not so much a matter of "control" as it is a matter of recognizing the capacity of a text, through the structures that emerge from it, to address the reader. While Iser's model has perhaps been implemented without proper attention to the responses of real readers, it does not follow that the model itself needs to be rejected.

Iser's ultimate interest lies not in so precisely distinguishing between implied and real reader, but in describing the *interaction* that takes place between them.[39] His theoretical concern for both poles—structures within the text that provide some constraint on possible readings, as well as those experiences and presuppositions which an individual or community bring to a text—achieves a helpful and realistic balance between them, as we shall see below.

The Reader and the "Authorial Audience"

Before moving to further discussion of Iser's model as it will be developed for this study, one other conception of the reader in the text which has emerged in recent work on Mark's Gospel needs to be addressed. Some interpreters have noted that contemporary literary theories, such as Iser's, have been developed with reference to modern literary forms and conventions, and thus need significant adaption when applied to an ancient text such as Mark's. That is, the implied reader of an ancient text must be explicated in terms of

---

[39]A helpful summary of his views on this interaction is found in his "Interaction between Text and Reader," in S. Suleiman and I. Crosman, eds., *The Reader in the Text: Essays on Audience and Interpretation* (Princeton, NJ: Princeton University Press, 1980), 106-119.

literary conventions and cultural codes contemporary with the
original author's.[40]

The most significant proposal for reading Mark in terms of its
own literary context has come from Mary Ann Tolbert. In Tolbert's
view, an analysis of the text of Mark requires that one work toward
an understanding of the original social and cultural milieu in which
the author wrote; her goal is to "articulate one possible interpretation
of the Gospel in all its parts *in the light of its authorial audience.*"[41]
Mark's simplicity and crudeness lead Tolbert to hypothesize that this
"authorial audience"—that is, the audience which, in the author's
mind, "could be expected to recognize the conventions, to follow the
plot structure, and generally to possess the necessary competencies
to understand the text"[42]—would have been one created and prepared
by Greco-Roman popular culture and popular literature, specifically
the Greco-Roman erotic novel.[43] According to Tolbert, the Gospel of
Mark shares many stylistic, linguistic, and rhetorical features with
these novels:

> Its mixing together of historiographic form and dramatic force, its
> synthesizing of earlier genres such as biography, memorabilia of a sage,
> aretalogy, and apocalypse, its stylistic techniques of episodic plot,
> beginning with minimal introduction, central turning point, and final
> recognition scene, and most of all, its fairly crude, repetitious, and
> conventionalized narrative display striking *stylistic* similarities to the
> popular Greek ancient novel.[44]

---

[40]See, e.g., P. J. Rabinowitz, "Truth in Fiction: A Reexamination of Audience,"
Critical Inquiry 4 (1977), 126; R. Scholes and R. Kellogg, *The Nature of Narrative*
(London: Oxford University Press, 1966), 83-91.

[41]Tolbert, *Sowing the Gospel: Mark's World in Literary-Rhetorical Perspective*
(Minneapolis: Fortress, 1989), 53.

[42]Tolbert, 53.

[43]See 60-64. Two examples of the genre prove especially important for
Tolbert's hypothesis: Chariton's *Chaereas and Callirhoe* and Xenephon's *An
Ephesian Tale.*

[44]Tolbert, 65.

Though she stops short of calling Mark an ancient novel of the erotic type,[45] Tolbert draws on the similarities between Mark and the ancient popular novel to interpret many of Mark's own features—features which have long perplexed modern readers of the Gospel. For example, Mark's repetition of words, scenes, and themes, which have usually either been explained away through generic hypotheses, or utilized in modern interpretations to impart a mysterious aura of "otherness" to Mark's text, is readily explainable in terms of the ancient novel. For one thing, such novels were written for largely illiterate audiences, and so would have been structured for oral recitation.[46]

Thus the most significant competency Mark's authorial audience would be expected to possess, according to Tolbert, is an understanding of Mark's *genre*. She rejects recent proposals for a genre for Mark—e.g., that Mark is to be seen as a "parable"[47]—which do not rely on criteria which the author of Mark's Gospel would have shared with his authorial audience. Such proposals rely instead on "modern" understandings and sensibilities foreign to Mark's conceptual world:

> [T]o describe the genre of Mark as parable is *not* a recognizable historical use of the term. However, "parable" has come to have a metaphorical meaning in current theology for the paradoxical, open-ended, and participatory nature of the Christian message. . . . Indeed, calling the Gospel of Mark a "parable" is thoroughly comprehensible, and perhaps even insightful, to contemporary theologians and students of the Bible who have already come to understand parable as a metaphor for Jesus' message and life. In other words, *Gospel as parable does fit the shared expectations of twentieth-century readers.*[48]

---

[45]65. Tolbert contends that it is enough "to confirm the plausibility of the authorial audience of the Gospel having some previous experience of the ancient novel in any of its types" (66).

[46]See Tolbert, 67, 72.

[47]E.g., Werner Kelber, *The Oral and the Written Gospel: The Hermeneutics of Speaking and Writing in the Synoptic Tradition, Mark, Paul, and Q* (Philadelphia: Fortress Press, 1983), 211-20; see also John Donahue, "Jesus as Parable of God in the Gospel of Mark," *Interpretation* 32 (1978), 369-86.

[48]Tolbert, 57; italics are author's.

While Tolbert admits that concern for the assumptions of a contemporary audience is legitimate in interpretation, her interest lies in reading the Gospel in light of its "authorial audience;" thus she feels free to bracket other proposals for understanding Mark and engage only those which attempt to do the same. Her argument for finding a generic model in the hellenistic popular novel rests on several features shared by Mark's narrative and the few extant popular novels; she finds most helpful two such novels, Chariton's *Chaereas and Callirhoe* and Xenophon's *An Ephesian Tale*. Both can be placed in the first two centuries of the Common Era, and so arguably form part of the cultural milieu of Mark's audience.

Other literary characteristics of ancient popular literature that affect a reading of Mark include the episodic, breathless way in which Mark narrates his story; such a narrative style is found in several of the ancient novels, and again reflects their popular origin. Further, modern interpreters err if they read Mark's verisimilitude in the same way they would understand modern realism; like most ancient literature, Mark's realism is "more stereotypical than typical,"[49] meant only to suggest reality rather than describe it. The use of a central turning point (8:27-30), and final recognition scene (16:1-8) were also conventional. And Tolbert contrasts our modern notion of character development, and the central place character study has in the modern novel, with the ancient practice of utilizing flat, representative characters: "static, monolithic figures who do not grow or develop psychologically."[50]

Two final features of ancient narrative prove especially significant for Tolbert's reading of Mark, and merit some discussion here: the use of plot summaries in the main rhetorical units of a work, and, most important, the more generalized assumption that, inasmuch as Mark wrote to people who shared knowledge of such literary conventions as those above, any opacity or obscurity encountered by modern readers (and utilized for theological or hermeneutical purposes!) results from failure to recognize these features.[51]

---

[49]Tolbert, 74.

[50]Tolbert, 77.

[51]See especially 87-89.

Like ancient novels, the Gospel of Mark, so Tolbert, contains major plot summaries which function to orient the reader in the overall story; they form, in other words, an entrance into the basic hermeneutical circle of the parts and the whole: through these summaries, the audience sees the entire action of story played out, and so can fit individual pieces into that larger framework.[52] Tolbert sees the structure of Mark in two principal rhetorical divisions: The Galilee section (1:14-10:52), and the Jerusalem section (11:1-16:8). Mark has placed plot summaries in key positions in each of these halves; Tolbert finds them in the Parable of the Sower (4:1-34) and the Parable of the Wicked Tenants (12:1-12). The ancient reader would have recognized in their elements guidelines for how everything else in the narrative is to be understood: "The two parables in Mark present in concise, summary form the Gospel's view of Jesus: he is the Sower of the Word and the Heir of the Vineyard. The first emphasizes his task and the second his identity; together they make up the Gospel's basic narrative Christology."[53]

Not only do these parables provide a general hermeneutical framework for the reader; elements in the parables correspond in a more specific way to characters and themes in the larger narrative. For example, the various "soils" on which the sower sows seed correspond to characters in the story and how they respond to Jesus' message: "The instant rejection of Jesus by the scribes and the Pharisees illustrates the first response; the immediate joy but ultimate failure of the disciples, the second; the wealth, too great to give up, of the rich man, the third."[54] She finds the fourth represented by the anonymous characters in the Gospel who, unlike all the rest, respond in faith and are healed.[55]

Obviously, to read the whole of Mark in light of these parables represents a significant hermeneutical move, not only formally, but also materially. That is, the particular way in which one reads and understands the parables will greatly impact one's view of the whole.

---

[52]Tolbert, 121-24.
[53]Tolbert, 122.
[54]Tolbert, 124.
[55]Tolbert, 124.

In the body of my study, I will have occasion to engage in some detail the substance of her reading.

Finally, one of Tolbert's basic contentions is that, when Mark is read in light of the literary conventions exemplified in the ancient popular novel, much of the oft-noted "obscurity" of Mark's narrative style is clarified. The interpreter must attune his or her ears to the conventions of such works, for they represent the shared cultural and literary "code" which Mark would have shared with his original audience. Obscurity and mystery are modern values, she notes, and are the result of reading the Gospel without an understanding of its rhetorical and literary features, which have their roots in ancient popular culture. Her approach "assumes that the Gospel writer intended to communicate something to an audience who had the necessary competencies to understand it."[56] The narrative "as a whole ought to be fairly obvious, straightforward, and repetitious rather than subtle and esoteric."[57]

Perhaps the clearest example of this assertion—and, in terms of interpretive conclusions, the most significant—is Tolbert's reading of Mark's ending. As noted above, one of the central features of Mark's authorial audience was that they understood literature rhetorically; thus, according to Tolbert, the central question the original audience would have brought to Mark's abrupt ending would not have been "What does this mean?", but rather, "What does this ending *do*?"[58] She draws on the work of J. P. Tompkins,[59] who distinguishes the contemporary reader, whose concern is for the meaning of a text, with the ancient reader, for whom "[t]he text as an object of study or contemplation has no importance, . . . for literature is thought of as existing primarily in order to produce results and not as an end in itself. A literary work is not so much an object, therefore, as a unit of force whose power is exerted upon the world in a

---

[56]Tolbert, 88.

[57]Tolbert, 88.

[58]See Tolbert, 45, 295.

[59]Especially his article "The Reader in History: The Changing Shape of Literary Response," in *Reader-Response Criticism: From Formalism to Post-structuralism* (ed. Tompkins; Baltimore: Johns Hopkins University Press, 1980).

particular direction."[60] Thus Mark's ending is "intended to move its hearers to respond, to excite their emotions on behalf of Jesus and the gospel message."[61] That excitement is based on the audience's realization that there is no one left in the story to tell the message. All the disciples, including now the women, who were the characters in whom the audience had placed their last hope for the story to produce the promised fruit of the gospel (4:13-20), had failed. The rhetorical goal of Mark's epilogue, therefore—and indeed of the whole Gospel—is to mold the authorial audience into the "perfect disciple" where the characters have failed.[62] "In the end," Tolbert concludes, "Mark's Gospel purposely leaves each reader or hearer with the urgent and disturbing question: What type of earth am *I*? Will *I* go and tell? Indeed, one's response to the seed sown by the Gospel of Mark reveals in each listener's heart, as did Jesus' earlier preaching, the presence of God's ground or Satan's."[63]

Again, I will have occasion to engage the substance of Tolbert's reading of Mark in subsequent chapters of this study; but her reading of the ending most clearly demonstrates the relationship between her understanding of the reader in interpretive method and the interpretive conclusions she draws. This is important to note at this point, because, though Tolbert's work presents a major and important proposal for understanding Mark, it has problems which render it less than fully useful in my study. There is no question that uncovering literary conventions of ancient works, lost to modern audiences, is crucial to interpretation; who fails to enjoy a Shakespearean play much more after studying its conventions, allusions, idioms, and so forth? Robert Alter's *The Art of Biblical Narrative*,[64] already a classic in literary approaches to the Bible, makes a strong case for the way in which an ancient text can come alive when we understand the aesthetic principles which influenced its creation. But left unaddressed in any explicit terms in her study, and others like it, is the issue of how the genre and the "authorial audience" ought to

---

[60]Tompkins, 204; quoted in Tolbert, 289.

[61]Tolbert, 296.

[62]Tolbert, 297.

[63]Tolbert, 299. These are the closing lines of her interpretation of the Gospel.

[64]New York: Basic Books, 1981.

figure in an interpretation focused on "this side of the text." That is, how does one employ the insights gained from this approach if the goal of interpretation is the preparation of a contemporary audience for a fruitful contemporary hearing of the text—if the goal is what a text *means*? An argument for a particular genre can influence interpretive options or expectations in an overly restrictive way; it can, as Frank Kermode puts it, "prematurely limit the possible sense of the work."[65] In essence, the emphasis on historical genre is an extension of previous historical-critical concerns to elucidate the text primarily in terms of what it *meant* to its original audience.[66] Such a quest is legitimate; but despite protests to the contrary, those engaged in this enterprise still seem to grant a priority to their reconstructions of the Markan context for interpretation.[67] While Tolbert is careful to point out that there is no one "correct" reading of the Gospel, there is an implicit yet unmistakable argument that such a reading geared to the "authorial audience" in fact *does* have normative significance; that is, contemporary audiences should be impressed by and influenced in their reading of the Gospel by a reading which purports to reflect the audience the author had in mind.[68]

The problem lies not with seeking to educate an audience with respect to a text's literary conventions itself, thus creating a better reader of Mark's narrative, something this study is attempting to do as well, but rather in finding an aspect of the text which can link a contemporary audience to it as opposed to highlighting the distance. As I will argue below, such a link exists when one recognizes that

---

[65] *Genesis of Secrecy*, 143.

[66] Form critics, of course, were looking at developments behind the text as it stands. On the "what it meant/what it means" distinction, see K. Stendahl's well-known article, "Biblical Theology, Contemporary," in *The Interpreter's Dictionary of the Bible* (5 vols; ed. G. A. Buttrick; Nashville: Abingdon, 1962), 1.418-32; see also the trenchant critique by B. Ollenburger, "What Krister Stendahl 'Meant'—A Normative Critique of 'Descriptive Biblical Theology,'" *Horizons in Biblical Theology* 8 (1986), 61-98.

[67] See, e.g., Tolbert, 55-57.

[68] As I will show later in this study, the interpretive and theological conclusions resulting from Tolbert's study have profound implications for how Mark is understood by a contemporary audience, conclusions which are in some ways diametrically opposed to those resulting from my reading.

Mark, and indeed all Christian scripture, attempts to address an audience which has been formed in response to the gospel, the message about Jesus Christ. The original audience of Mark's Gospel and a contemporary audience which views it as scripture are, in important ways, joined rather than separated. The contemporary Christian community is in continuity with that community addressed and constituted by the gospel and the Gospels. Both are constituted by the particular story of Jesus, as well as the larger story of Israel to which the story of Jesus forms the concluding and climactic chapter. Indeed, as I will show, only when one views the story of Jesus, and especially the conflicts which characterize the story, in light of that larger story can one feel the full effect of Mark's Gospel.

The Reader as Critic

I have noted that Stephen Moore's critique of reader-oriented Gospel scholarship is well founded, but that it does not necessarily lead to the conclusion that exegesis must turn to poststructuralism. Where Moore does remain extremely helpful, though, is in his concern for the reading experience as experienced by real readers. His observations about the cerebral, "unfeeling" reader of critical scholarship are helpful in that they point to the reality that, especially in Gospel scholarship, the reader is often construed as coextensive with the professional critic, who becomes a crucial mediating link between the text and any "real" reader. As noted above, the most common mode of reader-response criticism has been a sequential unfolding of the plot from a "reader's" perspective, resulting in a story of reading with its own plot. Rather than freeing a real reader up for a fruitful, unmediated engagement with the text, such readings result in limiting a text's possible actualizations and, in some ways, offer up interpretive conclusions that substitute for a first-hand experience of the text. An important methodological presupposition of my study is that the critic's role is to prepare an audience for a fruitful encounter with the text itself; some comments on this issue are appropriate here.

The literary critic who has been most vocal in debunking the professional critic is George Steiner. In his essay "'Critic'/

'Reader'"[69] and, more recently, in his book *Real Presences*,[70] Steiner attacks the critical guild for creating a "secondary city" in which the experience of the arts—literature, music, painting—is held hostage to a group of professionals who offer their interpretations of artistic works as indispensable mediators of the works themselves. The professional critic inserts him- or herself between a work and its audience by professing a "mastery" over the material unavailable to the lay audience in what he calls the "Byzantine dominion of secondary and parasitic discourse over immediacy, of the critical over the creative."[71]

At stake for Steiner is the disappearance of the "real presence" that underlies artistic expression: the experience of the transcendent, of God.[72] The ironic outcome of centuries of secondary discourse on artistic works, according to Steiner, is that "the very methodologies and techniques which would restore to us the presence of the source, of the primary, surround, suffocate that presence with their own autonomous mass. The tree dies under the hungry weight of the vines."[73] One of the principal causes of this situation, so Steiner, is the stance over against the work the critic feels compelled, by the sheer weight of the institutions of which she is apart, to assume. In the essay "'Critic'/'Reader,'" Steiner sets up a stark contrast between the two stances. The critic is characterized by his role as judge and master of the text, while the reader sets herself up as its "servant."[74] The critic's task is to achieve a magisterial pose of critical, object-ifying distance, standing over against the text in ways that Steiner

---

[69]George Steiner, "'Critic'/'Reader,'" *New Literary History* 10 (1979), 423-52.

[70]George Steiner, *Real Presences* (Chicago: University of Chicago Press, 1989).

[71]*Real Presences*, 38.

[72]*Real Presences*, 3: "This essay . . . proposes that any coherent understanding of what language is and how language performs, that any coherent account of the capacity of human speech to communicate meaning and feeling is, in the final analysis, underwritten by the assumption of God's presence. I will put forward the argument that the experience of aesthetic meaning in particular, that of literature, of the arts, of musical form, infers the necessary possibility of this 'real presence.'"

[73]*Real Presences*, 47.

[74]Steiner, "'Critic'/'Reader,'" 449.

describes as "adversative," and "competitive."[75] The reader, by contrast, assumes a more passive stance, allowing herself to become mastered *by* the text, collapsing, to the degree possible, any distance between text and reader.[76]

Most importantly, at the root of the proliferation of secondary discourse is the critic's need to make critical judgments about the text and transmit them to the public as evidence of his mastery over the text; the reader, on the other hand, does neither of these things.

One must admit that it becomes difficult, in the face of a study such this one, not to see oneself simply perpetuating the secondary discourse Steiner would like, in his "fantasy city" of the immediate, to eliminate completely. Indeed, he finds in the production of dissertations a prime example of the victory of the tertiary over the primary![77] While Steiner admits that his dream of completely eradicating secondary discourse is just that, his pronouncements are particularly germane to the study of Scripture. The stance of critical distance to which the guild compels an interpreter is, in fact, inimical to the rhetorical goals of a work like Mark's Gospel. The resulting domestication and secularization of the "mystery and summons"[78] of such a work needs, at the very least, to be acknowledged.

Robert Fowler incorporates Steiner's views helpfully in his discussion of the nature of the reader:

> I see myself striving to be both a reader and a critic of Mark's Gospel: a critical reader. . . To be a critical reader means for me: (1) to affirm the enduring power of the Bible in my culture and in my own life and yet (2) to remain open enough to dare to ask any question and to risk any critical judgment.[79]

---

[75] "'Critic'/'Reader,'" 433, 436.

[76] "'Critic'/'Reader,'" 438-9.

[77]*Real Presences*, 25.

[78]*Real Presences*, 39. When surveying the incredible volume of secondary work on Mark's Gospel, it is easy to conclude with Steiner that "we crave remission from direct encounter with the 'real presence . . . .' In the agency of the critic, reviewer or mandarin commentator, we welcome those who can domesticate, who can secularize the mystery and summons of creation" (39).

[79]Fowler, *Let the Reader Understand*, 30-31.

He recognizes "the prior claim of the text and the preeminence of reading over criticism."[80] Most helpful here is that Fowler is clearly trying to *be* a reader, not just to talk about the phenomenon of reading as a critic. In large measure, he achieves that goal, and his work will provide a helpful source of discussion for this study.

From Critic to Ideal Reader

Significant movement toward the goal of moving the interpreter from attempts at "mastery" of the text to a stance as its servant can be achieved, it seems to me, through focus on two aspects of interpretation. One involves a further refinement of the identity of the reader; the other, attention to the reading process.

One other way of conceptualizing the reader that Gospel critics, especially Fowler, have found helpful is that of the "ideal reader." He is that reader who possesses, as Jonathan Culler puts it, what a reader "must know implicitly in order to read and interpret works in ways which we consider acceptable."[81] This notion suggests that, in order to "realize" a text (see below) to the fullest potential possible, a reader ought to possess certain "competencies"—literary, linguistic, and rhetorical skills. Stanley Fish calls this reader the "informed reader." She is one who "is sufficiently experienced as a reader to have internalized the properties of literary discourses, including everything from the most local of devices (figures of speech, and so on) to whole genres."[82]

Fowler points out that the result of speaking this way about the reader ought to be that the "critic's" role as ideal reader, which he

---

[80]Fowler, 31.

[81]Jonathan Culler, *Structuralist Poetics: Structuralism, Linguistics, and the Study of Literature* (Ithaca, NY: Cornell University Press, 1975), 123-24; see the discussion of the ideal reader in Fowler, *Let the Reader Understand*, 36-40. Fowler points out that Iser rejects the notion of the ideal reader, replacing it with his version of the implied reader (Fowler, 37). That may be so in terms of terminology, but in relation to Iser's understanding of the reading process, the difference is moot; a concern for the reader's capacity to make the moves the text requires is very much at the heart of his understanding of the interaction between text and reader; see below.

[82]Stanley Fish, *Is There a Text in This Class? The Authority of Interpretive Communities* (Cambridge: Harvard University Press, 1980), 48.

assumes in order to address the critical community, is exposed as a fiction.[83] That is, an interpreter, when in discourse with her colleagues in the guild through works of interpretation, does much the same thing as an author of any text: she creates a literary version of herself, and employs rhetorical techniques in order to persuade the community of the value of her critical work.

Another way of understanding the importance of the ideal reader, I would argue, lies not only in convincing the guild to accept one's ideas about a text, but to prepare an audience for a fuller realization of a text in their own reading of it. Indeed, that is what a work such as Fowler's accomplishes; the value of Fowler's work on Mark is that he (very successfully) provides his own readers with competencies which they can then bring to the text in such a way that their own experience of that text is more fruitful. To be attuned to the rhetorical strategies of Mark's Gospel as Fowler unpacks them—how the author uses the narrator for explicit and implicit commentary, his use of indirection, etc.—serves precisely this end. Becoming Steiner's "critic" *par excellence*[84] means not only recognizing the fictive nature of that role, but utilizing it in service of an audience. That is to say, the goal of interpretation ought, in some significant measure, be to aid in the *creation* of ideal readers of a text. My study attempts to do this by focusing on one aspect of Mark's rhetoric.

The Ideal Reader and the Reading Process

A second way of addressing Steiner's concern for the reader's stance over against the literary work is through proper attention to the reading process. As the diagram above (p. 54) showed, the implied reader as conceptualized in Chatman's model lies within the content of the "message" the real author "sends" to the real reader. In other

---

[83]Fowler, *Let the Reader Understand*, 38-9. He is following Fish in this regard.

[84]It may be that Fowler himself misreads Steiner on this; as noted above, Steiner's "fantasy" is for a world without critics, a world in which audiences experience a literary or other artistic work more immediately. The exposure of the fictive nature of the role of critic represents a concession to the reality that this can (and perhaps should) never be. This is not, of course, a criticism of Fowler's work as a whole, which does serve precisely this end.

words, reader-oriented interpretation can simply remain within the realm of the objectivizing interpretations of narrative criticism; an interpreter can offer a reading of a text that is more or less the mirror image of the implied author. Indeed, as Stephen Moore has pointed out, much reader-oriented criticism in Gospel scholarship has done just that.[85] My interest lies not simply in the reader embedded in the text, but in how a real reader interacts with the textual structures that create the implied reader.

It is at this point that Iser's phenomenological understanding of the reading process becomes helpful. For Iser, a literary work's very existence emerges precisely in this interaction between text and reader. Despite what some critics have called his conceptual "fuzziness,"[86] Iser's understanding of the reader and reading process remains one of the most helpful, precisely because, in theory, at least, it accords a proper role to both text and reader. Simply to provide a story of reading, summarizing the implied reader's moves in response to the implied author, keeps the text at a distance. Conversely, allowing the individual reader or a community to impose a reading on a text without regard to any of the implied author's "intentions" does not allow the interpreter to be addressed by the text, and thus is an equally one-sided affair, though in the opposite direction.

Iser's understanding turns on how a work of art or literature comes to life through the interaction between the poles of the work and the reader.[87] As Iser puts it,

> the literary work has two poles, which we might call the artistic and the aesthetic: the artistic pole is the author's text, and the aesthetic is the realization accomplished by the reader. In view of this polarity, it is clear that the work itself cannot be identical with the text or with its

---

[85]This is the basic thesis of his chapter on reader-response criticism; *Literary Criticism*, 71-107; he asserts, e.g., that "reader-response criticism in gospel studies is largely an extension of narrative criticism, and both remain close to author-oriented redaction criticism. . . . A preoccupation with the unfolding plot of a gospel marks a substantial overlap between reader-response and narrative criticism in the New Testament context" (73).

[86]See, e.g., Susan Suleiman, "Introduction," in Suleiman, *The Reader in the Text*, 23-25; Staley, *The Print's First Kiss*, 32.

[87]Iser's views on this interaction are helpfully summarized in his essay "Interaction between Text and Reader," in Suleiman, *The Reader in the Text*, 105-121.

actualization but must be situated somewhere between the two. . . . [I]t cannot be reduced to the reality of the text or to the subjectivity of the reader, and it is from this virtuality that it derives its dynamism. As the reader passes through the various perspectives offered by the text, and relates the different views and patterns to one another, he sets the work in motion, and so sets himself in motion, too.[88]

As Iser himself admits, it is difficult to describe this interaction; it is far easier to analyze the two poles of the communication process separately—the text alone or the reader (in, for example, her psychological or social location) alone.[89] But, for all its conceptual difficulties, it is this idea of a "dynamism," a two-way flow of information, that makes Iser's model helpful and appropriate for reading in such a way that one becomes servant rather than master of a text.[90] Iser's model suggests that a certain disposition on the part of the reader is called for in order to bring a work into being; in a sense, the reader needs to place herself at the "mercy" of the implied author by identifying, to the degree possible, with the embedded implied reader. In describing Iser's understanding of the interaction between text and reader, Raman Selden observes that

the reader's existing consciousness will have to make certain internal adjustments in order to receive and process the alien viewpoints which the text presents as reading takes place. This situation produces the possibility that the reader's own "world-view" may be modified as a result of internalizing, negotiating and realizing the partially indeterminate elements of the text.[91]

Selden's remark helps delineate the two aspects of Iser's understanding of the reading process which are especially key, and do admit of some conceptual clarity. First, that the reader must internalize and negotiate "indeterminate elements" of the text brings

---

[88]Iser, "Interaction between Text and Reader," 106.

[89]"Interaction between Text and Reader," 107.

[90]The affinities with Husserl's phenomenological hermeneutics, especially as developed by Heidegger and Gadamer, are evident, though not often drawn out. See Anthony Thiselton, *The Two Horizons : New Testament Hermeneutics and Philosophical Description* (Grand Rapids, MI : Eerdmans, 1980).

[91]Raman Selden, *A Reader's Guide to Contemporary Literary Theory* (Lexington, KY: The University Press of Kentucky, 1989), 121.

to the fore Iser's notion that the process of literary communication involves the reader's filling in gaps left in the text; and second, that this gap-filling takes place in a linear, temporal sequence ("as reading takes place").

Reading as Gap-Filling

All reading involves, to some degree, the filling of gaps or blanks, large and small, left by a literary work. It is precisely this gap-filling activity on the part of the reader that draws her into the reading process; it "calls me out of myself," as Robert Alter has put it.[92] The necessity to fill gaps as one reads engages both a reader's cognitive and affective sensibilities and compels him to bring something of himself to the text; that which he brings is, in turn, shaped by the various structures, points of view, characterizations, etc., within the text itself. Meir Sternberg, a critic who also focuses much attention on the reading process, puts it well:

> To understand a literary work, we have to answer, in the course of reading, a series of such questions as: What is happening or has happened, and why? What connects the present event or situation to what went before, and how do both relate to what will probably come after? What are the features, motives, or designs of this or that character? How does he view his fellow characters? And what norms govern the existence and conduct of all?[93]

But the real "drama of reading" emerges from the reality that, as Sternberg continues,

> a closer look at the text will reveal how few of the answers to these questions have been explicitly provided there: it is the reader himself who has supplied them, some temporarily, partially, or tentatively, and some wholly and finally. . . From the viewpoint of what is directly given in the language, the literary work consists of bits and fragments to be linked and pieced together in the process of reading: it establishes a system of gaps that must be filled in.[94]

---

[92] *The World of Biblical Literature*, 9.
[93] Sternberg, *The Poetics of Biblical Narrative*, 186.
[94] Sternberg, 186.

The rhetorical power of gaps, their capacity to pull an audience in, is understood well by what is unquestionably the most rhetorical of media: advertising. Beer commercials, for example, often display beautiful people doing fascinating things while singers extol the virtues of the beer; the viewer is invited or even compelled to fill in the gap by inferring a cause and effect relationship between the beautiful people and the beer.

The interaction between text and reader is perhaps best considered in light of what each brings to this gap-filling activity. The real reader will bring to the text both his literary competencies and his lived experiences, all of which can influence how a particular gap is filled in the reading process. The ideal reader will bring a knowledge of literary conventions, rhetorical techniques, and, if necessary, linguistic and historical knowledge to a text. On the other hand, a real reader will bring his "stock of experience" which will, to some degree, affect his response to the work. With respect to biblical narrative, for example, a reader may bring to a story such as Mark's simply an awareness of first-century literary conventions which will aid in following the text's rhetorical moves; but if he also brings an experience of the things Mark's Gospel addresses—the reality of God, suffering, failure, etc.—the reading experience will be significantly different.

The varieties of competencies and experiences among real readers is, not surprisingly, the most significant factor in the production of different readings of a text. An example from Mark's Gospel will illustrate this well. One of the most well-known and controversial gaps is the hole left at the end of Mark's narrative: What has happened to the disciples? Does Jesus meet them in Galilee? Will they be reconciled to Jesus? Or have they failed utterly and hopelessly?[95] Two diametrically opposed fillings of this gap exist in contemporary Markan scholarship; one, represented by Mary Ann Tolbert (see above), involves filling the gap with the assertion that

---

[95]Of course, whether Mark actually ends with 16:8 has long been debated, and ancient attempts to fill this gap by narrating a reconciliation between Jesus and the disciples are generally included in modern editions of the Gospel (the "shorter" and "longer" endings). For a discussion of the textual difficulties surrounding the ending of Mark, see Juel, *Master of Surprise*, 107-10.

Mark has been using his narrative to prepare the "good soil" that all those associated with Jesus failed to be—i.e., in the audience of the Gospel.[96] Her reading calls for the audience to bear the flame none of the characters in the story was able to. As noted above, she arrived at this reading through attuning herself to Mark's first-century rhetorical milieu, in which texts invite a response involving action, not just a contemplation of meaning.

In contrast, this gap has been filled by others such as Andrew Lincoln and Donald Juel in such a way that a reconciliation between Jesus and the disciples is indeed presupposed;[97] the resulting experience of reading is quite different. For Lincoln, the final two verses of Mark's Gospel (16:7-8) represent the final instance of a pattern found throughout Mark's Gospel of human failure in the light of God's promises. It is, he says, certainly an austere ending, but one meant to provide encouragement:

> If, as disciples, the readers fail to stand up to the rigors of the way of the cross set out in the story, all is not necessarily lost. Christ's powerful word of promise will still prevail. . . . Mark's story allows for human failure even after the resurrection yet holds out the triumph of God's purposes despite this.[98]

Likewise, Juel maintains that Mark's ending is not about closing off possibilities (i.e., that the disciples were doomed), but rather of opening them up; the empty tomb forbids such closure—indeed any real closure at all:

---

[96]Tolbert, 297-299; see the discussion above. Variations of this view are also espoused by Thomas Boomershine, "Mark 16:8 and the Apostolic Commission," *JBL* 100 (1981), 225-39; Rhoads and Michie, *Mark as Story*, 61-62; and Pheme Perkins, *Resurrection* (London: Geoffrey Chapman, 1984), 121-22.

[97]Andrew Lincoln, "The Promise and the Failure—Mark 16:7,8," *JBL* 108 (1989), 283-300; Donald Juel, *Master of Surprise*, 107-21. The principal support for this presupposition is knowledge the reader of the Gospel would have gained from Chapter 13, in which the disciples are addressed in light of a future that, given the certainty of Jesus' promises and predictions in the Gospel, will certainly come about.

[98]Lincoln, 297; he also says that "[t]he importance of the command [to the women at the tomb] is the promise it contains and its fulfillment, not its obligation upon the reader to do the actual task the women failed to do" (297, n. 36).

Jesus is out, on the loose, on the same side of the door as the women and the readers. The story cannot contain the promises. Its massive investment in the reliability of Jesus' words becomes a down payment on a genuine future. . . . There will be enlightenment and speaking; the disciples will somehow play the role for which they have been chosen..[99]

It would be difficult to account fully for these diametrically opposing readings, I would argue, without delving into the theological presuppositions and life experiences of the interpreters (something I am not prepared to do in this context!). But on the other hand, this is not to go so far as to say that the text itself has offered nothing to these readings, that these interpreters have simply looked into a mirror. Each of these interpreters presents his or her argument in the form of Steiner's "critic" and Fowler's ideal reader: through textual argument, through demonstrating a mastery over the interpretive techniques developed by the community of interpreters. This presupposes that, though different, even opposing realizations of a text are possible, the text itself lays out in its structure some guides as to how it should best be read; at the very least, a text provides constraints on what readings are *plausible*. To return to Iser's model, the reader is not put into a position over the text, such that what a reader brings to a text essentially determines its meaning; rather, as Iser puts it,

> if communication between text and reader is to be successful, clearly the reader's activity must also be controlled in some way by the text. . . . Communication in literature . . . is a process set in motion and regulated . . . by a mutually restrictive and magnifying interaction between the explicit and the implicit, between revelation and concealment. What is concealed spurs the reader into action, but this action is also controlled by what is revealed; the explicit in its turn is transformed when the implicit has been brought to light.[100]

---

[99]Juel, 120.

[100]Iser, "Interaction," 110-111. See also Sternberg, who observes that "[t]o emphasize the active role played by the reader in constructing the world of a literary work is by no means to imply that gap-filling is an arbitrary process. On the contrary, in this as in other operations of reading, literature is remarkable for its powers of control and validation. . . . [T]o gain cogency, a hypothesis must be legitimated by the text" (*Poetics*, 188).

That is, as a reader moves through a text, what she has "learned" through what has been explicitly stated lays out possibilities for how any particular gap might be filled; how that gap is filled, in turn, colors the view of the explicitly stated, both retrospectively and in anticipation.[101]

Again, an example from Mark's Gospel will illustrate the point. The Gospel is notorious for its indeterminacy, for how much and how often it relies on the reader to fill in a blank between two events or scenes.[102] As suggested in the previous chapter, most of Mark's gaps have been explained away through generic theories which see them as evidence of Mark's composite nature. While such explanations reflect some truth about the way in which Mark's composition came into being, they cannot be said to aid in the actual reading of the narrative.[103] One need not argue that all of Mark's gaps are "intentional" literary devices any more than one need assert that for modern literature; the fact is, though, Mark's narrative does require that a reader fill in blanks as he reads or hears it, especially a reader not indoctrinated into the historical-critical view of Mark's composite nature. And it is clear that Mark's text does provide indications as to how these gaps might be filled in a way consistent with the overall point of view of the implied author. Perhaps the best example of such a gap is the centurion's response to Jesus' death on the cross: Mark leaves it entirely to the reader to discern the connection between Jesus' final, unintelligible cry of agony from the cross and the

---

[101]Of course, understanding the explicit involves taking into account the source of the information: the narrator (who may exist in varying relations to the implied author), a character, or some other means. This play of perspectives requires a constant sifting of information and disposition in order to arrive at a particular understanding of a text. See Iser, "Interaction," 113-20.

[102]There is the question of to what extent Mark's gaps are genuine literary devices, as Iser understands them in reference to modern literature, or simply the result of the composite nature of Mark's Gospel. Iser apparently does not concern himself with ancient literature, especially epic and allegory, precisely because it lacks this quality of structured gaps. Sternberg, too, has reservations about New Testament narrative, though finds the strategic gap to be a primary feature of Hebrew narrative.

[103]Heikki Räisänen's *The 'Messianic Secret' in Mark's Gospel* (tr. Christopher Tuckett; Edinburgh: T & T Clark, 1990) is the most recent work to challenge the notion that Mark's Gospel can be read from any other perspective than a historical-critical one.

centurion's confession that "Truly this man was God's Son!" (15:39).[104] Anyone who has ever taught this pericope to students is no doubt aware of how urgent is the desire to fill this gap with some obvious occurrence in the story-world that would evoke such a confession from the centurion: He must have seen the temple curtain tearing; he knew that Jesus would be raised, etc. Indeed, Matthew, one of Mark's first readers, succumbed to this impulse and inserted miraculous signs to accompany Jesus' death (Matthew 27:51-53). However, the reader who has placed himself at the mercy of Mark's poetics throughout the narrative is in a position to fill that gap in accord with the point of view of the implied author. From 8:27 on, Mark has attempted through various means to correlate Jesus' identity as the Christ to his destiny on the cross. Clearly he antici- pates resistance to this idea, as reflected especially in the disciples, but also in the mockers at the cross; what a reader has learned through the narrative up to this point ought to point him toward filling this gap with precisely this correlation between Jesus' identity and destiny. Though he is free to reject this point of view in terms of his ultimate real-life assessment of Jesus, the text does provide some constraints on how the gap should be filled.

The Temporal Experience of Reading and Meaning as Event

Two final and closely related methodological observations will guide the reading of Mark presented in this study. The preceding discussion has adumbrated the first of these; inasmuch as the gap- filling activity characteristic of the reading experience is influenced in any specific instance by what has come before (e.g., the example of the centurion at the cross), it is clear that reading is a temporal phenomenon. That is, as our reading progresses through time and we gain further information about events and characters and develop

---

[104]As is often noted, Matthew, as one of the first textual readers of Mark, felt the need to fill the gap with the visible apocalyptic signs which accompany Jesus' death in his telling of it, thus rendering the centurion's response much less ambiguous. But filling the gap in this way significantly alters the picture the reader forms of the significance of Jesus' death.

feelings toward and judgments about them, our perception of the text shifts accordingly.

Stanley Fish was one of the first critics to highlight the temporal aspect of reading, followed by Wolfgang Iser and others.[105] In his close readings of literary texts, Fish asserts that the interpreter's task is to ask what each component of a text—a word, phrase, sentence, paragraph, etc.—*does*, and then to analyze "the developing responses of the reader in relation to the words as they succeed one another in time."[106] Iser speaks of the "wandering viewpoint," observing that the whole of a literary work can never be grasped at any one time; in contrast to a subject-object model, in which the observing subject can perceive the whole of an observed object (a chair or a cat), the relationship between a reader and the text is characterized by "a moving viewpoint which travels along *inside* that which it has to apprehend."[107]

As Robert Fowler has put it, the temporal experience of reading can be summarized by speaking of the experience of "looking forward and looking back": [A]s we read we are constantly looking back and re-visioning what we have already read, while at the same time looking forward in anticipation of what might lie ahead. We re-view and pre-view constantly to make as much sense of our experience as possible at each individual moment.[108] Echoing Iser, Fowler continues by noting that "[t]his obviously visual metaphor invites us to consider how our view of the whole literary work changes ceaselessly, as we proceed step by step on our way through the reading experience."[109]

Two important implications follow from the temporal nature of the reading experience. The first regards the relationship between text and reader. Reader-oriented exegesis distinguishes itself from other models of interpretation, especially traditional historical-critical ones but also from narrative criticism, by its assertion that a literary work

---

[105]See Fish's *Is There a Text in This Class?*, a collection of his major essays from 1970-1980; Iser, *The Act of Reading*, 108-118.

[106]Fish, 26-27.

[107]Iser, *The Act of Reading*, 108-109.

[108]Fowler, *Let the Reader Understand*, 45.

[109]Fowler, *Let the Reader Understand*, 45.

emerges in the temporal process of reading itself. To return to Steiner's observations, the acknowledgment that the literary work can never be grasped in its entirety by the reader suggests that no reader can ever be the "master" of it in the sense that he can convey to an audience in discursive language the experience of an encounter with the text itself. To restate the central ideas of a text, to note themes and analyze the plot—none of these things can encompass or substitute for an immediate engagement with the text.

This is especially important for a text such as Mark's Gospel; simply to reiterate Mark's major christological themes—that he sees Jesus' messiahship constituted by his suffering, for example—circumvents an experience with the rhetoric by which Mark makes this point. Mark's rhetorical goal is a challenging one, to say the least. More than the other Gospels, he has chosen to rub the "scandal of the cross" in readers' faces, so to speak; there is no evasion of the cross and its radical challenge to human conceptions of power and of the nature and purposes of God. But the form in which Mark makes this argument is not simply a dispensable container; the Gospel begs to be read or heard, in order that it can pull the reader out of himself, compel him to sift through the various points of view offered in the story, fill the gaps in ways which make sense of it, and experience the conflict between "the things of God" and "the things of human beings" (8:33).

The second implication is closely related to this, and indeed implicit in what has been said. The meaning of a literary work can no longer be described solely in terms of its content, but needs to take into account this dynamic, temporal nature of the reading process. Robert Fowler's discussion of this aspect of reader-oriented exegesis is especially helpful and insightful.[110] I will only highlight some of the main features of this discussion here.

The shift from focusing on the text as a static container from which meaning is to be siphoned off to concentrating on the dynamic nature of the engagement of reader with text means that "we must speak not of the meaning of the text per se but of the meaning of the

---

[110]See Fowler, *Let the Reader Understand*, 47-58.

reading experience, and in dynamic, temporal terms."[111] He develops this idea in relation to three different models of language and communication. First, he notes the speech act theory of J. L. Austin and John Searle,[112] which stresses the performative nature of language; that is, language does not simply denote or connote, but has the capacity to effect something. The "I do" of the wedding ceremony is oft-cited example; it is an utterance which effects a change in reality for the person saying it. One could also point to certain understandings of the Eucharist (e.g., Lutheran), in which the words "the body and blood of Christ shed and broken for you" effect a change in the communicant's reality.

Second, Fowler points to the emerging realization that there is a distinction between oral and written language—indeed, between oral and literate cultures.[113] He relies here on the studies of Walter Ong[114] and, in relation to Mark's Gospel, Werner Kelber.[115] The most important difference between oral and literate cultures, according to Ong, is that for an oral culture, language is inherently rhetorical; speech was viewed as a means of power, not as a static denoter of meaning. In such a context, a speaker or a written work designed for recitation and aural reception will shape the presentation in such a

---

[111]Fowler, 47.

[112]J. L. Austin, *How to do Things with Words* (Oxford: Oxford University Press, 1962); John R. Searle, *Speech Acts: An Essay in the Philosophy of Language* (Cambridge: Cambridge University Press, 1969).

[113]Fowler, 48-52; Stephen Moore also highlights the orality-literacy distinction in his discussion of reader-response criticism (*Literary Criticism*, 84-88). See also Tolbert, *Sowing the Gospel*, 41-46. A helpful entry into the discussion is found in John Miles Foley, *Oral-Formulaic Theory and Research: An Introduction and Annotated Bibliography* (New York: Garland Press, 1985). My study will not explicitly emphasize these insights, but rather is informed by the general implications for understanding Mark's narrative raised by them.

[114] Walter Ong, *The Gutenberg Galaxy: The Making of Typographic Man* (Toronto: University of Toronto Press, 1962); and *Understanding Media: The Extensions of Man* (New York: McGraw-Hill, 1964).

[115]Werner H. Kelber, *The Oral and the Written Gospel*. See, however, the critique of Kelber in Tolbert, *Sowing the Gospel*, 44, n. 36. She rightly points out that what Kelber sees as a radical shift in meaning from the oral tradition which Mark inherited and the Gospel he wrote does not accurately reflect the observation that, inasmuch as Mark's cultural milieu itself was an oral one, he would have composed his text with aural reception and oral recitation in mind.

way that aural reception of the message is enhanced: i.e., through repetition of words, phrases, scenes, motifs, through the use of simple, easily graspable language, and so on.[116]

As Stephen Moore points out, the affinity between reader-oriented exegesis in its temporal understanding of the reading experience and the nature of literature in an oral culture is strong. Most of the methods associated with the historical-critical paradigm require that all of the words of a text be present at one time; redaction-critical analysis, for example, combs a text for precise appearances of particular words and phrases. Spoken words, on the other hand, "are events, not things: they are never present all at once but occur seriatim, syllable-after-syllable."[117]

Finally, Fowler follows the developments beyond and refinements of Roman Jakobson's basic communication model (see above, p. 54); Paul Hernadi's "Compass for Critics"[118] overlays Jakobson's Sender—Message—Receiver model with an axis which distinguishes between focus on the communication between sender and receiver and attention to the message itself. The latter, vertical axis he calls the "mimetic axis of representation." It is comprised of the literary work itself, which he breaks down into the language and verbal signs which comprise it, and the represented world and information to which it refers. Fowler observes that most historical-critical and even modern literary-critical approaches focus their attention here, with historical-critics especially interested in the information gleaned from the work (e.g., Mark's christological ideas or historical situa-tion). The former axis represents the "rhetorical axis of communication,"

---

[116]I do not agree, however, that attention to the oral nature of a text such as Mark's rules out concern for the form of the narrative (against Fowler, 51, and Moore, *Literary Criticism*, 86). It is possible to grasp form in aural reception, as form critics long have observed, and as any attentive listener to a well-formed symphony can attest. Though she perhaps stresses rhetorical structure to a greater degree than desirable, Tolbert is closer when she emphasizes that one needs to consider the oral milieu when attempting to discern the formal features of an ancient text.

[117]Moore, *Literary Criticism*, 86, quoting Ong, "Text as Interpretation: Mark and After," *Semeia* 39 (1987), 22.

[118]Paul Hernadi, "Literary Theory: A Compass for Critics," *Critical Inquiry* 3 (1976), 369-86; see Fowler, 54-58.

i.e., the means by which the sender/author makes his appeal to the receiver/reader.

In line with his previous observations concerning the performative nature of language as especially characteristic of ancient cultures, Fowler asserts that "the language of Mark's Gospel functions primarily along the rhetorical axis, with an emphasis on the pole of the reader and its associated pragmatic or conative function, and that we would do well to orient our criticism of Mark accordingly."[119] Doing so, according to Fowler, means paying attention not so much to what is written on the surface of Mark's text, or to that to which it ostensibly refers, but to the features of Mark's rhetoric, his appeal to his audience. How does Mark seek to engage the reader/hearer of his narrative? What rhetorical techniques does he employ that affect the reading experience? Fowler summarizes it very well:

> We could say that the Gospel is not so much designed to construct its own world as it is designed to construct its own reader; it is not designed so much to say something about its implied world as it is to do something to its implied reader; the narrative does not strive to convey meaning as referential content as much as it strives to achieve communion with its audience by means of a forceful even that takes place through time.[120]

From this starting point, Fowler proceeds to explore Mark's rhetorical devices, to explicate the rhetorical axis of the communication between author and reader. His work seeks to be a fairly exhaustive catalogue of Mark's rhetorical repertoire, moving from explicit and implicit commentary by the narrator,[121] through Mark's "rhetoric of indirection,"[122] especially his use of irony, to what he terms Mark's "moves of greater uncertainty,"[123] such as ambiguity

---

[119]Fowler, 57.

[120]Fowler, 57. Fowler notes that, in reality, even in their overt concern for the Gospel's "content," interpreters have been impacted by Mark's discourse in their engagement with the text; he sees this as a testimony to the power of that rhetoric (see 57 and 14-26).

[121]Fowler, 81-145.

[122]Fowler, 155-194.

[123]Fowler, 195-227.

and opacity. His insights throughout are extremely valuable, and reference will be made to them as appropriate in the rest of this study.

READER-RESPONSE CRITICISM AND THE CONFLICTS IN MARK: CONCLUSIONS

We are in a position now to begin to apply some of the preceding methodological reflections to this study of conflict in Mark. Fowler's work is important because it provides a "catalog" of Mark's principal rhetorical devices. I have attempted to argue that Fowler and others have demonstrated the fruitfulness of a particular understanding of reader-response criticism for both the literary and theological questions which emerge from Mark's Gospel; my goal in this study is to direct these methodological insights to the question of the rhetorical function of the three principal conflicts in the narrative. As I see it, an audience-oriented reading of Mark involves a particular understanding of the role of the interpreter and of the reading process. My understanding of the role of the interpreter is informed by reader-response criticism's focus on the way in which a work comes to life in the interaction between text and reader. My goal is to perform that role in such a way that what I bring to the text as a "professional" reader is placed in service of the text and its intended or potential audience; that is, though I do approach the text as a critic, my stance over against the text is that of a critical reader, one who is self-conscious about what he brings to the text, as well as intentional in placing himself in a position to be impacted by its rhetorical goals (cf. Steiner). The ultimate aim of such an approach is to bring the reader of my reading a bit closer to the "ideal" reader, and thus to enhance a direct engagement with Mark's text. That is, the goal of the critic is to show how an identification between the implied reader and real readers is invited by the rhetoric of the work in order to make agreement with/acceptance of the implied author's values and beliefs a genuine possibility for a real reader.[124]

I have rejected views of the reader which leave him embedded in the text, with or without concern for the historical conditionedness

---

[124]See Suleiman, "Introduction," 9.

of the construct. Likewise, I have found models which place the reader over the text to be inadequate to let the text have its way with the reader. My concern is for an audience composed of readers who turn to Mark's Gospel to hear good news, who understand themselves as part of the community addressed and constituted by that good news, and see themselves as participating in the larger story of God's dealings with humanity and creation to which Mark's Gospel is bound. Such a reader comes to the text with certain competencies, but may also need to have them enriched through the interpretive enterprise.

I have chosen to focus on the reading process as opposed to the story itself; doing so highlights the way in which a text pulls an audience into active engagement with its discourse, and attempts to avoid the objectivizing of the text that results from attention only to story. I have identified the metaphor of "gap-filling" as the most fruitful way of understanding this process. This means that I will attempt to elucidate the ways in which Mark's text attempts to guide a reader to fill gaps in the story in a certain way. As I read the conflicts in Mark, in other words, my attention will be not so much on what they are "about" on the story level, but what they *do* to the reader.

Thus I understand the rhetorical axis of communication to be the most important aspect of the narrative. As Fowler insists, Mark's Gospel is not "about" the characters and events which make up the story, but about its reader: "The Gospel writer's chief concern is not the fate of either Jesus or the Twelve in the story but the fate of the reader outside the story."[125] This holds true, I suggest, for the conflicts in the Gospel. Mark's concern is for the tension produced in and the resolution promised for the audience of his Gospel. That the reader's involvement in the narrative and in the conflicts which drive the story forward is Mark's principal concern becomes clear when one considers the fundamental nature of those conflicts. Mark presents Jesus from the opening verses as the Christ, the beloved son

---

[125]Fowler, 80; Fowler goes so far as to say that coherence at the story level is "sacrificed" to Mark's interest in the discourse (e.g., 155-56). This may be going too far, especially with respect to the role of the disciples in the Gospel, as I will suggest in Chapter 5.

of God, whom God has sent in confirmation[126] of God's promises of a redeemer to Israel. But Jesus encounters fierce opposition from religious leaders, those originally entrusted with tending the vineyard Israel; from powerful demonic forces, in whose death-grip humanity and creation clearly lie; and from his own chosen ones, who fail utterly to grasp the real significance of Jesus' messiahship, and to conform their lives to it. In other words, regardless of what a formal analysis of the conflicts might reveal about the literary interrelationship among them, it is clear that in the reader they serve a united purpose: each threatens, in very real ways, to undermine the very promises of God Jesus was sent to confirm. And in fact, viewed from a perspective outside of the Gospel's evaluative point of view of Jesus, that God was at work in him, God's promises *are* undermined: The religious leaders apparently succeed in their plan to do away with Jesus; Jesus succumbs to the very force of Satan over which he initially appeared to have power (e.g., 5:35-43); and the followers he chose to bear the fruit of the kingdom of God betray, deny, and desert him.

The essential conflict, in other words, lies *within* the reader who engages Mark's narrative argument that God's promises are confirmed in Jesus. A reader's acceptance of the Gospel's point of view on Jesus—Mark's goal—is threatened at every turn by forceful opposition to God's plan from all quarters. The power of Mark's narrative emerges from the author's willingness to acknowledge this conflict as real; there is correspondence between the world of the text and that of the reader, who comes to the text with the problem that

---

[126]I use the word "confirm" instead of the more traditional "fulfilled" because, first, it is probably more accurate with respect to Mark's particular use of the Hebrew Bible; as opposed to Matthew and Luke, Mark rarely speaks of Israel's Scriptures being "fulfilled" in Jesus (the exception is 14:49; he uses "it is written" in 1:1; 14:21; 14:27). Rather, Mark's principal aim is to show that what God accomplished in Jesus, and how God accomplished it, is in continuity with God's past dealings with Israel. Moreover, for Mark especially, "fulfillment" suggests a finality not in keeping the Gospel's orientation to the future, what God has yet to accomplish (see, e.g., Mark 13 and the ending). More on this in the following chapter.

the reality God promises and that which he experiences are in tension.[127]

In a sense, the conflicts in Mark involve the filling of one large gap in the narrative, the gap which emerges from the very first verse of the Gospel: Placing the name and the particular story of Jesus with the title Christ, Son of God.

Mark does more, of course, than simply lay the problem bare; his narrative attempts to convey to his audience the way in which God addresses this situation. Indeed, my study seeks to explore just what strategies Mark employs in service of this goal. The question becomes, then, how Mark pursues this goal through a narrative whose basic plot involves God's saving activity and intense opposition to it from every side. In the next three chapters, I will explore how Mark's narrative works to impact its audience, resulting in an experience of both the endangerment of God's promises and their ultimate reaffirmation.

---

[127]This is not to read the text in the light of a specific historical reconstruction of the audience, or to engage in such reconstruction. The assertion that Mark writes to address a situation of conflict in the reader or audience emerges from the poetics of the Gospel, from observing the centrality and nature of conflict in the Gospel, as will be argued below. One need not presume or seek to reconstruct a particular historical situation in such a reading, though attention to a text's poetics may often provide clues to the particularities of the rhetorical situation out of which the author wrote. (See Juel, *Master*, 123-46; for an example of reading Mark in order to construct with some precision the historical situation in which he wrote, see the study by Joel Marcus, *The Way of the Lord: Christological Exegesis of the Old Testament in the Gospel of Mark* [Louisville: Westminster/John Knox Press, 1992], e.g., his discussion of Mark 12:35-37 [130-52].)

CHAPTER 3

PREPARING THE WAY FOR THE READER: THE PROLOGUE OF MARK'S GOSPEL

> How do the Gospels persuade us? They force us to enter the world of the narrative. And they do this . . . not because of any excess of detail but by forcing apparent contradictions upon us and yet giving us the confidence that this and no other way was how it was. . . . We assent to narratives, as we do to people, to the degree that we grow to feel we can trust them. (Gabriel Josipovici, *The Book of God*[1])

Mark's Gospel is characterized by conflict; this conflict should be examined not solely in terms of its generic or historical referents (Chapter 1), or even solely through its form and structure, à la narrative criticism, but should be examined in terms of its rhetorical effect on an audience (Chapter 2). The Gospel presents the conflicts between Jesus and the authorities and Jesus and the disciples not in order to give a distant reader the satisfaction of a neat and structurally interesting resolution to these conflicts, but to engage the audience's own experience of conflict between the promises of God and the reality of an unredeemed world.

In the previous chapter I outlined a reader-oriented approach to Mark's Gospel which highlights the gap-filling activity of an ideal reader. I suggest that gap-filling is an especially appropriate focus for the experience of reading Mark, both because of Mark's laconic narrative style as well as the content of the narrative. The goal of this

---

[1]Gabriel Josipovici, *The Book of God: A Response to the Bible* (New Haven: Yale University Press, 1988), 229-30, 234.

chapter is two-fold. First, I wish to show through an exploration of the prologue of the Gospel how Mark sets up his narrative to focus on the reader's experience of the gap between Jesus' purported identity and his fate. Almost all studies of and commentaries on the prologue focus on the *information* it provides for the reader—information critical to understanding the remainder of the narrative (e.g., the identity of Jesus, his relation to John the Baptist, etc.). However, the prologue does much more than provide information for the reader to process cognitively; it is a principal vehicle Mark's text (indeed, any text) has at its disposal for drawing an audience wholly (i.e., not just cognitively) into the story so that the narrative can shape that audience. My examination of the prologue will try to show how profoundly reader-oriented is the Gospel as a whole; that is, I will show that it presents its narrative not as something that happened some time ago, but as something that impinges on the reader's present reality in an inescapable way. I will argue that the prologue's principal function, from a reader-oriented perspective, is to set forth both the central problematic of the Christian confession as well as foreshadow how that paradox will play itself out. That is, it presents the principal "gap" that the audience must fill in some way: how the beloved Son of God can be destined for both the glory, exaltation, and victory that traditionally attend this role, as well as rejection by the present tenants of the vineyard Israel and by his own followers, culminating in the humiliation of the cross—all of which would seem to be the antithesis of the Christ. The correlate to this gap in the audience's experience is how such a story of endangered promises becomes "good news."

Second, I will suggest that the prologue also sets up the grid through which Mark's story of Jesus is to be experienced; that is, by setting the story within a particular reading of the larger story of Israel, the tension or gap between expectation and reality becomes precisely the basis for the confidence that the story of Jesus confirms God's promises. Mark taps into a narrative pattern which is firmly entrenched in Israel's scriptures, namely, the conflict which emerges out of the consistent and seemingly insurmountable endangerment of God's promises, and the ultimate reaffirmation of those promises.

I will support these observations in the course of a rhetorical examination of the prologue by developing the following points:

(1) The prologue consists of Mark 1:1-15, and exhibits a two-part structure.

(2) The prologue introduces Mark's narrative in several ways as a narrative which is especially reader-oriented; that is, it clearly situates itself on the rhetorical axis of communication between author and audience:

• It establishes, first, the narrative voice, the ideological point of view from which an audience is invited to view the ensuing narrative. It seeks to collapse, insofar as possible, any distance between the discourse and the audience, allowing the audience to experience the story from the privileged point of view of the narrator.

• The prologue introduces the terse, laconic style that will characterize the mode of presentation of the whole narrative, a style which requires much gap-filling activity on the part of the reader.

• The temporal coordinates introduced in the prologue—the long-ago promise of God to redeem creation through Israel (1:2-3) and the promise that the Reign of God will be established through the work of Jesus (1:14-15)—envelop the reader's own time, and thus draw her into the story world. That is, in a sense Mark "intercalates" the reader's own story between the two terminal points of the story he narrates.

• The prologue engages the reader's experience of the gospel by beginning with baptism, an experience which, it can be assumed, Mark's audience would have shared. It compels the readers to interpret their baptism in light of the story of Jesus.

(3) The prologue sets before the reader the central paradox of the "gospel of Jesus Christ," and engages the reader in the work of seeing in the particular story of Jesus of Nazareth the working out of God's redemptive purposes. It brings into opposition traditional Messianic language and expectations with the particular nature of Jesus' Messiahship in such a way that the reader is compelled to search for ways to fill the gap between the two. It does this in a way that goes beyond providing information to be processed cognitively,

however; its climax is a moment of transcendence above the action of the story, one whose violent tearing of the heavens suggests that boundaries which keep humans safe from God's action are ripped away; the response Mark is looking for here, I will argue, is as much affective—a sense of awe and fear as in classic theophanies—as cognitive—i.e., conveying the "knowledge" of what God thinks about Jesus. Here again the narrative shows itself to be reaching to impact the audience and its entire sense of reality.

(4) The rich resonances of Israel's scriptures, more concentrated here than at any point in the Gospel outside of the passion narrative, invoke the stories of God's past dealings with Israel as a key to a fruitful encounter with this story; specifically, it invokes the pattern of God's endangered and reaffirmed promises as a principal source for the confidence that through the conflicts presented in the story, God is fulfilling God's promises.

THE SCOPE AND STRUCTURE OF THE PROLOGUE

The Scope

In Markan scholarship since the 1960s there has been an increasing recognition of the crucial function of Mark's opening verses for a proper understanding of the whole work.[2] Most commen-

---

[2]See, e.g., Leander Keck "The Introduction to Mark's Gospel," *NTS* 12 (1966), 352-70; James M. Robinson, *The Problem of History in Mark* (Philadelphia: Fortress Press, 1982), 69-80; Ulrich Mauser, *Christ in the Wilderness: The Wilderness Theme in the Second Gospel and its Basis in the Biblical Tradition* (London: SCM Press, 1963), 79-102; Norman Petersen, *Literary Criticism for New Testament Critics* (Philadelphia: Fortress Press, 1978), 49-54; Jack Dean Kingsbury, *The Christology of Mark's Gospel* (Philadelphia: Fortress Press, 1983), 55-71; John Drury, "Mark 1:1-15: An Interpretation," in *Alternative Approaches to New Testament Study* (ed. A. E. Harvey; London: SPCK, 1985), 25-36; Frank J. Matera, "The Prologue as the Interpretive Key to Mark's Gospel," *JSNT* 34 (1988), 3-20; Mary Ann Tolbert, *Sowing the Gospel: the Gospel of Mark in Literary-Historical Perspective* (Minneapolis: Fortress Press, 1989), 108-114; M. Eugene Boring, "Mark 1:1-15 and the Beginning of the Gospel," *Semeia* 52 (1991), 43-91; Morna D. Hooker, "The Beginning of the Gospel," in *The Future of Christology: Essays in Honor of Leander Keck* (ed. Abraham Malherbe and Wayne Meeks; Minneapolis: Fortress Press, 1993), 18-28.

tators agree that in a fundamental sense the author of Mark, in accordance with common literary conventions of his day, begins his narrative with an introduction designed to orient his audience to the main features of the story he is about to tell.[3] Aristotle suggested that a dramatic prologue should provide "a paving [of] the way for what follows,"[4] and this is precisely what Mark seems to have attempted in his introduction.

Critical opinion is divided, however, in terms of the scope of the prologue. The question is whether the prologue ends with v. 13[5] or v. 15.[6] This is certainly not the most crucial issue an interpreter of these verses faces (though most commentaries and many studies seem to treat it as such), but it is not irrelevant. As Mary Ann Tolbert (among others) has argued, a narrative's structure can provide an important clue to its rhetorical goals.[7] Especially in a narrative which, like Mark, with its paratactic, episodic style, provides few overt structural markers, it can make a significant difference whether one sees a section such as 1:14-15, the principal locus of disagreement with respect to the scope of the prologue, as conclusion to what precedes or prelude to what follows.[8] It may be, of course, that it does both; indeed, the temporal aspect of the reading experience, as

---

[3]On prologues as a part of ancient narratives, see Dennis E. Smith, "Narrative Beginnings in Ancient Literature and Theory," *Semeia* 52 (1991), 1-9; for an extended discussion of the relationship between Mark's Gospel and Greek tragedy, see G. G. Bilezekian, *The Liberated Gospel: A Comparison of the Gospel of Mark and Greek Tragedy* (Grand Rapids: Baker, 1977).

[4]Aristotle, *Rhetoric* 3.14.1; quoted in Smith, "Narrative Beginnings," 3.

[5]The first to argue for 1:1-13 seems to have been R. H. Lightfoot, *The Gospel Message of St. Mark* (Oxford: Clarendon, 1950), 15-20; he has been followed by a good many commentators, including Robinson, Mauser, and, more recently, Matera, Tolbert, Kingsbury (and Hooker; in terms of the major commentaries on Mark, see R.A. Guelich, *Mark 1-8:26* (Word Biblical Commentary 34A; Dallas: Word Books, 1989), 4. The Nestle-Aland 26th makes a break after v. 13.

[6]A slight majority has, since Leander Keck, opted for extending the prologue through 1:15; see below and Keck, Boring, Drury; most recent commentaries make the break here; again, see Guelich, *Mark 1-8:26*, 4; also Matera, 16 n. 9.

[7]See Tolbert, *Sowing the Gospel*, 106-108; also Joanna Dewey, *Markan Public Debate: Literary Technique, Concentric Structure, and Theology in Mark 2:1-3:6* SBLDS 48 (Chico, CA: 1980), 5-40.

[8]Another important example is where to make a break between the two "halves" of the Gospel, whether at 8:22 or 8:26.

discussed in the previous chapter, means that a careful reader will, when presented with new information, look back and evaluate what she has already encountered in the light of this information as well as anticipate what lies ahead.[9] I will argue, in fact, that this is precisely the case with 1:14-15: the reference to John's arrest and the recurrence of the word εὐαγγέλιον in these verses compel the reader to look backward at how John's fate might relate to his work as the Messiah's forerunner, and to anticipate how Jesus' own way on that path can be considered "good news."[10] This retrospective glance, as well as the nature of these two verses, as we shall see, argue for understanding them within the scope of the prologue. At the same time, though, the verses also point ahead as a programmatic summary of Jesus' impending Galilean ministry.

Perhaps the strongest argument supporting this dual function of vv. 14-15 emerges from the observation that current scholarship is again seemingly equally divided on whether they belong to the prologue or not. Until recently, Leander Keck's arguments for including them in the prologue have been seen as the consensus view;[11] recent commentaries and studies, however, have reasserted James Robinson's contention that the prologue consists only of vv. 1-13.

Interpreters who contend that the prologue ends with v. 13 argue that vv. 14-15 set themselves off from what precedes it by several things, both stylistic and substantive; vv. 14-15 thus form the opening to the Galilean section of the Gospel rather than part of the

---

[9]Jerry Camery-Hoggatt observes regarding these verses that "[t]here are times when Mark's transitions are so smooth that they create difficulties for interpreters who require that their outlines be tidy" (*Irony in Mark's Gospel: Text and Subtext* [Cambridge: Cambridge University Press, 1992], 99).

[10]There is also the issue of how one would perform the first fifteen verses orally, whether one would signal that the main body of the narrative begins with Jesus' appearance in Galilee or with his calling of the disciples. I will argue below that 1:14-15 constitute a climax and summary of the preceding verses; the move to Galilee itself is not sufficient to suggest a break, and the fact that no other named characters are present suggest that these verses continue the more direct address to the audience characteristic of the previous verses continues here. Like the epilogue (16:1-8), the reader is confronted with words of Jesus, words of promise.

[11]See, e.g., Frank Matera, "The Prologue as the Interpretative Key," 5; Boring, "Mark 1:1-15," 359.

prologue. James M. Robinson, for example, offers four principal observations which lead him to limit the prologue to the first thirteen verses.[12] First, he considers the prologue to deal essentially with John's preparatory activity, rather than Jesus' own work: the narrated activity of the prologue is circumscribed by the coming (v. 4) and going (v. 14) of John, and even vv. 9-13 form only a "transition" to Jesus' actual ministry, which does not commence until vv. 14-15.[13] Second, vv.14-15 set themselves off from what precedes by the verb tenses; in vv. 2-3, the language is oriented toward a future fulfillment, while vv. 14-15 contain Jesus' proclamation that the time "has been fulfilled." Robinson suggests that Mark leads us "to look in the intervening narrative (vv. 4-13) for an event of fulfillment."[14] He finds this fulfillment in the eschatological activity of John. And third, vv. 9-13, the baptism and temptation of Jesus, are both linked to what precedes and set off from what ensues by their relationship to John's activity. They are linked by the reference to Spirit in vv. 8, 10, 12, and set apart because Jesus' appearance fulfills John's mission of proclaiming the coming of one "stronger" than he who will baptize with the Spirit; John is cleared from the scene through his arrest, and Jesus' public ministry can begin in v. 14. Finally, Robinson points out that the baptism and temptation of Jesus, unlike the beginning of his preaching in v. 14, function as foundation for everything that ensues, especially the continuing battle with Satan reflected in Jesus' exorcisms.[15]

Thus, for Robinson, the burden of the prologue is to set forth the inauguration of eschatological time in John's ministry; with this time begun, and John moved off the stage, Jesus can appear with the message and ministry which emerges from this foundational occurrence: "This event marks the 'beginning' of the last hour and

---

[12]Robinson, *The Problem of History*, 69-80.

[13]He points to the stylistic similarity between the narration of John's baptizing activity in v. 5 and Jesus' own baptism in v. 9 (70).

[14]Robinson, 72.

[15]Robinson notes that, when viewed retrospectively through the exorcism debate (3:20-30), Jesus' encounter with Satan in the prologue proves to be the ground for Jesus' statement that the strong man has been bound (3:27); this binding is the necessary presupposition for Jesus' power over the evil spirits (79).

thus of the Christian history (1:1). The basis has been provided for the ministry of Jesus, which consists in proclaiming the new situation (1:15), and in carrying through the struggle against Satan in the power of the Spirit."[16]

More recently, these arguments have been expanded through literary and rhetorical observations. Frank Matera agrees that one of the principal burdens of the prologue is to distinguish between John and Jesus: it identifies John as the Messiah's forerunner promised in scripture, and draws a clear distinction between his power, worth, and baptism and those of the one whose way he prepares.[17] He furthers Robinson's observation about the distinction between vv. 14-15 and what precedes; not only does v. 14 introduce a sense of fulfillment which contrasts with the earlier sense of anticipation (vv. 2-3), but it narrates a change in locality as well.[18] Perhaps most important, Matera finds a change in the way the narrator speaks to the reader beginning at v. 14. Up to this point, the information about John and Jesus has been provided only to the reader, whereas from 1:14 the events narrated are public in nature: "From the point of view of the narrator, the events of these verses are different from those communicated in the rest of the narrative (1:14ff.) inasmuch as they are told solely for the reader's benefit."[19]

---

[16]80.

[17]Matera, 7.

[18]Matera, "The Prologue as the Interpretative Key," 5.

[19]Matera, 5-6; Morna Hooker makes a similar point, asserting that only vv. 1-13 provide information about Jesus not known to the characters in the story; from v. 14 on, she observes, the story unfolds from the viewpoint of those who are "on stage"; since there is nothing secret in vv. 14-15, the prologue ends at v. 13 ("The Beginning of the Gospel," 20; see also her commentary, 32). Mary Ann Tolbert also sees the grammatical and geographical shift in vv. 14-15 as a basis for arguing that these verses introduce the first major rhetorical division of the body of the narrative and are thus not part of the prologue itself, and she offers as well an elaborate rhetorical structuring of 1:1-13 as further evidence that these verses comprise the prologue (*Sowing the Gospel*, 108-116). For Tolbert, the Gospel as a whole is composed of two main rhetorical sections, 1:14-10:52 and 11:1-16:8; each begins with an introduction which suggests the predominant themes and activity which will characterize it: 1:14-15 introduces Jesus' Galilean ministry, and 11:1-11 does the same for his work in Jerusalem (114-15). She sees in the reference to John in 1:14 a "hook" with the prologue which helps distinguish Jesus' ministry from John's (116). Her analysis of the rhetorical structure of 1:1-13 leads her to see it as a unified section composed of

Leander Keck's arguments in support of including vv. 14-15 in the prologue are still persuasive, however. In his 1966 article "The Introduction to Mark's Gospel," a piece which anticipates in many significant ways the literary turn in gospel studies, Keck counters Robinson's view that only vv. 1-13 stand as the basis for Jesus' subsequent ministry, arguing that there is no real gap at all between vv. 13 and 14, but that the whole first fifteen verses function "to disclose (to the reader) the nature of Jesus in such a way that the basis of his work (the rest of the narrative) is rightly understood from the start."[20] Keck offers three compelling arguments for the unity of 1:1-15. First, he argues that the occurrence of εὐαγγέλιον in v. 1 is complemented by its appearances in vv. 14-15, and that this term "is clearly the rubric under which Mark wants to place his material. . . Mark 1:14f. not only complements the title of the book but rounds out the whole introduction in such a way that the entire fifteen verses stand as a genuine prologue to the whole subsequent text."[21] Keck understands the "gospel of God" which Jesus preaches to be the theme of the work as a whole; it stands as fulfillment and summons to the audience, calling the hearers to faith in the "word" of Jesus. In this sense, the "gospel of God" which Jesus proclaims is parallel to the phrase "the beginning of the gospel of Jesus Christ" in v. 1, which refers not just to John as the forerunner, nor simply to Jesus' own preaching, "but to the Christian gospel which has Jesus as its content *and* starting point."[22] Thus the introduction to Mark's Gospel encompasses these opening words of Jesus.

Keck's second principal argument for including vv. 14-15 in the prologue is also theological and represents perhaps the most important observation to make regarding the prologue as a whole. As I noted above, those who see the introduction only in vv. 1-13

---

four parts, each of which, after the opening section, begins with the impersonal *egeneto*; the four sections form a chiasm, whose inner and outer elements correspond, respectively, to the human and divine levels of the plot of Mark's Gospel (109-112). In addition, she asserts, each successive section is linked to the previous one through the use of a key word or phrase: "in the wilderness" links sections 1 and 2; "baptize" links sections 2 and 3; and "heaven(s)" and "spirit" link sections 3 and 4 (109).

[20]Keck, "The Introduction to Mark's Gospel," 354.

[21]Keck, 359-60.

[22]Keck, 359.

suggest that the ostensive break in v. 14 serves to separate the ministry of Jesus from that of John. Keck argues correctly, though, that Mark, both here and elsewhere in the narrative, wishes to guide the reader to see the profound way in which the figures are linked.[23] "What Mark has done," Keck asserts, "is to set the preaching and summons of Jesus into the divinely willed deathward work of John."[24] The key here is the passive verb παραδοθῆναι, which for Mark does not serve to separate biographically or historically the work of John and Jesus, but has rather a theological meaning.[25] Only here, and not in v. 8, is the work of Jesus' forerunner complete; the "way" John prepares for Jesus is the way of suffering and death. In fact, I would add that to the extent that a prologue serves to "pave the way for what follows" (Aristotle), setting forth the major themes which will be dealt with in the body of the narrative, it is clear that the "deathward work of John" represents one of those themes (see, e.g., 6:14-29; 9:11-13; 11:27-33; 15:33-35; I will return to this theme below).[26]

Finally, Keck points out that the complex of ideas surrounding τὸ εὐαγγέλιον have to do with the good news of *victory*; vv. 14-15

---

[23]Keck, 360-361. Others, of course, note that John the Baptist's fate foreshadows that of Jesus in some way (e.g., Tolbert, 116); still, it is surprising the extent to which many interpreters read the prologue as Mark's way of distinguishing between John and Jesus (again, Tolbert, 109-112; Hooker, *The Gospel According to Saint Mark*, 36-38; Robinson, 78; Matera, 6-7). This is perhaps an instance of reading Mark through the "grid" provided by the other gospels, which do spend more time on the relationship; see Fowler, *Let the Reader Understand*, 233-237. With respect to Robinson's initial ideas, one wonders whether he is not influenced specifically by Conzelmann's reading of Luke, who, in the latter's view, has a neat salvation-historical scheme which sees a decisive break between the time of John and the time of Jesus (e.g., Luke 16:16; see Conzelmann, *The Theology of St. Luke* (Philadelphia: Fortress Press, 1982).

[24]Keck, 360.

[25]Keck, 360-61.

[26]The importance of the idea of "delivering up" for Mark's understanding of the gospel was highlighted by Norman Perrin, who saw the Gospel structured around a three-fold sequence of preaching and being delivered up: first John, then Jesus, then, as Ch. 13 foreshadows, the disciples (Norman Perrin and Dennis Duling, *The New Testament: An Introduction* (New York: Harcourt Brace Jovanovich, Inc., 1982), 237-239. On the function of John the Baptist's death in Mark's Gospel, see below and Norman Petersen, *Literary Criticism for New Testament Critics*, 58-60.

announce the victorious conclusion to Jesus' encounter with Satan in
1:12-13, and show that "Mark's Jesus is the victorious Son of God
who returns from the testing-ground with the εὐαγγέλιον."[27]

Keck confirms these arguments by arguing that seeing 1:1-15
as the prologue makes sense out of Mark's principal concerns in the
Gospel as a whole.[28] Such a structuring of the prologue means that
the body of the narrative begins at 1:16, the calling of the first
disciples; clearly, what it means to follow Jesus is one of Mark's
major themes. Indeed, Keck suggests that the participation of the
disciples in Jesus' mission is the dominant theme, surpassing even
purely christological interests.[29] For Mark, so Keck, Jesus is
important not in himself but only and always in relation to his
disciples, both within and outside the story. As I noted above,
Keck's article anticipates later more explicitly literary concerns in
many significant ways, both in terms of text-oriented and reader-
oriented approaches. His concern to relate the prologue to the whole
of Mark irrespective of generic considerations, as well as his
recognition that the Gospel as a whole reaches beyond the story
world and into the audience's world render his study continually
helpful and insightful. Further details of his reading of the prologue
will enter into the discussion of its function below.[30]

---

[27]Keck, 362. Keck also argues here that the way in which Jesus shows himself
to be "stronger" than John (1:7-8) is not, as Robinson suggests, in his exorcisms,
which would make Jesus' encounter with Satan the logical climax of the prologue, but
rather in his word, to which all of his work is subordinated (360-362). Thus vv. 14-15
"are a climactic statement that fulfills the word of John about Jesus, while at the same
time it rounds out the over-arching interest in τὸ εὐαγγέλιον" (361)

[28]Keck, 362-367.

[29]Keck asserts that "no strictly Christological aim (in the narrow sense of
doctrine about the person of Christ) does justice to the peculiarity of Mark—namely
the steady emphasis on the disciples' participation in the work of Jesus" (363). The
whole Galilean section (1:16-10:52), Keck points out, is framed by calls to follow
Jesus (364).

[30]One final argument for the broader scope of the prologue is perhaps worthy
of (a) note. Norman Petersen, in his attempt to show that Mark's Gospel bears the
marks of an intentionally plotted narrative, sees the opening as introducing the major
plot device in Mark's narrative, namely, the suspense and anticipation provided by the
many predictions present in the Gospel (*Literary Criticism*, 49-54). The first fifteen
verses introduce this suspense; they are united by three predictions (one might also call
them promises): the narrative opens with Isaiah's prediction that the Messiah's

In sum, there are clearly elements of vv. 14-15 which complete themes and rhetorical techniques present in vv. 1-13 (the fate of John the Baptist; the gospel Jesus preaches; the word of Jesus which fulfills John's prediction). Just as evident, however, is the way in which these verses point ahead to what follows (Jesus' work in Galilee, centered around his preaching; the centrality of "the reign of God").[31] The attentive reader will be drawn to review what she has learned and experienced from the first 13 verses when she learns (or is reminded of) John the Baptist's fate; Jesus is not only said to be "stronger" and more "worthy" than John, but John says that the stronger one will come "after me" (ὀπίσω μου).[32] Likewise, the recurrence of εὐαγγέλιον in vv. 14-15 occasions a backward look at how the "gospel of Jesus Christ" relates to the "gospel of God" which Jesus preaches. Jesus' proclamation that "the time has been fulfilled" (v. 15), when contrasted with the language of prediction and promise with which the Gospel opens (vv. 2-3), compels an

---

forerunner would appear in the wilderness to prepare the way for God's final redemption; that prediction is fulfilled with the appearance of John the Baptist (vv. 4-6). John, in turn, foretells the "stronger" one who would come after him and baptize with the Holy Spirit; Jesus' appearance fulfills his prediction. Then Petersen suggests that Jesus' first words also implicitly contain a prediction: that the reign of God has drawn near implies that it will soon be fully present (50-2; cf. also 9:1). This last prediction, whose fulfillment is not plotted in the story itself, provides the suspense which draws the reader into Mark's narrative:

> [T]he unfulfilled prediction about the kingdom introduces to the reader an element of *suspense* that will only be relieved when the question of when the kingdom will come is in some way addressed or answered . . . In 1:1-15 this suspense is heightened by the fact that three predictions are made but only two come to pass: Isaiah predicted something and John's appearance fulfilled it; John predicted something and Jesus' appearance fulfilled it; Jesus predicted something and . . . and what? That is the suspense, and it has been plotted by naming three predictors, three predictions, but only two fulfillments, the last of the three having been suspended (52-3).

Petersen is actually a bit murky on what this means for the scope of the prologue, but the force of his observations speak for including Jesus' prediction in v. 15.

[31]Perrin considers 1:14-15 a "transitional summary;" such summaries provide for him the major clues to the structuring of Mark's Gospel. See Perrin, *The New Testament*, 239-40.

[32]Though this "preposition" can be understood temporally, in every other instance in Mark it is spatial (1:17,20; 8:33,34; 13:16); in all but 13:16 it refers to "coming behind," i.e. following, Jesus. See Bauer-Arendt-Gingrich-Danker, *A Greek-English Lexicon of the New Testament and other Early Christian Literature* (Chicago: University of Chicago Press, 1979), 575.

audience to consider what has happened in this opening scene which would have brought about this "turn in the ages." Both the appearance of John the Baptist as the promised forerunner Elijah and the tearing of the heavens and descent of God's spirit on Jesus would certainly come to mind, accompanied by the radically contrasting images of John's arrest and of Jesus appearing with "sinners" at John's "baptism of repentance for the forgiveness of sins" (v. 4). As I will argue below, far from simply giving information about Jesus' identity, Mark has placed before the reader the central paradox of his understanding of Jesus as God's promised anointed one.

But the reader must also look ahead in anticipation of the unfolding narrative. Jesus goes into *Galilee* with this pronouncement, the "backwaters" of Israel and the seat of revolutionary fervor against the Roman imperial power, just as all those who responded to John's preaching came *from* Judea and Jerusalem into the wilderness. Both settings locate God's ultimate redemptive activity outside the traditional holy sites of temple and outside of religious authority. With Jesus' proclamation that the reign of God has drawn near (v. 15), the stage is set for a fulfillment which runs contrary to traditional expectations: How does Jesus' ensuing activity in Galilee signal the nearness of God's reign?

The Structure

As Tolbert and others have observed, since Mark took shape in a predominantly oral culture, clues to the structure of Mark's Gospel should be sought in textual indications that seem to be designed to facilitate aural reception, especially repetition of key terms, phrases, and motifs.[33] In other words, attention to the structure of a text from a milieu such as Mark's is not necessarily anachronis-

---

[33]Tolbert, *Sowing the Gospel*, 106-108; Joanna Dewey, *Markan Public Debate*, 7-40; G.A. Kennedy, *New Testament Interpretation Through Rhetorical Criticism* (Chapel Hill, N.C.: University of North Carolina Press, 1984), 21-46. Tolbert notes that "[s]peaking and writing in the Greco-Roman world were done *for the ear, not the eye*. Many of the figures listed by rhetorical handbooks concern the *sound* of language, not the visual image presented, and since one is composing for the ear, many rhetorical strategies concern the use of repetition, in small and large ways, without eliciting boredom" (43).

tic and inappropriately text-centered, as some interpreters have recently suggested.[34] Much can be gained by an examination of structural markers in terms of determining how a text wished to be heard and received,[35] especially when one views the Gospel through the eyes of one who will "read" it for an audience. Whether one chooses to change the tone and pace of the narrative at 1:14 or at 1:16 can affect the connections an audience makes among various parts of the text. I suggest that such a break should not come before 1:16 if the prologue is to have its maximal effect.

As suggested above, both substantively and stylistically vv. 14-15 round off the first thirteen verses and provide the foundation for the ensuing narrative. And although I disagree with Tolbert concerning these verses, her inclusion of v. 1 in the prologue is to be preferred over the view that it functions as a title for the work as a whole.[36] Those who hold the latter view argue that ἀρχή is to be construed as the beginning or foundation of the whole Christian proclamation in the story about Jesus, rather than simply referring to the opening and foundational events of that story.[37] Although one may not rule out such a reading, in the immediate context the reference appears most logically to be to the events of the prologue. The strongest argument for this is the way v. 2 begins. As Guelich points out in his study of the prologue, καθὼς γέγραπται never begins a sentence in Mark (cf. 9:13; 14:21) or in any other New Testament document, and it always refers to what precedes rather than what follows.[38] Moreover, against Boring, who claims that ἀρχή

---

[34]See, e.g., Moore, *Literary Criticism*, 86.

[35]Tolbert cites Demetrius, the first-century B.C.E. rhetorician, who points out the necessity in rhetoric for "signposts and resting-places," for "the signposts act as guides, whereas a straight road without signposts, however short it is, seems aimless" ("Demetrius, *On Style*," in *Ancient Literary Criticism: The Principal Texts in New Translations* [ed. D. A. Russell and M. Winterbottom; Oxford: Clarendon Press, 1972], 202; quoted in Tolbert, *Sowing the Gospel*, 107.

[36]Boring, 50-1.; Matera, 6; Dieter Lührmann, *Das Markusevangelium* (Handbuch zum Neuen Testament 3; Tübingen: J.C.B. Mohr [Paul Siebeck], 1987), 30; (see Guelich, 7, for other commentaries which take this position).

[37]The various options as to how to understand the syntax of 1:1-3 are nicely laid out by Boring, 47-50.

[38]Guelich, 7; see also his article "'The Beginning of the Gospel'—Mark 1:1-15," in *Biblical Research* 27 (1982), 1-14; he is followed by Tolbert, 242-44. Tolbert

is never used in all Greek literature as a label for the introductory segment of a narrative,[39] Guelich adduces several examples of precisely such a usage.[40] Thus vv. 1-3 should be rendered "(The) beginning of the Gospel of Jesus Christ, Son of God, as written in the prophet Isaiah, 'Behold . . . .'"[41] The reader will understand that the principal character in the story is Jesus, and that the ensuing verses introduce his story.

Beyond the issue of the inclusion of v. 1, I follow Boring's structure, which brings into parallel the work of John and Jesus, inviting both comparison and contrast:

> 1:1-8: John
> > *Identified by off-stage transcendent voice (2-4)*
> > *John in the wilderness: baptizing (5-6)*
> > *Preaching: repentance/in terms of promise (7-8)*
> 1:9-15: Jesus
> > *Identified by off-stage transcendent voice (9-11)*
> > *Jesus in the wilderness: testing/being tested (12-13)*
> > *Preaching: repentance/in terms of fulfillment[42]*

The references to εὐαγγέλιον in v. 1 and vv. 14-15 frame the entire section.

The most important advantage of this structuring from a rhetorical perspective is that it conveys the strong sense in which John's and Jesus' ministries are linked. Obviously, Mark places Jesus above John, but the real key to understanding their relationship, as we will see, is the way in which John prepares the way for Jesus

---

takes the grammatical and rhetorical unity of vv. 1-3 as grounds for arguing that the scriptural citation in vv. 2-3 actually refers to Jesus, not John. If καθὼς γέγραπται refers back to verse one, then it must refer to Jesus! She overlooks the possibility (rather likelihood) that it refers to ἀρχή.

[39]Boring, 51.

[40]E.g., Isocrates, *Phil.* 1; Philo, *de Sob.* 1; *de Spec. Leg.* 1; Tacitus, *Hist. 1.1.1.* (Guelich, *Mark 1-8:26*, 7).

[41]With Guelich, 6; see also Joel Marcus, *The Way of the Lord: Christological Exegesis of the Old Testament in the Gospel of Mark* (Louisville: Westminster/John Knox Press, 1992), 18.

[42]Boring, 60-61; see also Keck, 367.

through his own arrest and death. The completion of John's ministry, as noted above, comes only with his arrest and death, alluded to in v. 14. It is on this ominous note that the one who comes after John lays out in a programmatic way the basic theme of his ministry, the gospel of God that "the time is fulfilled and the reign of God has drawn near" (v. 15).

THE FUNCTION OF THE PROLOGUE

In the course of our discussion of the scope and structure of the prologue, several indications of its function have already come into play. Several of the interpreters argue, in fact, that the prologue constitutes the "hermeneutical key" to Mark's Gospel.[43] We have seen that it sets itself off from the rest of Mark's Gospel in several ways; broadly stated, the prologue functions to provide the foundation for the rest of the narrative. The author provides in these opening verses the larger context in which his narrative is to be understood (the story of Israel, vv. 1-3); he "prepares the way" for the initial appearance of his protagonist through a divinely commissioned messenger (vv. 4-6); he clarifies the relationship between Jesus and that messenger (vv. 7-8); he sets forth the narrator's point of view on Jesus, through explicit commentary and by narrating a revelatory event (vv. 9-11); he sets up the context for the conflicts which will drive the ensuing narrative forward (vv. 12-13); and, if the prologue extends to vs. 15, he provides a programmatic statement for the mission of the protagonist (vv. 14-15).[44]

These aspects of the prologue work together to establish Mark's narrative as one that is especially reader-oriented, that is, one which, as Fowler puts it, situates itself on the rhetorical axis of communication between author and audience.[45] Although each of

---

[43]Matera, "The Prologue as Interpretative Key," 15; cf. Morna Hooker, who states that the prologue is "the key to the Gospel" ("The Beginning of the Gospel," 20); also Jerry Camery-Hoggatt, "the entire rest of the narrative will depend for its direction of movement on the character of its beginning" (*Irony in Mark's Gospel*, 94).

[44]See Matera, 6-14; Tolbert, 112-116; Keck, 367-8; Boring, 63-69.

[45]See Fowler, 57.

these themes could be set in relation to the narrative as a whole,[46] the most important observation to make about this opening material is that it is provided to the *audience alone*. Only the reader has access to this crucial information about Jesus' identity; the characters in the story do not. As Camery-Hoggart has observed, the crucial point of the prologue is not this or that detail of its text or vocabulary, but that it "from the very beginning places in the reader's hands interpretative keys which are denied the story's characters until very much later in the narrative."[47] Although most of the commentators discussed above point out that Mark addresses the reader in a special way in these verses, they emphasize almost exclusively the *information* the prologue provides to the reader—especially information about John's and Jesus' identity.[48] There is some measure of agreement about how that information functions to give the reader an advantaged position over the characters in the story so that, for instance, as the disciples continually grasp for understanding (4:41; 6:51; 8:16-21), or Herod tries to determine the relationship between Jesus and John the Baptist (6:14-16), the reader stands above it all, since he has possessed the information they lack since the opening verses of the Gospel. In other words, the audience is provided with the necessary information to make the *cognitive* moves necessary to understand what Mark is trying to say.

While granting that this is one of the central functions of the prologue, I would argue that the prologue does much more than simply provide information for the audience. This emphasis on the cognitive or mental aspects of reading, as Jonathan Culler points out, characterizes much contemporary audience-oriented criticism; the experience of reading is portrayed as "generally *cognitive* rather than *affective*: not feeling shivers along the spine, weeping in sympathy,

---

[46]This is what Matera sets out to do.

[47]Camery-Hoggatt, *Irony in Mark's Gospel*, 93; see also Matera, 4; Hooker, *The Gospel According to Saint Mark*, 32; Keck, 367; Kingsbury, 56.

[48]E.g., Matera, "The Markan prologue . . . presents the reader with information essential for understanding who Jesus is" (6); Hooker states that the first thirteen verses "give us certain information about Jesus which enables us to understand the significance of the events that follow," and that "we have [in the prologue] a concentration of christological material—information about the identity of Jesus and the meaning of his ministry" (*The Gospel According to Saint Mark*, 31-32).

or being transported with awe, but having one's expectations proved false, struggling with an irresolvable ambiguity, or questioning the assumptions upon which one had relied."[49] Especially in narratives which attempt to persuade and to shape an audience, the author must engage that audience on levels beyond the cognitive; he must seek to build confidence in the audience that this and no other way of viewing the events is true. The world created by the narrative has to appeal to and "ring true" to the readers/hearers and bring them to a point where embracing the view of reality projected by the text becomes both possible and desirable. In essence, this is what the "story-teller's craft," as Fowler puts it,[50] is all about: Engaging the audience and providing it with the confidence to accept the implied author's persuasive moves.

Thus the privileged position the reader of Mark's narrative receives vis-a-vis the characters does not simply serve to provide knowledge to make sense of the story. First of all, as I will show below, while the prologue does identify Jesus as God's agent of redemption by authoritative voices (the narrator's and God's), it also brings in imagery which seems to conflict diametrically with and complicate that conviction: Jesus' origin (Galilee) and his initial appearance among those who came to submit to a baptism of repentance for the forgiveness of sins; the violence of the theophany; his encounter with Satan; and the fate of his forerunner. The stark juxtaposition of these images with the more traditional messianic imagery suggests that Mark wishes to place the central conflict of the message he offers before the reader; he does not simply want to provide the reader with a sense of superiority over the conflicts in the narrative generated by the consistently failing characters such that the audience is in a position to accomplish what the characters could not.[51] Rather, Mark acknowledges the difficulty of embracing the

---

[49] Jonathan Culler, *On Deconstruction: Theory and Criticism after Structuralism* (Ithaca: Cornell University Press, 1981), 39; quoted in Moore, *Literary Criticism*, 96 (emphasis is Moore's).

[50] Fowler, 61.

[51] This is the view of many who view the Gospel from the standpoint of the distance between character and reader created by Mark's Gospel—e.g. Tolbert, Tannehill, even Fowler.

paradoxical and radical view of reality the narrative offers, and seeks to address the conflict in the reader and provide him with the confidence to embrace it (or perhaps to generate a conflict in complacent readers whose understanding of Jesus does not entail the conflicting imagery). The principal way in which Mark does this is by placing the conflict within the context of the larger story of God's endangered and reaffirmed promises.

In what follows, I will first briefly set forth some of the rhetorical strategies in the prologue by which Mark seeks to gain the confidence of his audience; then I will address more fully the substance of the conflict created by the contrasting images, and the way in which Mark addresses it through reading of Israel's scriptures implicit in the prologue.

Drawing the Audience in:
The Rhetorical Strategies of the Prologue

Mark seeks to engage and gain the trust of his audience in several ways: through the establishment of an authoritative and trustworthy narrative voice; perhaps somewhat paradoxically, through the narrative's terse, paratactic style and minimal overt commentary, which leaves an impression of realism and allows the reader to make connections among the various events and ideas; through the use of temporal coordinates which envelop the reader's own time and world; by beginning with baptism, an experience which, it can be assumed, Mark's audience would have known.

The Narrator. The prologue of the Gospel establishes the narrator's stance vis-a-vis the implied author, the narratee, and the implied audience, and sets up the conceptual point of view from which the ensuing story will be narrated. In his prologue, Mark sets up the relationship among these narrative components in such a way that the narrative voice,[52] the voice through which the reader actually experiences the narrative, emerges as unlimited, omniscient,

---

[52]Fowler makes this helpful distinction between point of view and voice, relying on Renee Genette, *Narrative Discourse*, 161-62, 185-86; see Fowler, 66.

authoritative and reliable.[53] Rhoads and Michie provide a helpful summary of the characteristics of Mark's narrator:

> The salient features of Mark's narrator are these: the narrator does not figure in the events of the story; speaks in the third person; is not bound by time or space in the telling of the story; is an implied invisible presence in every scene, capable of being anywhere to "recount" the action; displays full omniscience by narrating the thoughts, feelings, or sensory experiences of many characters; often turns from the story to give direct "asides" to the reader, explaining a custom or translating a word or commenting on the story; and narrates the story from one over-arching ideological point of view.[54]

This stance clearly implies a claim to ultimate authority concerning the narrated events; such a narrative stance is often called "God-like,"[55] and here the simile practically has literal force: the narrator claims to know how this story fits into God's design for creation and history as a whole (e.g., 1:2-4), what God's evaluative point of view on Jesus is (1:11), and the workings of the holy spirit (1:10, 12). Meir Sternberg, in his study of the narrative poetics of the Jewish Bible, aptly describes the rhetorical effect of such a narrator:

> The very choice to devise an omniscient narrator serves the purpose of staging and glorifying an omniscient God. . . .The Bible therefore postulates a narrator with such free movement through time and space, the public and the private arena, that he invests his dramatizations with the authority of an omniscience equivalent to God's own. Since this omniscience itself ultimately goes back to God, such tactics of validation may not survive logical analysis—but then rhetoric never does, or else there would be no need for it. Its proof lies in the swallowing, and the Bible's art makes resistance difficult, certainly to the implied audience of believers.[56]

---

[53]On Mark's narrator, see Rhoads and Michie, *Mark as Story*, 35-42; also Norman Petersen, "'Point of View' in Mark's Narrative," *Semeia* 12 (1978), 97-121.

[54]Rhoads and Michie, 36.

[55]See Fowler, 65 n. 12.

[56]Meir Sternberg, *The Poetics of Biblical Narrative: Ideological Literature and the Drama of Reading* (Bloomington: Indiana University Press, 1987), 90. Sternberg unfairly draws a sharp line between the rhetoric of the Jewish Bible and that of the New Testament, however, claiming that while Hebrew literature remains accessible to all through a calculated ambiguity in narration (see, e.g., his reading of the story of David and Bathsheba, 190-6), the New Testament rhetoric seeks to exclude any other

That is precisely what Mark's narrative strategy attempts to do: Make resistance to the "gospel of Jesus Christ" (which is the gospel of God) difficult, if not impossible.

The force of the narrator's stance is further enhanced in Mark's Gospel by the lack of any distinction between the implied author and the narrator, which carries with it the corresponding collapse between narratee and implied audience.[57] This strategy brings author and audience as close together as possible, again with persuasive effect. Moreover, there is a further alignment between the narrative voice and that of the protagonist. As Fowler points out, the narrator and Jesus "become virtually indistinguishable," sharing the same conceptual point of view.[58] This careful alignment of the points of view of the narrator, God's own self, and Jesus, almost always over against the characters in the story, serves to give the audience confidence that, among the various other points of view offered throughout the story, this is the one the audience is to embrace.[59]

The first fifteen verses of the Gospel clearly manifest this rhetorical situation. First, Jesus is proclaimed by the narrator to be "the Christ, the Son of God" in the opening sentence (1:1). There is no external, formal claim to authority here, but rather a simple but forceful declaration. The narrative continues, however, with the implicit assertion that this point of view on Jesus will be confirmed

---

possible reading of a story (49). I would argue that, at least with respect to Mark, there is also very much a rhetoric of indirection (Fowler) which works in much the same way.

[57]See Fowler, 78-80.

[58]Fowler, 73. Fowler claims that Mark does this in three ways: First, through the use of "inside views" on what characters in the story are thinking and feeling; Jesus and the narrator share this capacity (e.g., 2:6-7). Second, Jesus will often repeat the words of the narrator (e.g., 8:1-2), or vice versa (e.g., 1:17-18); finally, by giving over to Jesus the role of voicing the major norms of the narrative (74-6). As Fowler sums it up, "we can say that the narrator and his protagonist share not only the same perceptual point of view and the same voice but also the same conceptual point of view" (76).

[59]As Fowler puts it, "[I]n the course of reading the Gospel, a real reader is invited to play the role of the implied reader and also the role of the narratee, and from that position the reader is encouraged to move as close as possible to the narrator and the narrator's Jesus and to adopt their conceptual point of view" (80).

in terms of what, presumably, author and audience agree to be the criterion for authentication of such claims: Israel's Scriptures. The "beginning of the gospel"—i.e., the opening scene of the larger story[60]—unfolds according to the promise made in Israel's scriptures. John the Baptist, whose appearance as "Elijah" the narrator presents as confirmation of these promises (vv. 2-4),[61] and suggests that he, too, speaks for God, also testifies to Jesus' identity (vv. 7-8). Then God himself appears on the scene, accompanied by the violent tearing of the heavens, and lends ultimate authority to the claims about Jesus, setting forth what will be the normative evaluation of Jesus' identity: He is God's beloved son.[62] Jesus' own actions reveal his acceptance of his identity and mission: he submits to John's baptism (vv. 9-11); he engages in an initial and foundational confrontation with Satan (vv. 12-13); and emerges to proclaim the gospel of God in word and deed (vv. 14-15).

The interesting and most important question here, of course, is what Mark does with this rhetorical strategy. Such a close alignment among the principal authoritative voices, and the acceptance of these voices required of the reader, as noted above, brings about the potential for great distance between the reader and the characters in the story, most of whom lack this knowledge or, if they obtain it (e.g., in the transfiguration), remain uncomprehending. Almost all interpreters who note this potential assert that it serves to bring the reader in line with the author's point of view over against the failing characters, especially the disciples. Indeed, Fowler goes so far as to say that Mark "is so eager to secure the reader's adherence to the Jesus of his story that he is willing to sacrifice the disciples of his story."[63] That is, the function of the disciples, and all other characters who offer opposition to Jesus, is simply to provide a foil for the

---

[60]See the discussion above.

[61]As I argued above, Tolbert's argument that the opening scriptural citation refers to Jesus primarily, and John secondarily is not convincing (*Sowing the Gospel*, 239-248).

[62]It is interesting to note that when God speaks, it is with scriptural language, thus reinforcing the connection between God and scripture.

[63]Fowler, 80; see Tolbert, 297-299; Robert Tannehill, "The Disciples in Mark: The Function of a Narrative Role," in *The Interpretation of Mark* (ed. William Telford; Philadelphia: Fortress Press, 1985), 134-57.

rhetorical goals of the author. The reader is put in a position of moral and divine superiority over those characters, and in that position he is presumed to be able to embrace the redemption offered in God's saving work which is denied to those who opposed or misunderstood Jesus.

This will be an issue to be taken up more fully in a subsequent chapter; but here I wish to point out that such an understanding of Mark's narrative strategy would give the power offered through the narrative voice an almost abusive aspect. The failure of those whom Jesus called and to whom he granted special insight (the "mystery of the reign of God," 4:11-12 [see also 9:2-13]), indeed the failure of any human character to comprehend what it means to follow Jesus, cannot serve rhetorically to provide the grounds for embracing that message. In fact, it may even serve to repulse readers who see, on the one hand, the compassion Jesus has for the lost, which virtue the audience is to emulate, while on the other hand the audience sees God abandon those whom Jesus has called. The increasing distance between the authoritative point of view and the principal human characters, when combined with the compassion for the lost exhibited by the main character, will much more likely result in the audience's own experience of the clash between the "things of human beings" and the "things of God" (8:32). Again, the principal rhetorical goal of the intense conflict Jesus' ministry brings about is to address the audience's own situation of conflict with the gospel message; I will argue below that the stripping away of confidence in human capacity to respond faithfully to the gospel leaves the audience at the end of Mark's narrative only with a word of promise.

The Mode of Narration. I will develop this argument in my reading of the conflicts in Chapters 4 and 5. But it relates to the next point I wish to make about the prologue: the narrative voice presents itself as one who "knows all, but only tells some." That is, the prologue introduces the terse, paratactic style that characterizes the mode of presentation of the whole, and which compels the reader to fill gaps on his own. While, on the one hand, Mark offers clear and explicit commentary on Jesus' identity from the narrative's point of view (e.g., 1:1; 1:11), he leaves much of the "work" of setting that identity in relation to Jesus' fate, and the implications of his fate for those who would follow him, up to the audience. In other words, Mark's narrative is just as important for what it does not say as what it does.[64]

Mark's less than graceful style of narration has often given rise to the assertion that it must therefore lack literary or rhetorical sophistication. Previous Markan scholars saw it as either an indication that Mark is therefore reporting things "as they happened" or as he knew them (nineteenth century), or that he was simply compiling traditional units over which he was not master (e.g., Bultmann). Mary Ann Tolbert's work on Mark's rhetoric in its first-century context demonstrates, however, that the very "ordinary" literary style Mark exhibits ought not lead to these conclusions. As she notes, "That Mark lacks graceful periods, extended figures, or light pleasantries does not indicate that the narrative is without rhetorical development, if one understands the variety of styles available to a Hellenistic author."[65] Among the styles Tolbert adduces, principally from the rhetorical handbook of Demetrius (see above), is one which, in fact, sets forth the kind of style Mark exhibits: "the simple co-ordination of clauses with καί instead of the use of participles or subordinate clauses," and the absence "of the connecting links supplied by particles and conjunctions."[66] Demetrius notes in his rhetorical handbook (*On Style*) that such a style can be more persuasive than a self-consciously grand, ornate one. He suggests that

> not everything should be given lengthy treatment with full details but some points should be left for our hearer to grasp and infer for himself. If he infers what you have omitted, he no longer just listens to you but acts as your witness, one too who is predisposed in your favor since he feels he has been intelligent and you are the person who has given him this opportunity to exercise his intelligence. In fact, to

---

[64]As Donald Juel has pointed out with respect to Jesus' initial appearance, "The information the narrator fails to provide is at least as impressive as what he does" (*Master of Surprise: Mark Interpreted* [Minneapolis: Fortress Press, 1994], 33).

[65]Tolbert, *Sowing the Gospel*, 42. See also Fowler, 134-40.

[66]Vincent Taylor, *The Gospel According to St. Mark* (London: Macmillan/New York: St. Martin's Press, 1966), 48-9; quoted in Tolbert, 42.

tell your hearer everything as if he were a fool is to reveal that you think him one.[67]

Thus the features of Mark's gap-ridden style, Tolbert concludes, "all find a home in Greek rhetorical theory."[68]

When viewed from the perspective of Mark's rhetorical goal—to shape an audience which will embrace the crucified Messiah he presents—the force of these stylistic features emerges distinctly. It is the audience who must do the work of filling the gaps in the narrative, and it is thereby drawn further into the orb of the narrative world. The technique is especially appropriate for Mark's understanding of Jesus, which involves bringing together events, ideas, and images that cannot be presented coherently through explicit, explanatory language.[69] And, as noted above, the exercise is far from a purely intellectual one. The attempt to bring together the conflicting images and ideas also stimulates the audience's imagination and emotions.[70]

The prologue aptly introduces this mode of narration, for the reader is from the very beginning compelled to understand events in relation to each other whose connection is only inferred, and indeed whose "logic" would appear strained if explicitly spelled out. The very opening statement of the Gospel requires just such an effort. After the explicit declaration that the following events mark the beginning of the gospel of Jesus Christ, the Son of God, Mark lays before the reader a composite scriptural citation, introduced as though it were all from the prophet Isaiah (vv. 2-3), and then narrates the appearance of John the Baptist in the wilderness (v. 4). John is subsequently described in terms of the prophet Elijah (v. 6; see 2 Kings 1:8), preaches a baptism for the forgiveness of sins, predicts the coming of one "mightier" than himself, and, suddenly and mysteriously, is removed from the scene through his arrest.

---

[67]Demitrius, *On Style*, 221-22; quoted in Tolbert, 43.

[68]Tolbert, 43.

[69]Cf. Boring, "The Christology of Mark," *Semeia* 32 (1983), 125-53.

[70]See Juel's helpful discussion of the imaginative moves the baptism of Jesus in Mark encourages (*Master of Surprise*, 33-43); more on this below.

First, there is the question of the relationship between the scriptural citation and John's appearance.[71] The abruptness of the introduction leaves one wondering about whom the scripture is speaking. As noted above, καθὼς γέγραπται does most likely refer backwards to "the beginning of the gospel," which might lead one to associate the citation with Jesus himself.[72] In retrospect, however, Mark clearly wants the reader to associate John the Baptist with the Elijah-type figure God promised to "send before the face" of his final messenger "to prepare the way;" he is "the voice crying in the wilderness."

This mode of presentation has several significant implications. First, the opening verses signal to the reader that the unfolding story cannot be apprehended apart from the larger story of God's dealings with Israel. As many commentators have noted, the composite citation draws together motifs which were commonly associated with God's final, apocalyptic intervention in history; the notion that this consummation would take place in the desert, as Isaiah envisioned it, is reflected in the Qumran community's exegesis of this same passage from Isaiah (40:3).[73] Each of the Gospels makes the connection between the story of Jesus and God's dealings with Israel an indispensable feature of their presentations. What distinguishes Mark in this respect, however, especially over against, for example, Matthew's Gospel, is the way in which he compels the audience to make the connections between the scriptural "echoes" he invokes and the unfolding narrative. The retrospective connection the audience makes between the citation and John's appearance has a very different rhetorical effect from the more explicit, formulaic connection characteristic of Matthew (e.g., Matt. 1:23; 2:6, 15, 18, etc.). While the latter evinces a pattern of movement from the scriptural promise to its fulfillment in the present, Mark's presentation encourages a look from the present situation back to God's past actions and promises, and allows for a freer, more mutual interpreta-

---

[71]The citation, of course, is actually a composite; most interpreters find elements of Ex. 23:20 and Mal. 3:1 in v. 2; v. 3 comes from Is. 40:3 LXX. See Joel Marcus, *The Way of the Lord*, 12-17.

[72]Tolbert, 239-48.

[73]See, e.g., Marcus, 22-6.

tion of the two; in the explicit statement that "this happened to fulfill this scripture," the imagination is closed down in a more overt attempt to persuade by appeal to external authority, while in Mark the imagination is set free to make connections.[74] In fact, this is the only place that the Markan narrator himself quotes scripture; from here on, reference to scripture comes either in the form of allusion (e.g., 1:13; 14:3; 15:20) or placed in the mouth of characters, most notably Jesus (e.g.10:6-8; 12:10-11, 36; 13:24-25; 14:27, 62; 15:34).[75] The result, I would argue, is both more involvement on the part of the reader, as well as, in part because of this, a narrative argument that "feels" more authentic.[76]

Again, the particular kind of work the author gives over to the reader also speaks for the appropriateness and effectiveness of Mark's laconic style. Returning to Mark's presentation of John the Baptist, we can now see more clearly why it might be important to include vv. 14-15 rhetorically in the prologue, for, as noted above, only with the reference to his ultimate fate is his work as forerunner complete. The scriptural citation has identified him (or rather, the reader has made this association) as the one who will "prepare the way" for God's anointed one to bring about the final consummation of history; he himself has stated that one will come "after me" (ὀπίσω μου).[77] The next thing the reader hears about John represents a rather arresting development in the story.[78] The way in which this

---

[74]In this sense, Mark corresponds more closely to the pattern of earliest Christian reflection on the scriptures in light of Jesus as Messiah; see Nils Dahl, "The Crucified Messiah," and Donald Juel, *Messianic Exegesis: Christological Interpretation of the Old Testament in Early Christianity* (Philadelphia: Fortress Press, 1988).

[75]Other characters, including Jesus' opponents, also quote scripture (e.g., 10:6; 12:19); in the next chapter we will see, in fact, that the conflict between Jesus and the religious authorities turns in large measure on the interpretation of scripture.

[76]Gabriel Josipovici cites this freer appropriation of scripture in Mark as one of the things that makes it a more convincing narrative argument: "[T]he more we sense an author's desire to authenticate his narrative, the less likely we are to assent to it, while the less conscious he seems to be of the effect he is making, the greater will be that effect" (*The Book of God*, 217-18).

[77]See the discussion above.

[78]Of course, it might be argued that John's fate was already known to Mark's audience, as it would be to most contemporary Christians. This requires only a small

deathward turn in the fate of "Elijah" relates to his status as the divinely chosen forerunner in the final battle against the forces of Satan, however, is left to the reader to work out through the rest of the narrative.

When the story does return to amplify John's fate, it is in a manner very similar to the prologue; this is a good example of how the body of the narrative continues to require the kind of participation of the audience for which the prologue has prepared it. The actual story of John's fate (6:14-29), of course, is narrated in retrospect, "sandwiched" between the sending out of the disciples (6:7-13) and their return (6:30); it comes as an ominous foreshadowing of the implications of following the way John prepared.[79] But perhaps even more significant is the point at which, in response to the disciples' query about Elijah, Jesus relates his own fate to that of John's, and claims that both occur "as it is written" (καθὼς γέγραπται, 9:11-13). The disciples have asked why the "scribes" say Elijah must come first, and Jesus responds by saying that "Elijah does come first to restore all things; and how is it written of the Son of man, that he should suffer many things and be treated with contempt? But I tell you that Elijah has come, and they did to him whatever they pleased" (ὅσα ἤθελον 9:12-13). This passage hearkens back to the prologue's depiction of John the Baptist as Elijah, the fulfillment of the traditional understanding of the scriptural promises (e.g., Mal. 3:1, 22), but fills out the presentation by stating that his violent end was also in accordance with "what was written of him."[80] Here, however, there is no citation that lends specificity to

---

adjustment in how one evaluates Mark's rhetorical strategy; clearly, even if one is aware of his fate, Mark, by placing this comment in v. 14, closely associating Jesus with John, wants to point to this aspect of John's preparatory activity.

[79]For a summary of common interpretations of this intercalation, see Janice Capel Anderson, "Feminist Criticism: The Dancing Daughter," in *Mark and Method* (ed. Janice Capel Anderson and Stephen D. Moore; Minneapolis: Fortress Press, 1992), 118.

[80]See the helpful discussion of this passage in Marcus, *The Way of the Lord*; Marcus argues that the best way to understand the vague reference to scripture here is as an attempt to reconcile apparent contradictions in scripture, a phenomenon of Jewish scriptural interpretation (97-107).

this aspect of the Baptist's career.[81] Here again, Mark appears to leave it to the audience to fill in the significant gap between the traditional expectations and John's actual fate.

What emerges from this passage is a rather striking and paradoxical juxtaposition of "wills," the divine and the human. Jesus says that "they did to him whatever they willed" (ἤθελον 9:13), suggesting that John's death was a matter of human desires, not divine; but then the final clause, καθὼς γέγραπται ἐπ' αὐτόν, asserts that this was, indeed, a reflection of divine will as expressed in scripture. The hint the prologue gives regarding John's fate, cast in what is most likely a divine passive (παραδοθῆναι), also suggests divine agency.[82] As we will see in the next chapter, this paradox is at the heart of the conflict between God's saving action and the world God wills to save, a conflict which results in the death not only of the forerunner, but of the Messiah himself. Here it is important to note that Mark's style befits his rhetorical ends; the reader is confronted with this apparently unresolved tension, this gap, between the conviction that God, in both John and Jesus, is engaged in bringing about the final redemption of creation on the one hand, and the undeniable fact that significant elements within creation oppose this action and seem to have their way. This tension comes to the reader as radical challenge; again, the information about John's identity provided by the prologue does not simply give the reader a position of superiority over the characters in the story, but links up with the audience's own experience of the conflict between God's promises and the reality of a world whose power structures stand in apparently effective opposition to those promises.

As with the forerunner, so the "major player" in God's redemptive plan; Mark's presentation of Jesus in the prologue, which I will discuss at length below, reveals the same kind of tension and places the same type of challenges before the reader as the presentation of John the Baptist. As with John, Mark brings traditional messianic promises (especially in 1:11) together with ideas and

---

[81]The question of what scriptures Mark's protagonist has in mind has long vexed scholars. See Marcus, 97-98; the same question applies, of course, to 9:12 and 14:21.

[82]See discussion above and Keck, 362-3.

imagery which would seem to contradict these promises (e.g., Jesus' submission to John's baptism). The scriptural language of 1:11 encompasses both the promises Jesus fulfills and the way in which those promises are endangered by human and "super-human" opposition to and incomprehension of God's redemptive plan.

The Intercalated Audience. Before turning to a more substantive discussion of the prologue's presentation of Jesus, though, I wish to point out briefly two additional, significant ways in which Mark's opening serves to "hook" the audience into the story and prepare it for an effective reception of its rhetoric, and which represent strategies beyond simply providing the audience with information. The first has to do with the temporal coordinates the prologue sets up for the story. Mark's story begins *in media res*, sandwiched between God's past creative activity and promise of redemption and the final consummation of God's activity. The prologue opens with reference to God's past dealings with Israel; the composite scriptural citation in vv. 2-3 actually touches upon both the original "creation" of Israel in the first exodus (Ex. 23:20) as well as the "new exodus," the promise that through Israel, all creation would be redeemed.[83] (For all its vagueness in terms of the ensuing verses, ἀρχή certainly invokes the first verse of Genesis.) For Mark, the appearance of John the Baptist, and then Jesus, marks the turning point in history which God promised through Isaiah. These occurrences provide the foundation for Jesus' proclamation in 1:15 that "the reign of God has drawn near," which in turn provides the basis for the exhortation to "repent and believe in the gospel." But the completion of these events, the final, public advent of God's reign, still lies before the audience; that is, the actual end of the story Mark tells lies in the future, beyond the events Mark narrates in the Gospel.[84] The effect of setting these temporal coordinates is power-

---

[83]See Mauser, *Christ in the Wilderness*, 81-92.

[84]Norman Petersen applies this helpful distinction between "story time," which encompasses all the events and times referred to in the story, and "plotted time," which involves the events actually narrated within the Gospel, selected and arranged according to the designs of the author. That Mark does arrange the story time into plotted incidents serves as evidence that Mark is indeed an intentional narrative (*Literary Criticism*, 49-58).

ful; the story Mark tells envelops the time of the reader, making it clear that the story deals neither with some time in the distant past which bears no relation to the reader's time (as "Once upon a time" or its equivalent would do), nor even with a specific time such as Luke's "fifteenth year of the reign of Tiberius Caesar" (Luke 3:1), but rather with the reader's own time, between the "beginning" of the gospel and its consummation.[85] This location of the audience is confirmed as the narrative unfolds: Jesus makes several predictions or promises whose fulfillment lies beyond the plotted events, most of which have to do with the return of the "Son of man" in glory, his public vindication (e.g., 8:38-9:1; 13:24-27; 14:62; 16:7).

The rhetorical effect of this envelopment is potentially very powerful. Mark's presentation of Jesus provides the foundation, in the events of Jesus' career, for the future hope that God will complete the promised redemption of creation against the backdrop of forces opposed to God. Mark's story, from the prologue on, locates the audience in the tension between promises which have been fulfilled and promises which have not. Indeed, much of the plot of the body of the narrative revolves around a prediction-fulfillment scheme:[86] Jesus predicts his passion and resurrection (2:20; 8:31; 9:12; 9:30-32; 10:32-34); knows what the disciples will encounter when they go to prepare Jesus' entrance into Jerusalem (11:1-4); he predicts Peter's denial (14:30), Judas' betrayal (14:18-21), and the disciples' desertion of Jesus (14:26-27).[87] All of these predictions eventually come to pass in the course of the story, and serve to instill confidence in the audience regarding the things which have yet to come to pass. This rhetorical strategy extends in the other direction as well, serving to undergird the Gospel's conviction that the identity and destiny of Jesus confirm God's promises made to Israel in the past.

---

[85]Boring, "Mark 1:1-15," 68-9.

[86]As Juel has pointed out (see, e.g., *Master of Surprise*, 114-15); also Andrew T. Lincoln, "The Promise and the Failure—Mark 16:7-8," *JBL* 108 (1989), 283-300, pp. 293-296; Petersen, *Literary Criticism*, 54-80.

[87]Not surprisingly, the motif is especially prevalent in the Jerusalem section of the Gospel (11:1-16:8), where confidence in Jesus' word becomes the only means of seeing Jesus' violent fate as God's will.

The "intercalation" of the audience's time and experience into the larger story of God's dealings with Israel and humanity in fact may, as Frank Kermode has suggested, provide a clue to the structure and meaning of the whole Gospel. The insertion of one story into the frame of another is one of Mark's most frequently employed literary techniques. While previous scholarship has often attributed these intercalations to the composite nature of Mark's narrative, others have more recently explored them for their interpretive possibilities:[88] Mark inserts the healing of the woman with the flow of blood into the story of the raising of Jairus' daughter; the story of John the Baptist's fate is inserted into the disciples' evangelistic mission (6:7-30); the story of Peter's denial is sandwiched between the accounts of Jesus' arrest and trial (14:53-72); and, in fact, the whole of the narrative is encompassed by the frame of a violent epiphany and a "confession" of Jesus' identity (1:10-11; 15:38-39). In all of these instances, Mark invites the reader to interpret the intercalated material through the frame, thus opening up a whole host of interpretive possibilities, as well as constraints. Kermode's comments on this technique capture its effect well; its frequent repetition, he says,

> makes one wonder whether the intercalated stories do not exist to replicate, in particular episodes, some feature characteristic of the whole discourse. Should we think of the whole gospel as an intercalated story? It is inserted between another story and its end. It divides and joins the promises and the fulfillments. It is an insertion, at the most crucial point of impression, into the world-narrative. . . . It stands at the moment of transition between the main body of history and the end of history; and what it says has a powerful effect on both. . . . [T]he gospel stands between past and immediately future time, establishing a continuity which makes sense only in terms of that which interrupts it. All Mark's minor intercalations reflect the image of a great intervention represented by the whole book. And all such lesser interventions deepen and complicate the sense of the narrative;

---

[88]See, e.g., Rhoads and Michie, *Mark as Story: An Introduction to the Narrative of a Gospel* (Philadelphia: Fortress , 1982), 51; Janice Capel Anderson and Stephen Moore, eds, *Mark and Method: New Approaches in Biblical Studies* (Minneapolis: Fortress Press, 1992), 34-7; Donald Juel, *Messiah and Temple* (SBLDS 31; Missoula, MT: Scholar's Press, 1977), 66-69.

or, they are indications that more story is needed, as a supplement, if the story is to make sense.[89]

The effect, in other words, is to bring the audience into the narrative world in such a way as to enable it to see its own time and story in relation to the story's time, and, most importantly, to see in its own future the real completion of the story. The audience feels that it, too, is poised between the momentous events of Jesus' story, which represent a decisive turn in the larger story of God's creative and redemptive activity, and the impending consummation of that activity.[90]

What is more, Kermode asserts that these intercalations demonstrate how a narrative can "cultivate structural oppositions, bring together significantly antithetical persons or actions or even words."[91] As we have seen, such oppositions characterize both the prologue and the Gospel as a whole; while they may pose a challenge to making logical, coherent sense out of Mark's narrative, their ultimate aim is to make sense out of an otherwise "unfollowable world." As Kermode puts it,

> [The] device of intercalation in Mark's narrative is an emblem of many conjunctions and oppositions, which are found at all levels of the discourse. . . . [T]hese conjunctions and oppositions reflect something of what the Gospel presupposes of its own structure, and the structure of the world.[92]

Here, I would argue, lies a key both to Mark's strategy and to its effectiveness: the oppositions which characterize Mark's narrative, both in terms of the conflicts which drive the plot and the conceptual tensions, reflect the audience's world back to them; to the degree that the Gospel persuades the audience that this world is the arena of God's life-giving activity and the ground for the future, ultimate

---

[89]Kermode, *The Genesis of Secrecy: On the Interpretation of Narrative* (Cambridge: Harvard University Press, 1979), 134-35.

[90]Dan Via locates the narrative and its audience in "the middle of time;" see *The Ethics of Mark's Gospel: In the Middle of Time* (Philadelphia: Fortress Press, 1985).

[91]Kermode, 133.

[92]Kermode, 137.

resolution to these oppositions, the Gospel renders the world followable and the audience's present experiences meaningful.[93] To refer once again to the words of Gabriel Josipovici, "We assent to narratives, as we do to people, to the degree that we grow to feel we can trust them." Mark's Gospel earns this trust through its capacity to "see the thing as it is," as Luther put it, and offer hope precisely in this reality.

Through the Waters. One final observation about the way in which Mark's Gospel sets the stage for viewing the conflicts in the Gospel in relation to the audience's own time and experience is worthy of note. Interpreters of the prologue generally overlook an important aspect of the significance of Mark's starting-point: He begins with baptism, an experience, it is safe to assume, with which Mark's audience would have been familiar, perhaps intimately (and this is certainly the case with modern readers). While it may be difficult to determine what image of baptism the author presupposes,[94] clearly both John's preaching of baptism and Jesus' own summons to repent and believe link up with the defining experience of the "Christian" life. As we will see below, Jesus' own baptism is a theophany which marks the turning point in God's dealings with creation, and is hardly in that sense a "model" for Christian baptism *per se.* Yet even if it cannot be presupposed that Mark's audience already understood baptism as new life out of death, as Paul expressed it (e.g., Romans 6), Mark's narrative moves the audience to make such a connection; by beginning with the beginning of the Christian life, Mark's narrative seeks to move that life in a particular direction through his narrative.[95]

---

[93]For Kermode, of course, the perception of a followable world is an illusion; it is the light behind the door in Kafka's parable, which is finally closed forever (see, e.g., 27-8). The illusion of followability is the result of the trickery of interpretation (144-45). On this, see Juel, *A Master of Surprise,* 117-21.

[94]Hooker suggests that the audience perhaps was aware of, for example, Paul's understanding of baptism as expressed in Romans 6 (*The Gospel According to Saint Mark,* 45; see also Drury, "Mark 1:1-15," 30-1).

[95]As Drury puts it, "beginnings of text and of Christian life synchronize" (31).

I have maintained above that Mark's Gospel is not "about" Jesus in himself, but Jesus in relation to the disciples and to the audience.[96] As I will observe below, Mark sets Jesus' baptism in relation to his death, both by invoking the imagery of his baptism at the scene of his death (15:34-39) and by conveying to his disciples that his death is a baptism (10:38-40). To the degree that Mark's narrative moves its hearers to embrace the new reality opened up by God through Jesus' life, death, and resurrection, it encourages them to understand their own baptisms as the ground of their participation in that reality. This becomes especially important when viewed in relation to the conflicts in the Gospel. It is precisely Jesus' acceptance of his "commission" to live out of the new reality brought about by God that brings him into conflict with forces opposed to God, and results in his death. For Mark, because that reality stands in opposition to much of the rest of the world, those who participate in it will themselves encounter opposition and conflict—indeed, it is constitutive of the Christian experience for Mark (4:2-20; 8:34-37; 10:42-45; 13:9-13). Thus for Mark, both the proper understanding of Jesus' identity and fate as well as the proper orientation of the life of discipleship revolve around the conflict between God's reign and a world opposed to God, which leads to the cross. Mark wants his audience to understand that their baptisms represent an entrance into this conflict, that the conflicts which so characterized Jesus' story reflect the reality in which they find themselves. By beginning his narrative with reference to baptism, Mark thus provides another crucial link with his audience and their experience, and reveals how the audience is to view the conflicts in the body of the narrative.[97]

---

[96]Recall Keck's observation that "no strictly Christological aim (in the narrow sense of doctrine about the person of Christ) does justice to the peculiarity of Mark—namely the steady emphasis on the disciples' participation in the work of Jesus. . . . What makes the story of Jesus εὐαγγέλιον for Mark is not, to speak anachronistically, who Jesus is *in se* but who he is *pro nobis*; strangely (for us!), Jesus is good news because as the Son of God he calls men to follow him with their own crosses" ("The Introduction to Mark's Gospel," 363-64.).

[97]Drury puts it well when he observes that baptism serves to show the "binding of the fate of Jesus into the fate of his disciples. The narrative primacy of baptism, the Christian rite of passage, the death sacrament enabling new life, achieved this for him and his readers with disconcerting power and would have alerted them to the way the

THE PRESENTATION OF JESUS

The central feature of Mark's prologue, of course, is his presentation of Jesus, which dominates the second half of the introduction (1:9-15). The presentation of Jesus against the backdrop of the rhetorical techniques outlined above represents the ultimate aim of the prologue. As noted above, many commentators observe the way in which the introduction of Jesus in the prologue serves to give the reader information crucial to "making sense" out of the ensuing narrative, information provided only to the reader. Mark informs the audience that Jesus is, according to divine witness, the "beloved Son of God" (1:11). Armed with this information, the audience is able to view the unfolding narrative from a privileged vantage point; the readers know from the beginning what the characters in the story struggle, usually unsuccessfully, to discern: the religious leaders fail to comprehend Jesus' exorcisms because they do not know that Jesus is the spirit-empowered Son of God who "bound" Satan in the wilderness (3:22-30); the disciples first fail to comprehend Jesus' ability to heal and his power over nature (4:35-41; 8:17-21), and then are unable to understand his destiny (8:31-33; 9:35-40; 14:50); Herod confuses Jesus with John because he does not know how they are related in God's eschatological plan, as the prologue reveals (6:14-16). As Matera puts it, "[A]ll of these misunderstandings result from ignorance of information found in the prologue: the proper relationship between John and Jesus; the declaration of Jesus' sonship; the conflict between Jesus and Satan in the wilderness."[98]

---

narrative had to go on to the outcome which they knew" (34).

It is important to note here, as I will discuss in a subsequent chapter, that conflict and suffering do not represent the *goal* of God's redemptive action, as is often asserted. That is, the death of Jesus does not reflect God's will in the abstract, theological sense that God somehow requires blood to satisfy God's justice, but is rather the *result* of living within the reality of God's reign in a world as yet not fully redeemed, and in fundamental ways opposed to God. This holds true for the life of discipleship as well. (On this see the helpful study by Donald Senior, *The Passion of Jesus According to Mark* [Wilmington, DE: Michael Glazier, Inc., 1984], 139-42.)

[98]Matera, "The Prologue as the Interpretative Key," 12.

Although this is certainly the case, such a view represents an insufficient accounting of what Mark accomplishes in his introduction. I will discuss two things the prologue accomplishes. First, Mark does much more than provide unambiguous information for the reader; his presentation of Jesus is a complex mixture of traditional messianic imagery and a setting that, as Juel puts it, is "all wrong,"[99] as well as imagery which both confirms Jesus' messianic identity and calls it into question. There is no information about Jesus' background, other than that he comes from Nazareth in Galilee—nothing, in other words, which "qualifies" him in any sense as a candidate for Messiah. That is to say, Mark presents the audience with at least as many questions as answers. The reader may "know" who Jesus is, but how he is to understand Jesus' identity in relation to the elements which stand in tension to it, and which foreshadow his fate, represents a significant gap which must be addressed.

Second, Mark points the audience to the key to this gap through the rich resonance of Israel's scripture, suggesting that fruitful filling of the gap will require engagement with God's past dealings with Israel, that the conflict between Jesus' identity and his destiny can move toward resolution only when placed against the background of Israel's scriptures. As Joel Marcus has put it, "If Mark's understated, terse, enigmatic narrative is 'freighted with background,' that background is in large measure supplied by the narratives and poetry of the Old Testament."[100] By invoking Israel's wilderness experience, as well as designating Jesus as God's "beloved Son," Mark guides the audience to particular features of Israel's story which reveal the way in which the story of Jesus confirms God's promises to Israel.

The Tension Introduced

The clash between expectations and reality in Mark's presentation of Jesus begins from his very first appearance (1:9). Verses 1-8,

---

[99]Juel, *Mark*, 36.
[100]Marcus, *The Way of the Lord*, 46.

while containing some surprising elements,[101] suggests a figure in line with traditional expectations: the Christ, the Son of God (1:1), who will redeem God's people through the way prepared for him in the desert, and all nations will see and acknowledge him and the one who sent him.[102] John is Elijah, the preparer of that way (1:6); his description of the coming one calls attention to the tremendous difference in stature between the two figures: the Messiah is more powerful (ἰσχυρότερος) than John/Elijah, so much so that John declares he is not himself worthy to "stoop down and untie the thong of his sandals." Moreover, even the great eschatological task to which John was put will be surpassed by the stronger one: he will baptize not with water but with the Holy Spirit (vv. 7-8).

The words which come on the heels of this declaration, introducing Jesus, could not be more jarringly contrasting: "In those days Jesus came from Nazareth of Galilee and was baptized by John

---

[101]As noted above, the location of John's activity is surprising: Rather than being centered in the holy city itself, the crowds come *from* Jerusalem and Judea into the desert. This foreshadows the role that Jerusalem will play in the ensuing narrative (see, e.g., Juel, *Mark*, 31; Lührmann, 35).

[102]To speak of "traditional messianic expectations" does not suggest a monolithic, uniform conception of the messiah, or a messianic figure, in Second Temple Judaism. The various expressions of Judaism of the period evince diverse expectations of how, indeed whether, God would redeem Israel and the world by sending an "agent" of some sorts—be it prophet, priest, or king. It is possible, however, based on examination of Israel's Scriptures, and especially the literature of Second Temple Judaism, to speak of a broad set of characteristics which relate this figure to God's intervention in history on behalf of Israel (see, e.g., James Charlesworth, "From Messianiology to Christology: Problems and Prospects," in *The Messiah: Developments in Earliest Judaism and Christianity* [The First Princeton Symposium on Judaism and Christian Origins; ed. James H. Charlesworth; Minneapolis: Fortress, 1992] 3-35; see the list of eight points of consensus among contemporary scholars, esp. nos. 1-4). Moreover, as Juel has observed, one of the best sources for gaining a sense of first-century messianic expectations is from Mark's Gospel itself (not to mention other passages in the NT such as 1 Cor 1:18-25). That some expressions of first-century Judaism expected a royal figure of some power and stature—possessing, indeed, enough power to be a threat to the Roman empire—is clear both from the fact of his crucifixion as a messianic (i.e., royal) pretender as well as from the mockery which attends his crucifixion (e.g., Mark 15:16-20; see Juel, "The Origin of Mark's Christology," in Charlesworth, 449-60, esp. p. 453). Without such a conception in the background, notes Juel, Mark's passion narrative makes no sense (453); I would suggest the same holds true for the prologue, and the Gospel as a whole.

in the Jordan" (1:9). Perhaps other than the echo of the Septuagint in the phrase καὶ ἐγένετο ἐν ἐκείναις ταῖς ἡμέραις (see, e.g., Judg 19:1; 1 Sam 28:1), everything about Jesus' initial appearance contrasts with what one has been led to expect. He comes from Nazareth in Galilee, a town far removed from the religious and political power base. The other Gospels, by comparison, make it clear either that Jesus has close ties to more traditional messianic locations (Matt 2:1; Luke 2), or subordinate his earthly origin to his heavenly one (John 1:1-18). Further, in what is perhaps the first instance of situational irony in the Gospel, rather than appearing to baptize with the Holy Spirit, Jesus submits to John's "baptism of repentance for the forgiveness of sins," and himself receives the spirit.[103]

Jesus' submission to John's baptism is especially jarring; indeed, two of Mark's earliest "readers," Matthew and Luke, each recognize the inappropriateness of this scene and attempt to mute it, as does John's Gospel.[104] But Mark leaves the tension unadorned; as such, it prepares the reader for something that in fact becomes a signature feature of Jesus' Messiahship, his scandalizing traffic with "sinners" and outcasts (e.g., 2:3-12, 15-17). Thus, one can already begin to see the way in which the nature of Jesus' Messiahship leads to conflict, and that it is a conflict not simply between Jesus and the religious authorities, but in the audience itself, which must also face the scandalous implications of such a Messiah, one who transgresses the supposedly divinely-ordained boundaries that order the audience's socio-religious world.[105] As we will see in the next chapter,

---

[103]See Tolbert, *Sowing the Gospel*, 110.

[104]Matthew fills this significant gap by constructing a dialogue between John and Jesus in which the inappropriateness is acknowledged, and uses the opportunity to tap into one of his main themes, righteousness; only then does John "consent" to the baptism (Matt 3:13-15); Luke glosses over it by lumping Jesus' baptism in with "all the people's," and also inserts one of his favorite characteristics of Jesus, his frequent praying (Luke 3:21); John omits reference to it entirely; his Baptist notes only in retrospect that he "saw the Spirit descending from heaven like a dove, and it remained on him" (John 1:32).

[105]See Juel, *Master of Surprise*, 38-41; David Rhoads, "Social Criticism: Crossing Boundaries," in *Mark and Method*, 135-161; more on this in the subsequent chapter.

there is an integral connection between Jesus' boundary-transgress-
ing behavior and his arrest, trial, and death.

In the brief scene of Jesus' baptism, which follows "immediately" upon his entrance, Mark once again highlights the tension
between Jesus' identity and his destiny, as well as the boundary-
shattering nature of Jesus' messiahship. The audience is privy to the
events which accompany Jesus' emergence from the water—the
violent rending of the heavens, the descent of the Spirit, and the
voice from heaven—all of which confirm Jesus' identity as the
"Christ, the Son of God" by invoking apocalyptic and messianic
imagery and words from Israel's scriptures, which speak of God's
apocalyptic intervention against Israel's enemies. The rending of the
heavens echoes Isaiah's apocalyptic vision:[106]

> O that you would tear open the heavens and come down, so that the
> mountains would quake at your presence . . . to make your name known
> to your adversaries, so that the nations might tremble at your presence!
> (Isa 64:1-2 NRSV[107])

The Spirit's descent also has eschatological implications; the
outpouring of God's Spirit at the end of days plays a central role in
the events surrounding the last days (cf., e.g., Joel 3:1-5 LXX; Acts
2:16-21; Isa11:2; 61:1).[108] When taken with the Baptist's prediction
about Jesus' own baptizing activity, which was to be "with the Holy
Spirit" (1:8), Jesus emerges as both the bearer of God's end-time

---

[106]For a detailed analysis of the allusions to and citations of scripture in the
baptismal scene, see Marcus, *The Way of the Lord*, 49-56; though I will disagree below
with his interpretation of 1:11.

[107]The Hebrew and LXX have this as 63:19-64:1; the LXX renders the Hebrew
קרע, to rend or tear, as ἀνοίγειν, to open (see Matt 3:16; Luke 3:21). Hence, here
Mark's language is closer to the MT; see Marcus, 49-50; he points out that there are
contacts as well with Isa 63:11 (MT), which speaks of "bringing up from the sea" the
shepherd of the flock, and that God "put his Holy Spirit in" the shepherd.

[108]The belief that the Spirit is to be understood in terms of the Hellenistic
"Divine Man" concept has been thoroughly discredited; see Chapter 1 and Kingsbury,
The Christology of Mark's Gospel, 25-45.

Spirit and the one through whom it will be poured out to God's people.[109]

The voice from heaven forms the climax of the scene, and provides divine confirmation of Jesus' Messianic identity for the audience in scriptural language: "You are my beloved son (σὺ εἶ ὁ υἱός μου ὁ ἀγαπητός, which may also be rendered "You are my Son, the beloved one"); with you I have been pleased (ἐν σοὶ εὐδόκησα)" (1:11). I will discuss more fully below the possible sources of this language in scripture, but clearly it is calculated to associate Jesus with messianic imagery.[110] The most likely source for the first phrase (apart from the ὁ ἀγαπητός) is Ps 2:7; as Joel Marcus points out, Psalm 2 "was consistently understood in the Judaism of Jesus' and of later times, and in early Christianity, as a prophecy of eschatological events: the rebellion of Yahweh's enemies against him and his Messiah, and the latter's decisive defeat of those enemies."[111]

The narrative continues to set forth cosmic, eschatological images in Jesus' encounter with Satan (1:12-13). Here we see the Messiah, Son of God driven into the wilderness to face victoriously the principal adversary to God's redemptive plans. As we later learn, it is most likely in this encounter that Satan is "bound" in order that his "house" might be "plundered" (3:27), and this initial, foundational victory over Satan provides the basis for Jesus' power over the demons. Then, in a prefiguration of the eternal peace that will characterize the coming reign of God, the Messiah is pictured "with

---

[109]See Ernst Lohmeyer, *Das Evangelium des Markus*, 21-22; Guelich, *Mark 1-8:26*, 32.

[110]See Juel, *Messiah and Temple*, 77-125; Hans-Jorg Steichele, *Der leidende Sohn Gottes: Eine Untersuchung einiger alttestamentlicher Motive in der Christologie des Markusevangeliums*, (Biblische Untersuchungen 14; Regensburg: Pustet, 1980); Kingsbury, *The Christology of Mark's Gospel*, 60-68; 145; Frank Matera, *The Kingship of Jesus: Composition and Theology in Mark 15* (Chico, CA: Scholars Press, 1982), 147-151.

[111]Marcus, 59; see, e.g., *Psalms of Solomon* 17:21-46; 4QFlor 1:18-2:3; Rev. 11:15. Marcus goes on to show how the Psalm came to be viewed as reflecting the cosmic struggle between God and the demonic forces opposed to God (62-63); see also Juel, *Messianic Exegesis*, 62-77, for a discussion of 4QFlor.

the wild beasts," in apparent fulfillment of prophetic vision.[112] The prologue concludes with Jesus' entrance into Galilee, and his proclamation of the "good news of victory" over Satan which provides the ground for the conviction that the reign of God has drawn near (1:14-15).[113]

Thus Mark paints a picture of Jesus as Messiah very much in keeping with traditional expectations; indeed, much of the eschatological imagery in this passage is paralleled in post-biblical texts such as the *Testaments of the Twelve Patriarchs*; in the Testament of Levi, the coming of the Messiah is described using very similar imagery:

> The heavens will be opened, and from the temple of glory sanctification will come upon him, with a fatherly voice, as from Abraham to Isaac. And the glory of the Most High shall burst forth upon him. And the spirit of understanding and sanctification shall rest upon him.[114] And he shall open the gates of paradise; he shall remove the sword that has threatened since Adam, and he will grant to the saints to eat of the tree of life. The spirit of holiness shall be upon them. And Beliar shall be bound by him. And he shall grant to his children the authority to trample on wicked spirits (*T. Levi* 18:6-13).

But this is only half of the picture Mark presents; he sets all of this traditional, awe-inspiring imagery of God's ultimate triumph over the source of all opposition to God over against imagery which suggests the opposite. I noted above how the unexpected, even scandalous nature of his appearance from Galilee among sinners in need of repentance suggests that Jesus' Messiahship will run counter

---

[112]See, e.g., Isa 11:6-9; 65:17-25; Hos 2:18 (LXX 2:20); *2 Apoc. Bar.* 73.6; as Guelich puts it, "Jesus' peaceful coexistence 'with the wild animals' boldly declares the presence of the age of salvation when God's deliverance would come in the wilderness and harmony would be established within creation according to the promise" (*Mark 1-8:26*, 39). It has also been suggested that there is some Adam typology present in this scene (see Guelich, 39).

[113]See the discussion above on this interpretation of vv. 14-15.

[114]The extent text concludes this sentence with the phrase "in the water," most likely a Christian interpolation. See *The Old Testament Pseudepigrapha, Vol. 1: Apocalyptic Literature and Testaments* (ed. James Charlesworth; Garden City, NY: Doubleday & Co., 1983), 795; for a discussion of possible interpolations in the *Testaments*, see 776-78.

to expectations in significant ways. But the most surprising element, the greatest dissonance, emerges when one places the motifs of victory alongside the notes which point to Jesus' death. Here the associations of Jesus' baptism with his death come to the fore. As I observed above, Mark develops this association at two key points in his narrative: at the conclusion of the Galilean ministry, when he confronts James and John with the reality of his death and speaks of it in terms of a baptism (10:38-40), and at the scene of his death (15:33-39).

The latter scene is especially important because the imagery and vocabulary used will certainly allow an audience with any degree of interpretive sensitivity to recall the baptismal scene, and interpret it in light of Jesus' death, and vice versa. The twinned stories, indeed, provide a frame or inclusion around the whole of the Gospel narrative,[115] such that the two seemingly mutually exclusive features of Jesus' Messiahship—his divinely authenticated identity and his shameful death on the cross—become inseparable, standing alongside each other in unresolved tension.

Three unmistakable features link the two scenes: reference to Elijah (1:2-3, 6; 15:35), a violent rending (σχίζειν, 1:10; 15:38) and the pronouncement that Jesus is God's Son (1:11; 15:39).[116] Each of these points of contact releases a multitude of powerful interpretive and imaginative possibilities, and brings to a climax the dissonant aspects of Mark's presentation of Jesus as Messiah, Son of God. The invocation of Elijah as part of the crowd's mockery of Jesus[117] recalls John the Baptist's role as forerunner: the "way" which he prepared for the Messiah involved his own arrest, suffering and death (6:17-29; 9:11-13); as I observed above, Mark alludes to this aspect of John's mission near the end of the prologue, when he conveys that John had been "handed over" (1:14). The recapitulation of this theme

---

[115]As many commentators have pointed out; see, e.g., Matera, "The Prologue as the Interpretative Key," 14-15; Juel, *Master of Surprise*, 34, 100-02; Tolbert, *Sowing the Gospel*, 281; H. Jackson, "The Death of Jesus in Mark and the Miracle from the Cross," *NTS* 33 (1987), 16-37, 23-24; Boring, "Mark 1:1-15," 65.

[116]Matera, "The Prologue as the Interpretative Key," 14.

[117]On the ironic aspect of the mockery of Jesus, see Juel, *Master of Surprise*, 96-97; Matera, *Kingship of Jesus*, 21-34.

at the climax of the story, Jesus' death on the cross, compels a "backwards look" at the beginning of the story, indeed a reevaluation of the entire story from the perspective of Jesus' apparent abandonment by his followers and by God's own self. The rhetorical effect which results from such a reevaluation involves an experience of dissonance between the triumphant way in which John is introduced and introduces Jesus on the one hand, and the fate of both figures in the course of the story on the other.

The other two pairings are set up to elicit a similar response. The tearing of the heavens and of the temple curtain forms perhaps the most fascinating juxtaposition. From the perspective of the prologue alone, the tearing of the heavens belongs to those apocalyptic images which accompany the revelation of the Messiah and the outpouring of the Spirit. From the perspective of the end of the story, however, the rending suggests a much more complex constellation of associations. That the image of the tearing of the temple curtain (τò καταπέτασμα[118] 15:38) at Jesus' death has evoked such a wide range of readings among interpreters testifies to its power and effectiveness. The two most common responses associate the event with a removal of boundaries between the divine and human realms,[119] and with the impending destruction of the temple, which Jesus had predicted in 13:1-2 (and foreshadowed in 11:12-21).[120] Clearly the two are not mutually exclusive; indeed, as Juel has shown, the temple theme in the passion narrative may well suggest the supplanting of the fruitless Jewish leadership with a temple "not made with hands."[121] There is new access to God—or rather, God has new access to human beings—through the death of Jesus. From this

---

[118]Most likely the inner of the two curtains referred to by this term; see Taylor, *The Gospel According to St. Mark*, 596-97.

[119]This interpretation goes back at least to Lightfoot, *Gospel Message*, 55-56; see also Vincent Taylor, *The Gospel According to St. Mark*, 596

[120]See Juel, *Messiah and Temple*, 127-39; *Mark*, 225-26; Donahue, *Are You the Christ? The Trial Narrative in the Gospel of Mark* (SBLDS 10; Missoula, MT: Scholar's Press, 1973), 113-47; Robinson, *The Problem of History*, 63-67; Lührmann, *Das Markusevangelium*, 264. Tolbert suggests an association with the dividing of Jesus' garments as signaling Jesus' departure from the human world (*Sowing the Gospel*, 280-81).

[121]*Messiah and Temple*, 143-57.

perspective, the rending of the heavens at Jesus' baptism brings together the awesome theophany which portends God's end-time redemption with Jesus' shameful death on the cross. Likewise, it invites the audience to experience the rending of the temple curtain as a sign that Jesus' death is also a theophany.[122] The framing of the episodes again compels a reevaluation of the whole story and brings its contradictory features to the fore. It recapitulates the whole ministry of Jesus, which has been characterized by a scandalous disregard of traditional barriers between the divine and human, the holy and the profane, and reveals that such a disposition toward these barriers characterizes God's redemptive activity. As I will show in the next chapter, Jesus' death paradoxically marks both the human response to God's new access to human beings as well as the basis for overcoming that response.

Finally, the beginning and ending of Mark's story come together in the two pronouncements regarding Jesus' identity. Both theophanies culminate in the acclamation that Jesus is God's Son. In the first, as I observed above, God's pronouncement that Jesus is God's beloved Son forms a crucial component of the traditional messianic imagery with which Jesus is introduced. In the second, the centurion's statement, regardless of what motivation one ascribes to it, echoes God's evaluative point of view on Jesus, recalling the two other central points in the narrative when the reader was privy to the divine assessment of Jesus' identity (1:11; 9:7). This time, though, it is in response to nothing but Jesus' cry of dereliction and his death. The scene has baffled Mark's readers at least since Matthew and Luke, both of whom sought to deal with the incongruity of the centurion's statement in Mark, which comes only in response to Jesus' death. Matthew added unmistakable portents of the apocalyptic significance of the event, which the centurion sees (27:51-54), and Luke has the centurion state only that Jesus was "righteous" or innocent (δίκαιος 23:47). More modern interpreters have also had difficulty with the scene, insisting, for example, that in fact the centurion saw the tearing of the temple curtain.[123] Here again,

---

[122]See Donald Senior, *The Passion According to Mark*, 135.
[123]See, e.g., Jackson, "The Death of Jesus in Mark," 24.

however, Mark leaves the tension unresolved, and indeed highlights it: Jesus' death is constitutive of his identity as God's Son; he is the Christ not in spite of his death (Luke), nor is that death interpreted as his "glorification" (John), but precisely *because* of his death he is God's beloved Son.[124]

Thus as the imagery from the two stories merges, the audience is compelled to see that the weakness of Jesus displayed in his arrest, trial, and crucifixion belongs to his mission as much as does the glorious victory over Satan. As Juel has put it, "The baptismal scene introduces tensions into the narrative, which will be developed into a story that seeks to depict the reality of the 'good news about Jesus Christ.' And the tension central to the narrative arises from the difference between Jesus the Christ and traditional messianic speculation."[125] This tension which is created by the prologue is not resolved in the story itself, but rather is magnified as Jesus' way to Jerusalem and the cross becomes inevitable. Thus Mark sets before the audience in the prologue radically conflicting images, images of manifest power and submissive weakness; holiness and the breaking of boundaries. That is, the audience is confronted both with the promise of redemption and with its endangerment. The rhetorical goal of the prologue, then, clearly is not simply to provide the audience with information necessary to understand the identity of Jesus and create distance between the audience and the characters, who fail to understand. The ironic potential that arises out of the discrepancy between audience and characters works not solely at the expense of the characters, but exercises its effect on the audience as well.[126] The audience cannot be smugly confident in what they know, because it must somehow come to terms with the tremendous clash

---

[124]Donald Juel has recently suggested that the centurion's remark might best be viewed as sarcasm, in keeping with the mockery of the Roman soldiers throughout the scene (*Mark*, 227-28); this may very well be, but if so, the centurion, like the other soldiers, still proclaims a truth that the audience cannot evade.

[125]*Master of Surprise*, 102.

[126]As Camery-Hoggatt notes, the reader, too, may have begun with inadequate or inappropriate expectations; "As he reads, if he does so with any level of skill or sympathy, he may discover that his own points of view have been blind or obtuse, that the narrative is in its own way passing judgment on its readers" (*Irony in Mark's Gospel*, 93).

between Jesus' identity and his fate. Readers cannot view the opposition to Jesus from a safe distance, but are drawn into the cosmic conflict and are confronted with a radical challenge. They are compelled to fill the gap between the traditional Messianic expectations ascribed to Jesus and the particular nature of Jesus' fulfillment of those expectations. As they move through the story, this tension only increases, and it becomes clear that the principal conflicts in the story have ultimately to do not with the narrative itself, but with the audience: How is it that God's final messenger is rejected by the very ones to whom he was sent? How is it that the disciples whom Jesus chose so utterly fail him? How is it that, though Jesus exercises supreme authority over the demons, he nevertheless succumbs to their power and dies a painful and humiliating death on the cross? All of these speak to the audience's question: How can the Messiah have come and God's promises of a world redeemed not be manifestly confirmed?

THE CRUCIFIED MESSIAH AND THE ENDANGERED PROMISES: THE BELOVED SON OF GOD

In order for the story of Jesus to encounter the audience as "good news," Mark needs to persuade his audience that both halves of the equation—the glory and the humiliation, the victory and the apparent defeat—are fully acknowledged in the proclamation of the gospel. We have seen how a central goal of the prologue is to envelop the audience by linking it to the larger story of God's dealings with creation and Israel from the beginning. In what follows, I will argue that it is precisely by doing so that Mark provides the audience with material to fill the gap in their understanding and experience. He does this, however, not by adducing scriptural citations which "prove" this conviction, but by compelling the reader to see and to feel how the tension inherent in the message, in the narrative world within which the reader is enveloped, corresponds to the real world of the audience, and how both are continuous with God's dealings with creation from the beginning.[127] In order to have a fruitful engagement with Mark's story, the audience must be capable of making connections between the story of John and Jesus and God's past actions, connections which are only imp-licit in the text.[128]

That is to say, to use modern parlance, Mark's narrative is a prime example of intertextuality;[129] it is, in effect, a reading of another narrative—Israel's story. It is a particular reading of that narrative, of course, but the effect of explicitly inserting a story within a larger story is to open up a wide range of interpretive possibilities through quotation, allusion, and the repetition of patterns and motifs; and indeed, inability to make such associations renders the inserted story open to misunderstanding at best, and incomprehensible at worst.[130] My argument in what follows is that the prologue not only begins to set up a grid through which to read

---

[127]This is the problem with most studies of Mark's use of the Old Testament, which tend to focus on Mark's explicit scriptural citations and not on the broader patterns and motifs which are build into the Gospel's very structure.

[128] That Mark assumes this competency on the part of his readers is clear from the opening verses. Juel, *Master of Surprise*, 133-36; Fowler, 87-88. I have noted in my teaching a tremendous difference between introductions to the Bible as a whole and courses devoted only to the New Testament in terms of students' ability to make associations on broader levels between the testaments. Though covering the entire Bible in one semester necessarily limits the depth to which one can explore individual parts, when students come to the New Testament having just read the stories of Israel's founding and history they make many more connections between the two testaments than those who start the semester in a New Testament course.

[129]There is a growing body of literature devoted to the study of this phenomenon; indeed, for deconstrutionists in particular, intertextuality is a characteristic of all narrative; see, e.g., Harold Bloom, *The Anxiety of Influence* (New York: Oxford University Press, 1973); Frank Lentricchia, *After the New Criticism* (Chicago: University of Chicago Press, 1980); the ideas have been explored in biblical studies by, among others, Michael Fishbane, *Biblical Interpretation in Ancient Israel* (Oxford: Clarendon, 1985); Richard B. Hays, *Echoes of Scripture in the Letters of Paul* (New Haven: Yale University Press, 1989); Ched Meyers, *Binding the Strong Man: A Political Reading of Mark's Story of Jesus* (Maryknoll, NY: Orbis Books, 1988), 97-99.

[130]It would be like watching *Return of the Jedi*, the final film in the Star Wars trilogy, without having seen the previous films, and hence not to know, for example, that Darth Vader is Luke Skywalker's father, who had been turned to the "dark side of the force!"

Israel's Scriptures, but just as important, it reveals the narrative's reliance on familiarity with Israel's stories to render the Gospel intelligible and life-giving good news.

The two explicit invocations of scripture which accompany the introductions of John and Jesus will be the primary focus: the composite quotation attributed to Isaiah in vv. 2-3, and the *bat kol*[131] in v. 11 which identifies Jesus as God's "beloved Son." Both passages tap into the precise same conflicting elements in Israel's experience with God as characterize Mark's narrative: the promise of God's redemption and the endangerment of that promise through opposition which comes both from within Israel and from sources external to it.[132]

Israel in the Wilderness

Mark's Gospel opens by recalling foundational events in Israel's history as God's people, events closely linked to Israel's time in the wilderness. The composite quotation from Exodus and Isaiah encompasses, in fact, both the original exodus from Egypt, the event which formed Israel out of the waters of the Red Sea, as well as the "new exodus" proclaimed by Isaiah, in which God would lead Israel triumphantly through the desert, and all nations would see the glory of Israel's God and worship that God.[133]

Mark's ideal reader will be familiar with the stories and themes associated with Israel's time in the wilderness. Its forty-year sojourn there, which occupies the attention of a major portion of the Pentateuch (Exodus, Leviticus, Numbers, and Deuteronomy), and is

---

[131]See Taylor, *The Gospel According to St. Mark*, 161; Bruce Chilton, *A Galilean Rabbi and His Bible: Jesus' Use of the Interpreted Scripture of his Time* (GNS 8; Wilmington, DE: Michael Glazier, 1984), 126-27.

[132]Nils Dahl has identified this pattern as a possible key to the continuity between the testaments, one which avoids the impasse brought on by the tension between modern historical exegesis of scripture and first-century employment of it ("The Crucified Messiah and the Endangered Promises," in *Jesus the Christ: The Historical Origins of Christological Doctrine* [ed. Donald Juel; Minneapolis: Fortress Press, 1991], 65-80).

[133]See Mauser, *Christ in the Wilderness*, 82-83.

continually hearkened back to by the psalms and prophets,[134] was a time of both deep despair and judgment, as well as of the foundational experiences of God's grace and salvation. Indeed, Israel moves directly from the glorious defeat of the Egyptians to the frightful and menacing wilderness, leading it continually to question and finally turn against Moses and God (e.g., Exod 16:2-3; 17:1-3; 32). This pattern is developed contrapuntally in the Pentateuchal accounts of Israel's time in the wilderness, alternating among the people's distress, God's threat of judgment, and God's saving acts. As Mauser has put it, "The wilderness is the place that threatens the very existence of Yahweh's chosen people, but it is also the stage which brightly illumines God's power and readiness to dispel the threat."[135]

Through the exodus from Egypt and the giving of the Law on Sinai, God had formed Israel to be God's "treasured people out of all the peoples" and "a priestly kingdom and a holy nation" (Exod 19:5-6), in fulfillment of God's promise to Abraham that through his descendants "all the families of the earth shall be blessed" (Gen 12:1-3; cf. Gen 15; 17:1-22; 22:15-18). In other words, God had chosen Israel as that entity through which God would bring all of creation into proper relation with the Creator; Israel was to have a priestly, i.e. a mediating role in God's relationship with the whole world.[136] Therefore, when Israel's existence is threatened, the very fate of the world hangs in the balance. And indeed, Israel's existence is threatened in the wilderness both by its own disobedience and rebellion (e.g., Num 25:1-9, etc.), as well as by external forces, both natural and human, which recognize neither Israel nor its God (e.g., Num 14:39-45; 20:2-8, etc.). (In fact, the wilderness experience itself

---

[134]E.g., Pss 78; 95; 106; Hos 2:14; 11:1-3; Ezek 20:36; 34; and of course Isaiah 40. For a helpful examination of the theme in the Psalms and prophets, see Mauser, *Christ in the Wilderness*, 36-52.

[135]Mauser, 21. Joel Marcus objects to seeing as much of the "first exodus" in Mark's composite citation as Mauser does, because the new exodus proclaimed by the prophets, especially Isaiah, shows a predominance of grace over judgment with its hope of eschatological victory in the wilderness (*The Way of the Lord*, 24); the objection is unwarranted, however, at least in terms of the Pentateuchal tradition taken as a whole, as Mauser's study shows.

[136]See, e.g., Jacob Neusner, *The Way of Torah: An Introduction to Judaism* (2d ed.; Encino, CA: Dickenson, 1974).

is a result of Israel's disobedience.) Each time, the very promise of God is endangered as well, often to a point beyond which any human effort or disposition could save it. With that same regularity, however, God enters the fray on Israel's behalf, sending the people food and water, rescuing them from their enemies, and restoring them to their place in God's redemptive plan—reaffirming the promise.

When the prophets envision God's future action as a return to the wilderness (e.g., Ezek 34), they recapitulate these motifs precisely because they so characterize Israel's identity and history. They take on added significance here, though, inasmuch as it is Israel's failure to live as God's people and to fulfill its role in God's purposes for creation in the land which God gave them that occasions the prophetic warning that Israel will once again be taken into the desert (Amos, Hosea), both for judgment and salvation. The wilderness is recalled for its time of Israel's absolute dependence upon God, so that, paradoxically, the state of being which was to characterize Israel in the promised land can be achieved ultimately only through a return to that state of dependence on God which characterized the wilderness period; there God will purge Israel of its sins and fulfill the promise of redemption of the whole world through Israel.[137]

It is against this backdrop, then, that Mark's narrative of the good news of the dawning of God's salvation begins. Intimate familiarity with the themes of the promise, its endangerment, and its reaffirmation contained in the wilderness traditions of Israel's scriptures provides an indispensable medium through which an audience may experience Mark's story as one which recapitulates and brings to a climax God's redemptive activity. As Mauser has aptly observed, "The wilderness in Mark 1:3 carries with it the full

---

[137]See Mauser's discussion of H. W. Wolff's understanding of שוב; Israel's return to Yahweh is made possible only by Yahweh's return of Israel to the wilderness; the word "does not denote basically the freedom of the human will to make an ethical decision in turning to God, but it points to a certain status in which alone Israel's filial relationship to God can be renewed and which God, through his judgment, will reestablish in the future—the status of Israel in the wilderness" (Mauser, 48; see H. W. Wolff, "Das Thema 'Umkehr' in der Alttestamentlichen Theologie," *Zeitschrift für Theologie und Kirche* 48 [1951], 129-48).

weight of a great religious tradition embracing high hopes and promises as well as the deep shadows of judgment and despair, and this is imposed upon the succeeding verses, molding them as counterparts of Israel's experience in the desert."[138]

The picture Mark paints of John's ministry thus represents a confirmation of God's promises as reflected in the composite quotation, but also recalls the way in which those promises have been jeopardized throughout Israel's history. The movement with which Mark's audience is swept along here represents a repetition of Israel's foundational experience: Entering into the desert and going through water to receive the promise of God.[139] And indeed, as Mark tells it, "people from the whole Judean countryside and all the people of Jerusalem were going out to him" (v. 5). But despite the boldness and hopefulness of this scene, Mark's ideal reader will recall that God's redemptive acts in the past were accomplished over against and in spite of tremendous and willful opposition from within God's own people. As Israel's history and the prophetic interpretations of it reveal, God's salvation comes to a people and to a place which are both inhospitable. Most commentators agree that Mark exaggerates the effect of John's ministry not a little bit here; but he obviously does so with a rhetorical effect in view. The report concerning the "exodus" of Judea and Jerusalem to the wilderness carries with it a studied ambiguity: the picture of all Israel being called into the desert to experience God's salvation confirms Isaiah's promise; but the movement away from the holy places interjects an ominous theme, which is developed as opposition to Jesus comes from Jerusalem (3:22; 7:1) and the movement of the story reverses itself in the direction of Jerusalem (10:32-33).[140] Jesus' way to Jerusalem for the climax of the story, the reader soon learns (if he, as a believer, did not already know), also brings to a climax Israel's history of rebellion against God; and though Mark does not contain Jesus' lament over Jerusalem per se (Matt 23:37-39; Luke 13:34-35), the

---

[138]Mauser, 82.

[139]Drury, "Mark 1:1-15," 31.

[140]See Elizabeth Struthers Malbon, *Narrative Space and Mythic Meaning in Mark* (San Francisco: Harper & Row, 1986), 44-46; Myers, *Binding the Strong Man*, 126.

parable of the wicked tenants clearly shows that Mark understands Jerusalem to be the city that "kills the prophets and stones those who are sent to it" (Matt 23:37).[141]

We can begin to see, then, how Mark's intertextuality, the interweaving of his story with that of Israel's, provides the audience with a means of filling the gap between the seemingly mutually exclusive elements of Jesus' Messiahship and the way in which John fulfilled his role as Elijah. The violent deaths of both, as noted above, occur "as it is written of them" (9:12-13; 14:21), as does the abandonment of Jesus by the followers he chose (14:27). Salvation does still come in the way through the waters, into the desert, and climaxing in Zion; but, as Israel's history reveals, it comes only because God is able to turn willful opposition and evil—from the very tenants to whom God entrusted the vineyard—to good (Gen 50:20). Both the opposition to God and the failure of God's chosen followers are rooted in Israel's story, as read through the grid of Mark's story; as we will see in the next two chapters, reading the conflicts which form the heart of Mark's narrative through the grid of Israel's story, while not resolving the tension, provides the audience with the sense that, indeed, God's action in Jesus is continuous with the history of endangered and reaffirmed promises.

God's Beloved Son

The second invocation of Israel's scriptures which merits examination along these lines is the heavenly pronouncement at Jesus' baptism that Jesus is God's beloved son, in whom God is well pleased (1:11). The verse is also a composite quotation/allusion, and it has received a tremendous amount of attention from scholars, most of whom have found in it some sort of key to Mark's understanding of Jesus. In fact, the history of the exegesis of this passage over the past century and a half or so represents in microcosm the history of Markan interpretation.[142] Nineteenth-century scholars viewed this

---

[141]I will develop this point in the next chapter.

[142]See Chapter 1; Sean P. Kealy, *Mark's Gospel: A History of its Interpretation* (New York: Paulist Press, 1982); Frank Matera, *What are they saying about Mark?* (New York: Paulist Press, 1987), 18-37.

scene as reflecting an actual historical turning point in the biography of Jesus—the beginnings of his messianic self-consciousness.[143] Form critics and the History of Religions school saw the passage against the background of the movement of Christianity from the soil of Palestinian Judaism to Hellenism; Jesus as υἱὸς θεοῦ was understood to be a transformation of the original Jewish concept into a Hellenistic divine man type.[144] Redaction critics by and large accepted the Hellenistic derivations of the Son of God language, but insisted that Mark's purpose was actually to "correct" and polemicize against such a view, especially with the Markan motif of the suffering Son of Man.[145]

A consensus of sorts has emerged in recent Markan study, however, that the most likely source for the language Mark employs here is Israel's scripture itself.[146] Yet the consensus has not resolved the controversy surrounding the passage, since the language is allusory enough to call to mind several different passages. As noted above, Ps 2:7, Gen 22:2, and Isa 42:1 are the sources most frequently adduced. Most interpreters have argued for the predominance of one association over the others; that is, Mark had in mind one prevailing type of imagery with which he wished to associate Jesus. Thus some have asserted that the royal imagery of Psalm 2 is the most significant;[147] others that the Aqedah, the binding of Isaac in Genesis 22, forms the controlling imagery, suggesting a link between the twin

---

[143]The work of H. J. Holtzmann was especially important in this regard; see Kealy, *Mark's Gospel*, 81-83.

[144]Recall Bultmann's understanding of the purpose of Mark: "*the union of the Hellenistic kerygma about Christ*, whose essential content consists of the Christ myth as we learn of it in Paul . . . with the *tradition of the story of Jesus*" (*History of the Synoptic Tradition* [tr. John Marsh New York and San Francisco: Harper & Row, 1963], 347-348); see also his discussion of this pericope (247-253).

[145]E.g., T. Weeden, *Mark: Traditions in Conflict* (Philadelphia: Fortress Press, 1971); Norman Perrin, "The Christology of Mark: a Study in Methodology," in *The Interpretation of Mark* (William Telford, ed.; Philadelphia: Fortress, 1985), 95-108.

[146]All the recent studies cited thus far concur.

[147]So Kingsbury, Matera, Steichele; see also Paul Vielhauer, "Erwägungen zur Christologie des Markusevangeliums," in *Aufsätze zum Neuen Testament* (Tübingen: J.C.B. Mohr [Paul Siebeck]), 1965), 199-214.

sacrifices of Isaac and Jesus;[148] and still others maintain that Mark highlights the so-called Suffering Servant of Isaiah 42 and the other servant songs, and thus that Mark wants the reader to understand Jesus primarily in light of this figure.[149]

It seems unwise, however, to view the matter in terms of correct and incorrect choices. The very fact that the language is allusory and has so many possible points of contact suggests that the evocation of a constellation of images is more what Mark "had in mind." Moreover, the very nature of this kind of intertextual echo serves to unleash imaginative associations, not merely to impose limits on them.[150] This is not to say, of course, that there ought to be no controls whatsoever on possible scriptural contacts; though first-century scriptural exegesis operated by very different rules from modern critical exegesis, rules did exist, and were an important part of determining the persuasiveness of a given scriptural argument.[151] When arguing for a particular understanding of how a New Testament author employs scripture, it is important to be able to show that such an association would have been available to author and audience.

Rather than entering the fray on behalf of one particular point of contact for this verse, then, I wish first of all to register agreement with those who see here a combination of images which, taken together, function to provide the foundation for Mark's radical appropriation and reinterpretation of traditional messianic understandings in light of the way Jesus was understood to fulfill the

---

[148]So, e.g., Kazmierski, *Jesus, the Son of God*, 67-71; Juel suggests this possibility as well; see *Mark*, 36; *Master of Surprise*, 36-37, 100-101.

[149]See, e.g, Lührmann, who argues against royal imagery on the grounds that "Son of God" is not found as a messianic title in Jewish literature, and is used in the Old Testament in many different contexts (*Das Markuseveangelium*, 37-38). Those who rule out this association note that Isa 42:1 in the LXX translates the Hebrew רצה as προσεδέξατο, whereas Mark uses ευδόκησα; see, e.g., Hooker, *The Gospel According to St. Mark*, 46-7. Others question whether the "Suffering Servant" was a recognizable figure available for Mark to invoke (e.g., Juel, *Messianic Exegesis*, 118-133; Juel does not, however, rule out an association with Isaiah 42 itself; see *Master of Surprise*, 101).

[150]See Hays, *Echoes of Scripture*, 14-21.

[151]See Juel, *Messianic Exegesis*, 31-58.

messianic role. That is, Mark continues here what he has set out to accomplish in the portions of the prologue we have already examined: Setting traditional messianic imagery—Ps 2:7—alongside of imagery which is traditionally non-messianic, but equally scriptural—the binding of Isaac and God's faithful, suffering servant.[152] In doing so, he both sets up the conflicts which will characterize the story as well as challenges the reader to see those conflicts as integral to Jesus' identity as Messiah.

I also wish to suggest that the allusory nature of Mark's use of scripture here opens up the possibility not only of allusion to specific scriptural passages, but to broader patterns and motifs as well. Specifically, I suggest that in designating Jesus to be God's "beloved Son," the narrative recalls the many stories from Israel's scriptures which reveal that the fate of those so chosen by God for God's redemptive purposes has always involved a paradoxical combination of glorification and humiliation, triumph and tragedy. That is, in its attempt to persuade its audience of the continuity between God's climactic work in Jesus and God's past promises to and dealings with Israel, the narrative taps into the motif of God's endangered and reaffirmed promises.

The Death and Resurrection of the Beloved Son

Several scholars have argued plausibly for a link between 1:11 and the story of the binding of Isaac in Genesis 22.[153] In fact, the connection of the phrase ὁ υἱός μου ὁ ἀγαπητός with Gen 22:2 forms perhaps the clearest link of any in the passage. Gen 22:2 (LXX) reads λάβε τὸν υἱόν σου τὸν ἀγαπήτον; Mark nowhere else uses the second attributive position. Moreover, the repetition of

---

[152]Others have suggested such a combination, of course; see Juel, *Master of Surprise*, 101; Marcus, *The Way of the Lord*, 76; Matera, "The Prologue as Interpretative Key," 18, n. 31. As Matera puts it, it is not "inconceivable that the narrator intends the reader to see an allusion to all of these texts. Thus, Jesus is the royal Son of God who comes as the Lord's Servant to surrender his life" ("The Prologue as the Interpretative Key," 18, n. 31). Juel's *Messianic Exegesis* provides helpful insight into how such untraditional scriptural associations might have been made in early Christian exegesis.

[153]See, e.g, Kazmierski, *Jesus, the Son of God*, 43.

the phrase at key points in the Gospel—the transfiguration (9:7) and the Wicked Tenants parable (12:6)—reflects its great importance for the narrative's presentation of Jesus. And Nils Dahl, in an examination of Rom 8:32, has amply demonstrated that there are indeed solid grounds for positing the availability of an association between the fatherly acts of Abraham and God, their willingness to give up their beloved sons to accomplish God's purposes, in early Jewish and Christian exegesis.[154]

Jon Levenson, in his fascinating study, *The Death and Resurrection of the Beloved Son*,[155] has shown that the story of the binding of Isaac is but the first and best remembered sacrifice, or near sacrifice, of those chosen by God to carry out God's plan. In this work, Levenson sets out to question the "universal assumption" that ancient Israel early on abolished the idea of the ritual sacrifice of the first-born, as Genesis 22 is usually understood to reflect. While the actual act of child sacrifice, rooted in the Canaanite culture alongside which Israel developed its religious traditions, did fall out of favor, according to Levenson "the *religious idea* associated with one particular form of it—the donation of the first-born son— remained potent and productive."[156] In fact, he continues,

> it proved central to Israel's efforts to render account of its origins and character, and it was, again with modification, to prove at least as central to the efforts of the early church to do likewise. . . . [W]ithout reference to the ancient myths associated with child sacrifice, certain biblical narratives about the origins and character of the people Israel and of the Church cannot be properly understood.[157]

---

[154]Dahl, "The Atonement: An Adequate Reward for the Akedah?" in *Jesus the Christ*, 137-151

[155]Levenson, *The Death and Resurrection of the Beloved Son: The Transformation of Child Sacrifice in Judaism and Christianity* (New Haven: Yale University Press, 1993).

[156]Levenson, ix; emphasis is the author's. Regarding the idea that Genesis 22 was designed to abolish child sacrifice, Levenson observes that "it is passing strange to condemn child sacrifice through a narrative in which a father is richly rewarded for his willingness to carry out that very practice" (13).

[157]Levenson, ix, 37.

Levenson suggests that the practice of child sacrifice actually underwent two transformations. On the one hand, the ritual of the sacrifice of the first-born son was transformed into several ritual substitutes: e.g., the "first-fruits" (e.g. Exodus 12; Deut 15:19-23), the substitution of the Levites for the first-born (Num 8:16-19), and perhaps even by circumcision.[158] But alongside this ritual sublimation of child sacrifice, Levenson argues, there exists a parallel transformation of the phenomenon in the narratives of Israel's—and the church's—scriptures. His central thesis is that "a basic element of the self-understanding of both Jewry and of the Church lies in stories that are the narrative equivalent of these ritual substitutions—narratives, that is, in which the first-born or beloved son undergoes a symbolic death."[159]

Thus the motif lies close to the heart of nearly every major turn in Israel's story as God's people. Levenson traces the theme all the way back to Cain and Abel, a story which shows already "the horrific price that the favor of God entails."[160] The motif provides the central drama of the three cycles in Genesis; the exodus, in which Israel as a whole is identified as God's "firstborn son" (Exod 4:22), brings Israel to the brink of death before its redemption through the waters—and then back into a time of testing. The continuation of David's line involves the death of his son and his rebirth in Solomon.[161]

The heart of Levenson's study, though, involves readings of the central patriarchal cycles in Genesis in light of this motif, and the post-biblical traditions which develop around them and figure prominently in the self-definition of Rabbinic Judaism and Christianity. Each of the central, favored figures in Genesis—Abraham, Isaac, Jacob, Joseph—undergoes humiliation as a necessary precondition for their promised exaltation and their role in the fulfillment of God's plans; and each reiterates the accompanying theme of the mysterious nature of God's election. God's choosing of particular sons to carry out God's plans is inexplicable and mysterious, and is usually the

---

[158]Levenson, 44-48.
[159]Levenson, 59.
[160]Levenson, 78.
[161]Levenson, 29-30.

very act that issues in the conflict which threatens to undermine those plans. So no sooner has Abraham been promised Canaan than he is forced into exile in Egypt (Genesis 12). After finally receiving the promised offspring, Abraham is asked to sacrifice him. Thus it is Abraham's willingness to undergo the loss of his beloved son which paradoxically insures the promise which depends on Isaac.[162] And, as the post-biblical traditions surrounding the Aqedah develop, attention increasingly turns to Isaac's role and attitude, about which the biblical account is silent, such that he is eventually seen as willingly giving himself up to a sacrifice which does, in fact, occur.[163]

Jacob likewise undergoes humiliation and a symbolic death as prelude to the fulfillment of his role in God's plan. His trickery and audacity make him an unlikely choice, and Esau's rage over Jacob's supplanting of his birthright and his father's blessing brings the story to the brink of fratricide; indeed, Levenson sees Jacob's journey as the narrative substitution for his death at the hands of his brother.[164]

The Joseph story plays on the very same themes, bringing them to an even fuller development: seemingly unmerited favoritism, as well as Joseph's audacious predictions about his exaltation over his brothers, results in conflict, which in turn leads to the endangerment of Joseph's dreams, and those of Jacob for him. When he reaches "bottom," having been cast into prison, Levenson notes that "the cost of chosenness has never been clearer: the chosen son has become the rejected brother, his life has turned into a living death, and the exaltation of which he dreamt has become a nightmare of humiliation from which it seems impossible that he will ever awaken."[165] There follows, however, a corresponding ascent to his ultimate exaltation, which serves to legitimate his chosenness; in the end, "The chosenness of Joseph proves more an asset than a liability, and the wisdom and justice of the God who chose him, so easily doubted at the beginning of the tale, are richly vindicated at its end."[166]

---

[162]Levenson, 141.

[163]Levenson, 125-142; on this see Shalom Spiegel, *The Last Trial* (tr. Judah Goldin; New York: Schocken Books, 1969).

[164]Levenson, 65-66.

[165]Levenson, 152.

[166]Levenson, 168.

As Levenson summarize it, "Justice is not done to the complicated role of the first-born son if we fail to note both his exalted
status and the precariousness of his very life. The beloved son is
marked for both exaltation and for humiliation. In his life the two are
seldom far apart."[167]

Levenson concludes the book with chapters devoted to the role
of the motif in the formation of early Christianity and Rabbinic
Judaism. He sees the emergence of these two great religions as a
recapitulation of the sibling rivalry which characterized the stories of
Israel's history.[168] Of most interest to the present study is his
discussion of the Christian transformation of the motif, undertaken
to make sense of the conviction that Jesus was God's promised son,
the Messiah, despite or even precisely because of his brutal death.
His observations in this regard are more suggestive than fully
realized, but their potential for shedding light on Mark's particular
story of Jesus, especially on the conflicts which form the heart of it,
is very significant.

With respect to the specific pronouncement at Jesus' baptism
on which we are focusing, Levenson asserts that

> [w]hen, in the synoptic gospels, a heavenly voice declares, just after
> Jesus' baptism, "You are my beloved son . . . with you I am well
> pleased". . . a reference to that other beloved son, Isaac, is surely to be
> understood. And a Jewish audience, versed in Torah and perhaps even
> in the Septuagint as well, would have recognized the dark side of the
> heavenly announcement: that the destiny of the son so loved and so
> favored included a symbolic death at the hands of his loving father.[169]

One would want to add that the resonance with the tradition of
Isaac's sacrifice would also be felt by a non-Jewish audience versed
in the Septuagint, which is more likely in Mark's case, and certainly
true of Mark's subsequent readers. The verse, according to Levenson,
clearly taps into the whole tradition of the humiliation which comes

---

[167]Levenson, 59.

[168]See also Alan Segal, *Rebecca's Children: Judaism and Christianity in the
Roman World* (Cambridge: Harvard University Press, 1985).

[169]Levenson, 30-31.

to those chosen by God in a sense for which the Isaac story is a foundation, but hardly the only instance; as he puts it,

> The midrashic equation underlying the heavenly announcement of Mark 1:11 and its parallels makes explicit the theology of chosenness that lies at the foundation of the already ancient and well-established idea of the beloved son: the chosen one is singled out for both exaltation and humiliation, for glory and for death, but the confrontation with death must come first. . . . Jesus' gory death was not a negation of God's love (the Gospel was proclaiming), but a manifestation of it, evidence that Jesus was the beloved son first prefigured in Isaac.[170]

Levenson also notes the contacts this passage makes with the suffering servant motifs of Deutero-Isaiah. He entertains the possibility that the interweaving of the two themes may even antedate Christian exegesis;[171] but regardless, he points out the appropriateness of the midrashic combination of the two themes: The Isaac tradition, which, as noted above, increasingly attributes to Isaac an active willingness to give his life, and becomes further associated with the Passover sacrifice,[172] has much in common with the traditions about the servant of God who willingly goes to be slaughtered like a sheep (Isa 53:7).

Levenson attributes to early Christian exegesis the crucial combination of the beloved sonship motif and the servant imagery with the tradition of royal, Davidic sonship.[173] As noted above, the baptismal pronouncement opens by identifying Jesus as God's royal son; and it is on the Christian claims that Jesus is to be identified with the promised Messiah that his authority rests. In the creative, midrashic interweaving of these two categories of sonship, so Levenson, early Christian exegesis lays the foundation for addressing the tremendous conflict between Jesus' identity and his fate: "[T]he two vocabularies of sonship, that of the beloved son and that of the Davidic king as the son of God, reinforce each other powerfully.

---

[170]Levenson, 202, 200.

[171]Levenson, 201.

[172]Levenson, 11-12; he cites *Jub.* 17:15-18:19 as evidence for this association.

[173]Levenson, 203-06.

They yield a story in which the rejection, suffering, and death of the putatively Davidic figure is made to confirm rather than contradict his status as God's only begotten son."[174]

Mark's Gospel, I suggest, is precisely such a story, one that emerges out of the tension between traditional expectations of a powerful figure from the line of David and the inglorious fate of Jesus, God's beloved son. Thus Levenson's work is extremely helpful in supporting the idea that Mark relies on his audience's ability to feel the rich resonances with Israel's scriptural traditions, albeit in new and challenging combinations, in order to address the central tension of the message he is proclaiming. Though the proclamation of a crucified Messiah contains a tremendous scandal and challenging surprises, precisely in this way it conforms to God's past dealings with Israel and represents the confirmation of God's promises.

Moreover, as in the narratives of God's previous "beloved sons," the mysterious, even preposterous claim to Davidic sonship made on behalf of Jesus is precisely what issues in misunderstanding, opposition and conflict. Thus the invocation of the theme of the humiliation and exaltation of God's beloved son provides a helpful grid through which to view the conflicts between Jesus and the religious authorities, as well as those between Jesus and his disciples. As I will show in the next two chapters, both of these story lines threaten to the core the conviction set forth in the opening of Mark's Gospel, and yet both serve paradoxically to confirm that conviction.

CONCLUSIONS

My examination of the prologue has had two principal goals, both related to the overall thesis of this study. First, I have tried to show that the prologue reveals Mark's Gospel as especially oriented to its audience's experience of the clash between expectations and reality. Through the rhetorical techniques exhibited in the opening verses—the structure, the gap-ridden style, the envelopment of the audience's time and experience—Mark directly addresses and even

---

[174]Levenson, 206.

highlights the tension between traditional hopes and the surprising, scandalous way in which Jesus fulfilled them. The prologue prepares the audience for a reading experience in which the conflicts which unfold cannot be viewed from a safe distance, but rather must be entered into as constitutive of the Christian confession and Christian existence. The opposition which Jesus faces from both external and internal sources addresses and challenges the audience's experience of conflict between the promises of God and their endangerment.

Second, Mark's introduction also sets up the grid through which the audience might see and experience the conflict as a confirmation of those promises. By invoking fundamental features and patterns of God's past dealings with Israel, Mark lays the basis for seeing the redemptive work of God precisely in the present struggles. Indeed, only with the capacity to fill the gap between Jesus' identity and his fate by seeing it in continuity with God's activity in the past—i.e., only when one encounters it as Mark's ideal reader—can the story of Jesus truly be experienced as good news.

The next two chapters will demonstrate how these two aspects of my thesis are developed in the major story-lines of the Gospel: The conflict between Jesus and the religious authorities, and the struggles between Jesus and his disciples. In each case, I will attempt to show how and why the conflicts develop, their potential rhetorical impact on an ideal audience, and the way in which each exhibits and develops the intertextual echoes established in the prologue.

CHAPTER 4

THE PROMISE ENDANGERED FROM WITHOUT: JESUS AND HIS OPPONENTS

The truth of God is not given as didactic exposition, but as the result of conflict, attained through effort, and as evidence of a break-through in the attack against evil. (James M. Robinson, *The Problem of History in Mark*[1])

A GOSPEL OF TENSIONS

The thematic and dramatic tension between expectations and reality which arises out of the prologue is carried into the body of Mark's narrative. Mark tells a story which has at least two levels in tension with each other.[2] On the one hand is the story of promise, the pronouncement that God's end-time reign has drawn near precisely through the ministry, death, and resurrection of Jesus, the good news of God's promised redemption of creation and victory over the forces of evil and enslavement. Jesus shows that he possesses God's power and authority in his healings, exorcisms, and in his control over the forces of chaos in nature. This dimension of Mark' story, however,

---

[1]James M. Robinson, *The Problem of History in Mark and other Marcan Studies* (Philadelphia: Fortress, 1982), 91.

[2]Robert Fowler describes this tension as that between two plots driven by two different conceptions: There is the plot of causality, which emphasizes the human characters in the story as willful actors; this plot culminates in Jesus' crucifixion. Then there is the plot of predestination, in which the outcome is predetermined by God's sovereignty. See *Let the Reader Understand: Reader-Response Criticism and the Gospel of Mark* (Minneapolis: Fortress, 1991), 153.

is not closed; its denouement lies beyond the story Mark narrates (8:38-9:1; 13:26-27; 14:62). Though Jesus himself is vindicated through his resurrection, and thus emerges ultimately victorious, the Easter event does not bring closure to the story, but rather makes possible its continuation.[3] Within this dimension of the story, the resurrection of Jesus functions as the basis for hope and trust that the story will resolve itself as promised.

Diametrically opposed to this level of the story is another in which the very forces with which Jesus was sent to do battle—the power of Satan and the human claims to authority which oppose God's coming rule—in fact appear to "do whatever they please" (9:13) with God's agents. The tension between these two narrative levels is developed through the story, as the audience is presented both with seemingly incontrovertible evidence of Jesus' divine commission and authority as well as with the increasing inevitability of Jesus' death at the hands of his opponents. God's promise and its endangerment are held in unresolved tension. Mark's rhetorical goal is thus formidable: He must present both aspects of the story in a credible, convincing way. From Mark's point of view, the ultimate resolution of the conflict is not at issue; God will accomplish God's redemptive purposes (cf. Jesus' initial victory over Satan and the predictions of his future coming in glory). But in order to present this conviction credibly, the authenticity of the hope in the ultimate fulfillment of God's promises must be firmly grounded in the reality of its endangerment. If the "fairy tale," comedic level of the story overwhelms or discounts the reality of those forces opposed to God, the audience will not be persuaded to embrace its promise; the dissonance between promise and reality will be simply too great. Yet unblinking engagement with the audience's experience of a reality which endangers God's promises—rubbing its face in reality, even waking sleeping dogs—carries with it the opposite danger that the audience will conclude that God's promises cannot in fact be trusted, at least insofar as they are related to Jesus.[4]

---

[3]See Dan O. Via, Jr., *Kerygma and Comedy in the New Testament: A Structuralist Approach to Hermeneutic* (Philadelphia: Fortress, 1975), 82.

[4]Precisely this tension between the tragic and the comedic leads Via to argue that Mark's story is a "tragi-comedy" (*Kerygma and Comedy*, 99-108).

Mark's presentation of the opposing sides of the conflict must reflect this tension. That is, his presentation of Jesus must show that Jesus does in fact represent God's divine authority, but it must also account for his death at the hands of Satan's representatives. Likewise, Mark must present the religious authorities in a way that keeps their apparent capacity to "do whatever they please" with Jesus in tension with the necessity to expose their power as illegitimate and ultimately ineffectual.

In the final two chapters of this study I wish to argue that Mark accomplishes exactly this balancing act, and therein, in fact, lies the Gospel's appeal and rhetorical power. Although, as we saw in the prologue, the cosmic struggle between God's redemptive activity and Satan's opposition to it forms the backdrop for the story,[5] unlike many contemporaneous works with apocalyptic themes, Mark's Gospel does not remain on the cosmic, super-human level. Rather, after setting the apocalyptic background for the story, Mark "immediately" brings the reader into the realm of historical existence, and it is here that the conflict plays itself out.[6] By examining first the conflict between Jesus and the religious authorities, and, in the next chapter, that between Jesus and the disciples, I will attempt to substantiate the argument I have been making thus far: that the rhetorical goal of the conflicts in Mark is to acknowledge and address the audience's experience of conflict between God's promises and the reality of an apparently unredeemed world, and that the narrative evokes the familiar pattern from Israel's traditions of God's endangered and reaffirmed promises in service of this goal. The structure and shape of the redemption offered through Jesus correspond both to reality as experienced by Mark's audience and to God's past activity on behalf of a beleaguered creation.

Though I will discuss each conflict separately, along the way I intend to point out the ways in which these conflicts which give shape to the story are closely interwoven and reveal a common

---

[5]See Rhoads and Michie, *Mark as Story: An Introduction to the Narrative of a Gospel* (Philadelphia: Fortress Press, 1982), 73.

[6]See Robinson, 81-101.

thread.[7] Both, I will argue, set before the audience a clear juxtaposition between "thinking in human terms" and "thinking in divine terms" (e.g., 8:33). Both reveal, however, that the latter alternative is impossible apart from radical trust in God's promise and in the forsaking of the seemingly comfortable but death-dealing power structures erected by illegitimate human conceptions of power. That is, Mark sets before the reader both the necessity and the apparent impossibility of thinking in divine terms. Both story lines thus work toward the same rhetorical end, namely, to persuade the audience that only by setting its mind on "divine things" can it participate in the promised eschatological redemption, but, paradoxically, only by trusting in God's promise of redemption can this occur.

JESUS AND HIS ADVERSARIES

It has become common to observe that it is through the story of the disciples that Mark most directly addresses the reader.[8] As we will see in the next chapter, Jesus' struggle to cultivate a community of faithful followers does emerge as the central focus of the narrative, though there are divergent ways of understanding Mark's goal in presenting the disciples as utterly failing in their calling to follow Jesus. The goal of Mark's portrayal of the conflict between Jesus and the religious authorities, however, has generally been seen to be the creation of cognitive and emotional distance between the audience and the authorities, leading to the rejection of their point of view on Jesus and their claims to authority.[9] There is without question much

---

[7]Rhoads and Michie point out that the "conflicts in Mark's story interweave and even overlap at significant points, yet each conflict has its own direction, content, ambiance, and resolution" (*Mark as Story: An Introduction to the Narrative of a Gospel* [Philadelphia: Fortress Press, 1982], 73), but do not go on to illustrate precisely how that is the case.

[8]This was recognized already by Bultmann; see *History of the Synoptic Tradition* (tr. John Marsh; San Francisco: Harper & Row, 1976), 350.

[9]See, e.g., Jack Kingsbury, *Conflict in Mark: Jesus, Authorities, Disciples* (Minneapolis: Fortress Press, 1989), 14-21; *idem*, "The Religious Authorities in the Gospel of Mark," *NTS* 36 (1990), 42-65; Elizabeth Struthers Malbon, "The Jewish Leaders in the Gospel of Mark: A Literary Study of Marcan Characterization," *JBL* 108 (1989), 259-281; Rhoads and Michie, *Mark as Story*, 117-122.

truth to this assertion, as will be seen below; but I wish to argue in this chapter that the nature and shape of the conflict between Jesus and the Jewish leaders serves to engage the audience's own struggle to "think the things of God." It does this, I suggest, in at least three ways. In the "tragic" component of the story, Mark is acknowledging that the human authorities who oppose God's reign as manifested in Jesus, though ultimately illegitimate, continue to be the center of worldly power—that is, they continue to exercise power in the real world experienced by the readers (cf. Chapter 13). The narrative may portray the religious authorities in a nearly unremittingly negative light, but the issues on which they ground their opposition to Jesus, and which ultimately lead them to desire his death, are precisely the issues with which an audience which makes itself open to Mark's rhetoric also must deal: Is Jesus a blasphemer or the Son of God? Does his freedom vis-a-vis the "traditions of the elders" render him a menace to society or provide the foundation for a new, life-giving community? Is his power from Satan or from God? Indeed, the questions all boil down to one: Does Jesus possess the authority to speak and act for God?

Second, the characterization of the religious authorities attributes their opposition to their "hardness of heart," and their actions reflect an alliance with Satan. As the conflict with the disciples reveals, hardness of heart is a disposition that can be associated with those who consider themselves "insiders" as well. Thus the audience cannot completely distance itself from the opponents to Jesus, because they are forced to consider hardness of heart not as a choice but as a condition from which humans need to be liberated—a condition which needs to be exorcized.

Third, the shape of Christian existence presented as the alternative to the way characterized by "thinking in human terms" points to the fact that Mark understands conflict and opposition to continue beyond the time of Jesus and in fact to characterize the life of the church.

This chapter will get at these concerns by examining the following questions: Who are Jesus' opponents? What is at issue in their opposition to Jesus? How does Mark present the development of the conflict? How and why do they endanger the promise? Each of these questions will be addressed with an eye toward the ways in which the conflict may work rhetorically on the audience.

THE IDENTITY OF JESUS' OPPONENTS

The character group that forms the most consistent and unified opposition to Jesus in Mark's narrative is, of course, the "religious leaders," a group which consists of several distinguishable sub-groups corresponding to several of the better-known expressions of first-century Judaism: scribes, Pharisees, chief priests, elders, Sadducees, and the so-called "Herodians."[10] From the very beginning of Jesus' public ministry, Jesus' work is set over against and engenders opposition from various combinations of these groups. Most frequently mentioned are the "scribes," who form the basis for the initial comparison voiced by the crowd in the synagogue upon hearing Jesus' teaching (1:22), oppose and dispute with him in his Galilean ministry alone (2:6) as well as with the Pharisees (2:16; 3:22; 7:1,5), and once with Jesus' disciples (9:14), and they are listed among the Jerusalem groups actively participating in the events which bring about Jesus' death, both in Jesus' predictions of the passion (8:31; 10:32-34) and in the narrative itself (11:18, 27; 14:1-2; 14:43, 53; 15:1, 31-32). The Pharisees appear most frequently in the Galilean section of the Gospel. In the series of controversy stories in 2:1-3:6, they dispute with Jesus about matters of Jewish law (2:16-17, 18-20; 24-28; 3:1-6), leading them to conspire with the Herodians to "destroy" Jesus (3:6), and continue their attacks in 7:1-

---

[10]The Herodians are the only group whose extra-textual existence is difficult to discern; see Arland J. Hultgren, *Jesus and His Adversaries: The Form and Function of the Conflict Stories in the Synoptic Tradition* (Minneapolis: Augsburg, 1979), 154-56; also Samuel Sandmel, "Herodians," *Interpreter's Dictionary of the Bible* 2: 594-95. Kingsbury is probably correct in his judgment that in Mark's narrative, the Herodians "appear to be thought of as agents of Herod Antipas (cf. 3:6 and 12:13 with 8:15), who stands out as a character in his own right (6:14-29). Nonetheless, because Mark associates the Herodians so closely with the Pharisees, they function in effect within the circle of the 'religious authorities'" ("The Religious Authorities in the Gospel of Mark," 42 n. 8). One might add that the addition of the Herodians to the circle of opponents suggests Jesus was opposed by every religious and political power center of his time: Jewish leaders, Herod, and the Romans.

13 and 10:2-9; they also request a sign from heaven to authenticate his ministry (8:11-13); in the Jerusalem section they are sent by other authorities with the Herodians to trap Jesus with the question about taxes (12:13-17), but otherwise do not play a role in Jesus' arrest, trial, and crucifixion. The chief priests are almost always mentioned as part of the core group working to bring about Jesus' death in Jerusalem, along with the elders and scribes (8:31; 11:27-33; 14:43, 53; 15:1), or with the scribes only (10:33; 11:18; 14:1-2; 15:31-32), once with the "whole council" (14:55), and twice alone (14:10-11; 15:3).

As these references show, Mark structures the conflict between Jesus and the religious authorities in such a way that it is in view from the opening of Jesus' public ministry in Galilee (1:22), and is continually flashed before the eyes of the reader until it culminates in the events in Jerusalem. As will be seen later, there are two concentrations of controversies between the parties (2:1-3:6; 11:27-12:44), each of which serves to give shape to the two principal sections of the narrative (Galilee and Jerusalem).[11] And while the focus shifts to the struggle between Jesus and his disciples in the central portion of the Gospel (Chapters 8-10), the intention of the authorities to thwart Jesus' mission remains ever in view (cf. 3:6; 7:1-13; 8:31; 9:31; 10:2-9, 32-34). Moreover, much of the substance of Jesus' teaching apart from the controversies clearly suggests that the kingdom of God, whose shape and appearance form the center of Jesus' preaching and teaching, comes only through intense conflict (e.g., 4:1-20; again, see below).

Before exploring in detail the nature and development of the conflict, however, we need first to deal with the question of the identity and function of Jesus' opponents. This is a question which can, of course, be addressed on several different levels. As I noted in

---

[11]Peter von der Osten-Sacken points out that the two cycles of controversies form a bracket around the whole public ministry of Jesus; see "Streitgespräch und Parabel als Formen markinischer Christologie," in *Jesus Christus in Historie und Theologie: Neutestamentliche Festschrift für Hans Conzelmann zum 60. Geburtstag* (ed. Georg Strecker; Tübingen: J.C.B. Mohr [Paul Siebeck]: 1975], 375-94, p. 376; as I will discuss below, this framing invites the audience to interpret Jesus' intervening struggles with his disciples in light of the conflict with the authorities, and highlights both the similarities and points of contrast between the two conflicts.

the first chapter, most previous studies of the conflict in the Gospels have taken as their point of departure some aspect of the historical question: How does the Markan depiction of the Jewish leaders reflect the historical "realities" of either Jesus' ministry[12] or the situation of Mark's community?[13] While this is a very important question for many reasons,[14] as I suggested in chapter 1, historical

---

[12]See, e.g., Joachim Jeremias, *New Testament Theology: The Proclamation of Jesus* (tr. John Bowden; New York: Charles Scribner's Sons, 1971), 142-151; Leonhard Goppelt, *Theology of the New Testament, Vol. 1: The Ministry of Jesus in its Theological Significance* (tr. John Alsup; Grand Rapids, MI: William B. Eerdmans Publishing, 1981), 84-105; Robert Banks, *Jesus and the Law in the Synoptic Tradition* (SNTSMS 28; Cambridge: Cambridge University Press, 1975).

[13]On this question, see especially Michael Cook, *Mark's Treatment of the Jewish Leaders* (NovTSup 51; Leiden: E.J. Brill, 1978); Cook's examination of the Jewish leaders seeks to determine the relationship between Mark's portrayal of them and historical reality; he concludes that "[t]he Evangelists *themselves* were unclear as to who all these Jewish leadership groups had actually been in Jesus' time; they did not adequately define and describe them or adequately distinguish among them because they *could* not. Moreover, some of the group titles ('chief priests,' 'Herodians,' 'elders') are merely general constructs, i.e., literary devices serving the convenience of the Synoptists themselves and lifted from their sources; they are not reflective of leadership groups actually functioning Jesus' time or later" (1). See also Dieter Lührmann, "Die Pharisäer und die Schriftgelehrten im Markusevangelium," *Zeitschrift für neutestamentliche Wissenschaft* 78 (1987), 169-85, whose concern is to examine how the conflicts between Jesus and the religious authorities reflect the experience of Mark's community in its relationship to the contemporary Jewish authorities. Also Anthony J. Saldarini, "The Social Class of the Pharisees in Mark," in *The Social World of Formative Christianity and Judaism: Essays in Tribute to Howard Clark Kee* (ed. J. Neusner et al.; Philadelphia: Fortress Press, 1988), 69-77. Saldarini suggests that in broad outline, Mark's portrayal does comport with historical reality as known from other sources: the Pharisees were the group to reckon with outside of Jerusalem, while the chief priests, elders, and the Sanhedrin held the power in Jerusalem; this corresponds to the distribution of references in Mark's Gospel. See as well the dissertation of Moston Robert Mulholland, Jr., "The Markan Opponents of Jesus" (Harvard University, 1977), which argues that the conflicts reflect the situation of Mark's community as it faces expulsion from its contemporary Jewish community.

[14]Not least of these is the determination of the historical role of the Jewish authorities in Jesus' death. On this, see Juel, *Messiah and Temple: The Trial of Jesus in the Gospel of Mark* (SBLDS 31; Missoula, MT: Scholars Press, 1977); Ellis Rivkin, *What Crucified Jesus?* (Nashville: Abingdon Press, 1984); John Donahue, *"Are you the Christ?" The Trial Narrative in the Gospel of Mark* (SBLDS 10; Missoula, MT:

studies in the past have tended to move too quickly from text to history, without sufficient attention to the role of the groups in Mark's Gospel; moreover, such historical study may answer genetic questions about the origin of Mark's narrative, but they leave important aspects of the narrative itself unaddressed.

More recent studies have affirmed this observation, and have sought to examine and clarify the literary features of Mark's characterization of the Jewish leaders and the development of the conflict in the narrative.[15] There is general agreement among such studies that Mark's principal concern in his portrayal of the religious authorities is to show that, in spite of their division over particulars of first-century Judaism,[16] "at the most elemental level, Mark leads the reader to look upon the various groups of authorities as forming a united front . . . bent on effecting the death of Jesus."[17] As a single character group, they receive a broad-stroked, flat characterization in the narrative, and exhibit the same basic, consistent traits, all of which set them at odds with Jesus' identity and mission. As Rhoads and Michie describe them, they are

> thoroughly untrustworthy characters. . . . The opponents have no faith, are blind to the rule of God, and are hardened against Jesus. Ironically, they think of themselves as guardians of God's law, but unknowingly they are God's enemies because their use of authority and their narrow legalism runs contrary to the way God rules. They are self-serving, preoccupied with their own importance, afraid to lose their status and power, and willing to destroy to keep them. As those who "think the

---

Scholars Press, 1973); most recently, John Dominic Crossan, *Who Killed Jesus? Exposing the Roots of Anti-Semitism in the Gospel Story of the Death of Jesus* (San Francisco: Harper Collins, 1995).

[15]E.g., Kingsbury, *Conflict in Mark* and "The Religious Authorities in the Gospel of Mark;" Rhoads and Michie, *Mark as Story*, 73-100, 117-122; Malbon, "The Jewish Leaders in the Gospel of Mark;" Robert Tannehill, "The Gospel of Mark as Narrative Christology," *Semeia* 16 (1979), 57-95; Joanna Dewey, *Markan Public Debate: Literary Technique, Concentric Structure, and Theology in Mark 2:1-3:6* (SBLDS 48 Chico, CA: Scholars Press, 1980); Mary Ann Tolbert, *Sowing the Gospel: Mark's World in Literary-Historical Perspective* (Minneapolis: Fortress Press, 1989), 127-299.

[16]E.g., Mark notes that the Sadducees do not believe in the resurrection (12:18).

[17]Kingsbury, "The Religious Authorities," 44-45; see also Malbon, 270-272; Rhoads and Michie, 117.

things of men," they echo Jesus' depiction of the gentiles great ones who "lord over" people. In the characterizations of the story, the authorities embody the opposite of Jesus and illuminate his character through contrast. Their presence in the story also highlights the failures of the disciples because of their similarity to the disciples.[18]

This is a very helpful description of the authorities as a group, and the observation that this portrayal serves to cast the characteristics of Jesus and the message he brings into sharper relief for the audience will be developed below. Two points, however, require further discussion. First, the judgment that the differences among the Jewish groups which oppose Jesus is insignificant, and that the narrative makes no meaningful distinction among them, is overstated. Second, the relationship of the conflict between Jesus and the authorities needs to be understood more explicitly against the backdrop of the larger story of which Mark's Gospel is a part. In discussing these two points, I will argue that the key to Mark's characterization of Jesus' opponents is his careful balancing of their concrete historical existence on the one hand and their role as Satan's allies in the cosmic conflict between God and Satan on the other.

The Distinctiveness of Jesus' Opponents

Jack Kingsbury's remarks are representative of the view that Mark makes no meaningful distinction among the various groups which oppose Jesus:

> Mark's overriding goal in portraying these groups is to stress, not the distinctiveness of each, but their solidarity with one another. Hence, to claim peculiarity for any of these groups within the story-world of Mark by wrongly or unduly stressing differences in doctrine, disposition, geography, or issues debated with Jesus is to ignore Mark's fundamental description of them as forming a united front and constituting a collective character.[19]

Several observations speak against this assertion. There is, first of all, a broad distinction discernible between the groups whose geograph-

---

[18]*Mark as Story*, 117-18.
[19]Kingsbury, "The Religious Authorities," 45.

ical sphere of influence lies outside Jerusalem and those which exercise power within Jerusalem. The Pharisees, as noted above, appear in conflict with Jesus almost exclusively in Galilee, and often in a synagogue (e.g., 3:1-6), while in Jerusalem the opponents are the chief priests, elders, and the Sanhedrin, who square off with Jesus in the temple.[20] This observation has both historical as well as literary-rhetorical implications; the latter concern us here.[21] As Elizabeth Struthers Malbon notes, the shift in the groups designated as Jesus' opponents thus corresponds to the spatial shift from Galilee to Jerusalem; the result is a "narrative escalation" of the conflict from the first half of the Gospel to the second.[22] As we will see below, this helps focus the conflict in Jerusalem on the issue of the chief priests' stewardship of the temple, the center of religious activity and power; as Malbon notes, "The Pharisees and scribes may protest Jesus' teaching and his 'impurity,' whereas the chief priests, scribes and elders can judge and condemn him."[23]

Moreover, within the Galilean portion itself the controversies with the various groups do appear to admit of a broad correlation between the issues raised and the groups who raise them, as Moston Mulholland has argued. In his dissertation, "The Markan Opponents of Jesus," he lays out the following correlations:[24]

---

[20]Malbon, "The Jewish Leaders in the Gospel of Mark," 272-73; *idem*, *Narrative Space and Mythic Meaning in Mark* (San Francisco: Harper & Row, 1986), 106-140

[21]See Saldarini, "The Social Class of the Pharisees in Mark," 74-75, who notes how this distinction probably reflects the reality of pre-70 C.E. Judaism.

[22]Malbon, "The Jewish Leaders in the Gospel of Mark," 274.

[23]Malbon, "The Jewish Leaders in the Gospel of Mark," 273. This distinction is also reflected in 3:6, where the Pharisees must conspire with the "Herodians" to destroy Jesus, perhaps reflecting their lack of power to do away with them on their own.

[24]Mullholland, 1; quoted in Malbon, "The Jewish Leaders in the Gospel of Mark," 267 n. 30.

Scribes	2:1-12	3:22-30	9:11,14
	Jesus' nature	*Jesus' nature*	*Jesus' nature*
	and activity	*and activity*	*and activity*
	(healing)	*(exorcism)*	*(exorcism)*
Scribes	2:13-17	7:1-23	(lacking in the
and	*Ritual cleanli-*	*Ritual cleanli-*	third appearance
Pharisees	*ness in eating*	*ness in eating*	of the opponent
			cycle)
Pharisees	2:18-28	8:11-12	10:1-12
	Fasting and	*Seek a sign*	*Lawful activity*
	lawful activity		
Pharisees	3:1-6	8:15	12:13-17
and	*Plot to*	*Jesus warns*	*Seek to entrap*
Herodians	*destroy Jesus*	*followers*	*Jesus*

Although Mulholland seeks to show that such a pattern reflects the historical situation facing Mark's community at the time of the Gospel's writing,[25] these observations also have important rhetorical implications. Though the groups are united in their opposition to Jesus, the distinction among them in terms of their particular concerns serves to highlight the various "options" for understanding and appropriating Israel's heritage as God's elect. With but two exceptions (7:3-4; 12:18), Mark's narrative presumes familiarity with some of the particulars of the debate within Judaism over issues of scriptural interpretation and the criteria for making valid claims to interpret the tradition.[26] The Pharisees are concerned primarily with Jesus' freedom vis-à-vis the law as interpreted by the "tradition of the elders" (7:3-5) and with preserving the "holiness" of the community of Israel through appropriate table fellowship (2:15-17) and proper observance of the holy days—especially, of course, the sabbath (2:23-28; 3:1-6).[27] The interest of the Sadducees lies in arguing for their claims that the resurrection cannot be substantiated

---

[25]See above, n. 13.

[26]As Juel notes, the various parties "appear as interest groups, people with a particular point of view about the tradition set off from the rest of the community" (*A Master of Surprise: Mark Interpreted* [Minneapolis: Fortress Press, 1994], 137; see 136-38).

[27]On the Pharisees, see Jacob Neusner, *From Politics to Piety: The Emergence of Pharisaic Judaism* (Englewood Cliffs, NJ: Prentice-Hall, 1973).

on the basis of the scriptures they hold as authoritative.[28] And, as noted, the chief priests, elders, and the council are interested in preserving their authority over the temple, which they view as the locus of God's interaction with Israel and the central identifying feature of Israel (Jesus' attack on the temple becomes the immediate occasion for his arrest).[29]

The scribes are perhaps the most interesting "group" in that they span the entire narrative: they figure in Jesus' first public teaching and action, in the synagogue in Galilee (1:22), and are the first to question Jesus' claims to authority (2:6-9); they are also the subject of Jesus' final public teaching, in which he warns of their hypocrisy (12:38-40). In between, they appear with each of the other groups, and their initial charge of blasphemy (2:7) becomes the charge on which Jesus is finally condemned by the High Priest and the council (14:63-64).[30] The importance of this "umbrella" group in Mark's narrative becomes clear when one considers their function in first-century Judaism. Though historically they did not comprise a separate party—each of the major parties apparently had their own scribes[31]—they operated as professional and authoritative interpreters of scripture, especially the Law. As Guelich points out, they exercised at least three tasks with respect to the Law: "a) to develop and interpret the Law pertinent to the times, b) to teach students the Law, and c) to act in judicial situations."[32] Their consistent appearance in the conflicts between Jesus and the religious authorities thus serves to highlight and clarify the degree to which interpretation of Israel's scripture lies at the heart of the conflict. Their opposition to Jesus is based in large measure on their understanding of scripture and the law and on their objection to Jesus' interpretation of the same (e.g., 2:7; 7:1; 11:18; 11:27-33).

---

[28]On the Sadducees, see David Rhoads, *Israel in Revolution 6-74 C.E.: A Political History Based on the Writings of Josephus* (Philadelphia: Fortress Press, 1976), 39-43.

[29]See Jacob Neusner, *Judaism in the Matrix of Christianity* (Philadelphia: Fortress Press, 1986).

[30]See von der Osten-Sacken, "Streitgespräch und Parabel," 376-81.

[31]See Robert Guelich, *Mark 1-8:26* Word Biblical Commentary 34A (Dallas: Word Books, 1989), 56.

[32]Guelich, *Mark 1-8:26*, 56.

Even more significant, the manner in which they voice their initial complaint holds at least one key to the entire opposition to Jesus. In the first controversy story, the healing of the paralytic (2:1-12), Jesus forgives the sins of the man who would be healed (2:5). In their objection to this action, the scribes judge this to be "blasphemy," asking, "Who can forgive sins but God (εἷς ὁ θεός)" (2:7). The words εἷς ὁ θεός clearly evoke the central Jewish confession, the Shema (Deut 6:4), that God is one.[33] The scribes' objection is thus that Jesus is claiming for himself an authority and a role rightly reserved for God alone, as scripture clearly teaches. When Jesus is finally condemned for blasphemy before the High Priest, the same objection is implied: Jesus actually replies to the High Priest's question with the divine name itself (ἐγώ εἰμι), and claims that he will be "seated at the right of the Power," thus exercising God's role as eschatological judge and savior (14:62; Jesus is quoting Ps 110 and Dan 7:3). Further, in the fascinating exchange with a scribe in the temple (12:28-34), the confession of God's oneness is confirmed by both Jesus and the scribe as the first and most important of God's commandments. Clearly, the question of the way in which faith in Jesus relates to Israel's central confession lies close to the heart of Mark's portrayal of the conflict between Jesus and the other representatives of Israel's heritage.[34]

---

[33]See Joel Marcus, "Authority to Forgive Sins upon the Earth: The *Shema* in the Gospel of Mark," in *The Gospels and the Scriptures of Israel* (eds. C. A. Evans and W. R. Stegner; JSNTSup104/Studies in Scripture in Early Judaism and Christianity 3; Sheffield: Sheffield Academic Press, 1994), 196-211. Marcus points out concerning this passage, as well as in 10:18, where the precise same phrase is employed by Jesus in conversation with the rich young ruler, that "in neither case is the word *heis* really necessary for the sense; in 2:7 the scribes could just as easily, and less awkwardly, have asked, 'Who is able to forgive sins except God?'" (197). See also Rudolph Pesch, *Das Markusevangelium* (2 vols.; HTKNT 2; Freiburg/Basel/Wien: Herder, 1976), 1:159; 2:138-39; J. Gnilka, *Das Evangelium nach Markus* (2 vols; EKKNT 2; Zürich: Benziger/Neukirchener, 1978), 1:100.

[34]Concerning the oneness of God as one of the central issues in the conflict between emerging Christianity and rabbinic Judaism, see Alan Segal, *Two Powers in Heaven: Early Rabbinic Reports about Christianity and Gnosticism* SJLA 25 (Leiden: Brill, 1977).

Thus the concerns of the scribes, as well as those of the Pharisees, Sadducees, and Chief Priests,[35] go to the heart of the interpretation and appropriation of the principal "cornerstones" of Judaism—God, Torah, Israel[36]—and each of these appears from the distinct perspectives of the various groups.[37] For Mark's implied audience, these are issues about which conflict is expected. The presentation of them in the narrative serves to highlight the distinctiveness of Jesus' own radical, new, and eschatologically-charged alternative; and the tension between the two poses the alternatives clearly and urgently for the audience.[38]

The Unity of Jesus' Opponents

The second point at which most literary treatments of the religious authorities in Mark require modification concerns the relationship of the conflicts to the larger story in which Mark's narrative is set, and may at first glance appear to contradict the first point. Obviously, Mark's goal is to persuade his audience that Jesus' alternative is the only one that leads to life, and thus, as we will see below, Mark

---

[35]On the possibility that Mark even deals with the so-called "revolutionaries" or Zealots, see Joel Marcus, *The Way of the Lord: Christological Exegesis of the Old Testament in the Gospel of Mark* (Louisville: Westminster/John Knox Press, 1992), 117-18; also "The Jewish War and the *Sitz im Leben* of Mark," *JBL* 113 (1994), 221-248. Marcus sees Mark's σπήλαιον λῃστῶν in 11:17 as a reference to the revolutionary bands active in the Jewish revolt against the Romans, and understands Mark to be rejecting their activity.

[36]See Hayim Donin, *To Be a Jew: A Guide to Jewish Observance in Contemporary Life* (New York: Basic Books, 1972), 3-38.

[37]As Juel notes, the contrast between Mark and John is especially illuminating; John refers to Jesus' opponents collectively as "the Jews" (more than 70 times); for John, the designation symbolizes opposition to Jesus on the part of the "children of the devil" (John 8:44), over against whom believers in the work and word of Jesus as God's divine son are to understand themselves (*Master of Surprise*, 137). On the "Jews" in John's Gospel, see J. L. Martyn, *History and Theology in the Fourth Gospel* (Nashville: Abingdon, 1979); also Epp, "Anti-Semitism and the Popularity of the Fourth Gospel in Christianity."

[38]Though they are never shown in outright conflict with one another, it may strike some readers (as it did me) that the inability of witnesses from the various groups to agree on testimony against Jesus at his trial before the High Priest (14:56-59) represents an instance of a "house divided against itself" (3:24-25).

develops the conflict in a way that drives this point home. For Mark, and for his implied audience, all other options for understanding the nature and identity of Israel are foreclosed. Insofar as this is the case, the judgment that Mark treats the various opponents of Jesus as a single character is valid: Though they express concerns corresponding with their group affiliation, they are united in being characterized by Mark as without divine authority, as oriented, instead, to maintaining an illusory and death-dealing authority over people at any cost. In this, as well as in their failure to acknowledge Jesus' divine authority, Mark portrays them as allies of the "supernatural" forces opposed to God's redemptive purposes—the larger context which the narrative sets up in the prologue and which is punctuated by the frequent appearance of "unclean spirits" in the first half of the Gospel. That is to say, in dealing with the question of the identity of the opponents in Mark, one must address the question of the way in which Mark portrays them as being, in some sense, in league with Satan, and thus manifesting the cosmic conflict which forms the larger context for Mark's story of Jesus.[39] As Robinson has put it, their opposition represents a historicizing of the cosmic conflict which the prologue introduced .[40] Mark develops this aspect of the

---

[39]This question must be addressed with caution in Mark; the dualism between "children of Satan" and "children of God" that appears, for example, in the Fourth Gospel is, in Mark, not nearly as fatalistic (or at least not in the same way). As I noted above, the controversies do deal with substantive issues for Mark's implied audience; the point is not merely to demonize the opponents. Moreover, for Mark it is the condition of "hardness of heart" which seems to issue in opposition to Jesus (e.g., 6:52; 7:6; 8:17; 10:5), which suggests that opposition to Jesus stems from a condition from which humans must, and can be, liberated (see Dan O. Via, Jr., *The Ethics of Mark's Gospel: In the Middle of Time* [Philadelphia: Fortress Press, 1985], 45; Robinson, *The Problem of History*, 98-99; Juel, *Master of Surprise*, 70-75). And, as Malbon concludes in her discussion of the "exceptions" among the Jewish leaders (Jairus, the "friendly scribe," and Joseph of Arimathea), "being a foe of Jesus is not simply a matter of one's social or religious status and role, but a matter of how one responds to Jesus" ("The Jewish Leaders in the Gospel of Mark," 280). One might say that, whereas in John, the opposition to Jesus on the part of "the Jews" is a manifestation of their prior identity as children of Satan (e.g., John 8:42-44), in Mark it is the action itself which leads Mark's Jesus to condemn opposition—even from his disciples—as having its roots in Satan (8:33).

[40]Robinson, *The Problem of History*, 91-94; he concludes that the debates are a continuation of the cosmic struggle initiated at the baptism and temptation and

authorities' character in several ways: through explicit commentary about their motivations from the narrator and the "reliable" character, Jesus; by juxtaposing incidents within and between scenes which lead the audience to infer a connection between the authorities and Satan; and by the similarity in form between the exorcisms and the debates.

First, as noted above, Mark sets the stage for the conflict between Jesus and the authorities in his first public action, his teaching and exorcism in the synagogue (2:21-28), when the crowd contrasts Jesus' authority with that of the scribes (1:22). When the man with an "unclean spirit" cries out to Jesus, he does so with words that represent programmatically Jesus' "plundering" of the "strong man's house" (cf. 3:27), which has been made possible by his encounter with Satan in the wilderness (1:12-13):[41] "What have you to do with us, Jesus of Nazareth? Have you come to destroy (ἀπολέσαι) us? I know who you are, the Holy One of God" (1:24). The statement both describes a central aspect of Jesus' mission and defines response to that mission in stark, either-or terms, forming a parallel to the contrast drawn by the crowd between Jesus and the scribes in 1:22; this parallel leads the reader to see opposition to Jesus and his mission in the light of the cosmic conflict between Jesus and the demons.

This association is strengthened as the narrative moves almost immediately to a fleshing out of the conflict between Jesus and the authorities in 2:1-3:6. The section follows what can be seen as a paradigmatic "day in the life" of Jesus,[42] as Mark sets out to show the intensity and relentness nature of Jesus' "battle." He moves breathlessly from one place to another, "proclaiming the message in their synagogues and casting out demons" (1:39; cf. 1:34), which, Jesus says, represents "what I came out to do" (1:38)—again reflecting the

---

carried into the narrative of Jesus' public ministry first by the exorcisms" (94). In her study of Markan characterization of the Jewish leaders, Malbon neglects to explore this important aspect ("The Jewish Leaders in the Gospel of Mark").

[41]Cf. Robinson, 85.

[42]von der Osten-Sacken, *Parabel und Streitgespräch*, 377.

programmatic nature of this section.[43] At the end of the first cycle of controversy stories (which I will discuss more fully below), Mark describes the resolve of Jesus' opponents to bring an end to Jesus in terms reminiscent of the demon's cry in 1:24: "The Pharisees went out and immediately conspired with the Herodians against him, how to destroy (ἀπολέσωσιν) him" (3:6). This ominous note makes explicit that the mounting opposition to Jesus is to the death, and that in seeking to destroy Jesus, the one who would destroy the demons which possess human beings and thus liberate them (1:24), the leaders ally themselves with Satan's minions in the cosmic conflict.

Mark further develops the characterization of the opponents of Jesus in the controversy over the source of Jesus' power over the demons (3:22-30). In a scene replete with irony, the "scribes who came down from Jerusalem" (3:22)—they are thus acting in their role as authoritative judges of "sinful" behavior according to the law—ascribe Jesus' authority to Satan (3:22). In doing so, they set themselves against the "Holy one of God" who bears the Spirit of God, and are thus themselves guilty of an eternal, unforgivable sin—indeed, apparently the only such sin (3:28-30).

The parable of the sower and its interpretation, which follows this section, yields (so to speak) another occasion for developing the association between the authorities and Satan. As Mary Ann Tolbert has argued, the parable may well provide an interpretive key for much of the action of the Galilean portion of the Gospel.[44] That is,

---

[43] As many commentators note, Mark's frequent use of εὐθύς underscores the intensity and urgency of Jesus' work (1:18, 20, 21, 23, 28, 29, 30, 42, 43; see, e.g., Tolbert, *Sowing the Gospel*, 117). Also important here, as I will discuss below, is the close association made here between Jesus' word and action.

[44] *Sowing the Gospel*, 121-124; 148-164. Tolbert argues that Mark, in accordance with common contemporary literary-rhetorical practice, has positioned the parable of the sower so that it functions as a "plot synopsis" for the first main rhetorical division of the Gospel (in her reading, 1:14-10:52). She finds the parable of the vineyard (12:1-12) to have the same function for the Jerusalem section (11:1-16:8). As Tolbert puts it, "Each of these parables . . . appear to reflect the basic actions of Jesus and the other characters in its respective division" (122). As in Xenophon's *An Ephesian Tale*, which contains poetic oracles which function to summarize the plot and orient the audience, the synopses in Mark "are located far enough into the story for their elements to be identified but near enough to the beginning to function as guides for how everything is to be understood. . . . The two parables in Mark present in

the parable provides an orienting "synopsis" of the plot of the Gospel, which aids the audience in its interpretation of the action. To a great degree Tolbert's interpretation of the typology presented by the various kinds of "soil" provides a helpful orientation to the action of the narrative (though not perhaps in the same way as she expresses it). The parable deals with the nature and fate of the Word sown by the Sower, and does focus in a certain fashion on human response to it (note the emphasis on "hearing" and "listening" [ἀκούειν]: 4:3, 9, 12, 15, 16, 18, 20, 23, 24, 33). The preceding narrative (Chapters 1-3) has clearly presented Jesus as the proclaimer of the "word" (1:38 [κηρύξειν], 2:2 ["he was speaking [ἐλάλει] to them the word [τὸν λόγον]"; cf. διδάσκειν, 1:21, 22; 2:13; 4:1-2), and, as we have seen, Mark wastes no time in setting up various responses to Jesus and his message: the first disciples follow him "immediately" (1:16-20); the crowds flock to Jesus to hear him and be healed (1:32-34, 45; 2:1-2,

---

concise, summary form the Gospel's view of Jesus: he is the Sower of the word and the Heir of the Vineyard. The first emphasizes his task and the second his identity; together they make up the Gospel's basic narrative Christology" (122). While Tolbert's understanding of the function of these parables has much to commend it (as she notes, Mark himself gives the parable of the sower such a key function in 4:13), her particular reading of the parables—especially the sower—does not reflect accurately *how* the parables orient the audience. As I will discuss further below, Tolbert's view that the parable of the sower should be better termed an "earth parable," i.e., that it has more to do with delineating the different types of soil (149-50), and functions ultimately to encourage the audience to "be good soil" (e.g., 299), misunderstands in a fundamental way the rhetoric of Mark's Gospel as I read it. True, the parable does put weight on the interpretation in terms of the different types of soil; but such a typology does not issue naturally in an exhortation to be a certain kind of soil. In each case, it is an *external* influence which affects the fate of the seed as the word (Satan, trouble or persecution, the cares of the world). Even in the interpretation (vv. 13-20), the emphasis is on the fact that, in spite of all this, the seed yields a miraculous harvest. The rhetorical implication seems to me to be much more that the audience must rely on God's promise of the harvest in such a way that the external factors which hinder a fruitful response to the Gospel are removed—by God.

For alternative readings of the parable along these lines, see Donald Juel, *Mark* (Augsburg Commentary on the New Testament; Minneapolis: Augsburg, 1990), 68-64; John Donahue, *The Gospel in Parable* (Philadelphia: Fortress Press, 1988), 29-51. Others have seen the parable of the sower as a key to the plot of the Gospel as well; see, e.g., John Drury, *Parables in the Gospels: History and Allegory* (New York: Crossroad, 1985), 51-52; Bernard Brandon Scott, *Hear Then the Parable: A Commentary on the Parables of Jesus* (Minneapolis: Fortress Press, 1989), 346-47.

13, etc.); and the authorities challenge him (2:1-3:6) and quickly resolve to do away with him (3:6). As Tolbert points out, the parable of the sower, especially in its interpretation, can be seen to interpret the responses developed so far in the narrative, and to do the same, in an anticipatory way, for the ensuing narrative.[45] The parable explains the "roots" of the responses, and promises that in spite of the seemingly overwhelming forces that inhibit the seed from yielding a harvest, it will, in fact, do so, and abundantly.

Our concern here is for the interpretive lens provided by the parable through which the audience is to view those who have overtly expressed their "hardness" toward Jesus, the religious authorities. If the audience has missed the preceding examples of Mark's more subtle characterization of the authorities as manifestations of Satan's opposition to God's redemptive plans, the parable ought to make this identification a "reasonably easy task for the audience," as Tolbert puts it.[46] The parable speaks of seed which "fell on the path, and the birds came and ate it up" (4:4). In other words, the seed never had the opportunity to germinate, but was snatched up immediately. In the interpretation, Jesus says of this seed, or rather of the earth on which it fell, "These are the ones on the path where the word is sown: when they hear, Satan immediately comes and takes away the word that is sown in them" (4:15).[47] This identification clearly suggests a group that responds to Jesus with hostility from the beginning, whose disposition leads it to attempt to prevent the word of Jesus from bearing any fruit. And in fact, as Mark portrays it, the authorities' (at first the scribes') first response to Jesus comes when he is "preaching the word" (2:1-12), and they accuse him of blasphemy.[48] The interpretation of the parable suggests

---

[45]*Sowing the Gospel*, 153-59.

[46]*Sowing the Gospel*, 153.

[47]The problem of the syntax here is well known; the Greek seems to make the identification of the responders with the seeds sown, rather than the earth; see, e.g., Vincent Taylor, *The Gospel According to St. Mark* (London: MacMillan, 1959), 258-262; Joel Marcus, *The Mystery of the Kingdom of God* (SBLDS 90; Atlanta: Scholars Press, 1986), 26 n. 29. Ultimately, though, this does not obscure Mark's basic point that various groups of people are to be identified with the sown seed (see Tolbert, *Sowing the Gospel*, 153 n. 42).

[48]Marcus, *The Mystery of the Kingdom of God*, 65 n. 186.

that this response is the work of Satan himself, and thus the authorities become the instruments of cosmic opposition to Jesus' mission.

As the narrative continues beyond Chapter 4, it confirms this characterization of the authorities' opposition. On three further occasions, reliable commentary informs the audience explicitly that the motivation of the authorities' opposition is "Satanic." In 8:13, the Pharisees approach Jesus, seeking from him a sign from heaven to validate his authority. Again, the irony is unmistakable; Jesus refuses their request, but the surrounding narrative is replete with just such signs: healings (7:24-37), miraculous feedings (6:30-44), authoritative teaching (7:6-13). Before these signs have a chance to take root in the authorities, the possibility of their fruitful hearing is prevented by Satan: the narrator characterizes the Pharisees' request for a sign as a "testing" of Jesus (πειράζειν), recalling Satan's testing of Jesus in the wilderness (1:13).[49] Mark portrays the Pharisees' question about divorce (10:2) in the same way. Finally, when the Pharisees and some Herodians approach him in the temple to "trap him in the word" (ἵνα αὐτὸν ἀγρεύσωσιν λόγῳ—recalling again the parable of the sower?), Jesus characterizes their attempt as a testing: τί με πειράζετε; (12:13-14).

A further way in which Mark portrays the authorities' alliance with Satan is through the similarity in form between Jesus' exorcizing activity, which serves to keep before the audience the cosmic implications of Jesus' ministry, and the controversies with the authorities.[50] Mark invites the audience to view the debates between Jesus and the authorities in the light of Jesus' exorcisms in several ways. First, the opening, paradigmatic scene of Jesus' first public teaching, as noted above, closely links Jesus' authority to teach with his authority over the demons (1:21-28); and the scene includes violent "debate" between Jesus and the demon.[51] As in this instance, most of the exorcisms open with a hostile challenge on the part of the demon, which is silenced by Jesus' authoritative word (1:23-26; cf.

---

[49]This association is unfortunately lost in most translations, which render πειράζειν in 1:13 as "tempt," but the other occurrences as "test."

[50]Robinson, *The Problem of History in Mark*, 92-94; cf. Martin Albertz, *Die synoptischen Streitgespräche* (Berlin: Trowitsch, 1921), 152-53.

[51]Robinson, 92.

the summary of Jesus' exorcizing activity, 3:11-12).[52] The debates between Jesus and the authorities begin in similar fashion, with the authorities accusing Jesus of breaking the law, acting out of Satan's authority, etc.; Jesus' reply effectively silences their protestations.[53] Occasionally Jesus' reply results in a further challenge from his opponents, as in 10:2-9; 11:27-33; 12:13-17; still the exchange culminates in an authoritative and silencing word from Jesus. This pattern is also found among the exorcisms, especially the Gerasene demoniac (5:6-13). Another variation of the pattern is common to both the debates and the exorcisms: at times the conflict begins with Jesus' disciples and the authorities, but is finally resolved by Jesus himself (2:16-17, 18-20, 23-27); this occurs as well in the failed attempt by the disciples to exorcize a demon from the epileptic child (9:14-29).[54] In this case, too, the scribes are on hand, arguing with the disciples (9:14).

Robinson's summary statement concerning the significance of these formal similarities is illuminating:

> The cosmic struggle has here reached a more subtle form and is stated in more immanent language than was the case in the exorcisms. But just as was the case there, Mark is not concerned either with purely immanent temptations, nor with purely inward and mental temptations; rather the concept is that of the 'trials' instigated by Satan and consisting in a historical encounter in a specific situation. It is therefore evident that Mark not only presents the debates in a form similar to that of the exorcisms, but also envisages the meaning of the debates in a way similar to the exorcisms. The debates are a continuation of the cosmic struggle initiated at the baptism and temptation and carried into the narrative of Jesus' public ministry first by the exorcisms.[55]

---

[52]Robinson, 92.

[53]Robinson, 92; see 2:6-11, 16-17, 18-22, 24-28; 3:2-5; 7:5-15; 8:11-12; 12:18-27. The clearest and culminating example of this comes in the final debates in the temple, after which "no one dared ask him any question" (12:34).

[54]Robinson, 92-93. Robinson also points out the similarities between the exorcisms and Jesus' struggles with his disciples, citing "the pointed attribution of the disciples' attitude to Satan (8:33), and the designation of the danger to which they are exposed in view of the passion as 'temptation' (14:38)" (93). On this, see Chapter 5.

[55]Robinson, 93-94.

Robinson's observations are especially significant for this study because he is able to show how the Gospel balances the cosmic and historical realities which comprise Mark's narrative. He argues correctly that Mark's understanding of the apocalyptic significance of Jesus does not involve a flight from history, but rather signals an urgent engagement with present history as the arena in which the cosmic battle is waged.[56] He suggests that Mark's narrative operates on three closely interwoven levels.[57] There is, first, the overtly cosmic level of the struggle between the Spirit (God) and Satan, as introduced in the prologue. The second level involves the Son of God in conflict with the demons/demoniacs; the exorcisms are significant for the way in which they form a bridge between the Gospel's cosmic level and the more immanent, historical level. As Robinson observes, the historical nature of the exorcisms is evident from the fact that the demons Jesus encounters are "in possession of humans through whose organs they speak."[58] That is, the struggle is over the historical existence of a human being, not simply over disembodied spirits. Further, the scenes are public, and often go along with and underscore the concrete teaching and preaching of Jesus.[59] The third level is that of the conflict between Jesus and his opponents, whose relationship to the cosmic struggle comes through the narrative's characterization of his opponents as acting in league with Satan.

Robinson's thesis underscores the rhetorical function of the conflict between Jesus and the authorities in Mark: namely, it serves to acknowledge and/or engender a sense of urgency, of crisis, in the audience. By characterizing the authorities in both historical and cosmic terms, indeed, in refusing to allow a distinction between these two levels, the narrative acknowledges the historical reality of the conflict between the promises of God and their endangerment, and interprets what the historical encounter with opposition to God's purposes as expressed in Jesus is about. Conflict in one's historical existence is not, in other words, the antithesis of God's promises, but rather the very means by which the truth and reliability of God's

---

[56]See especially 102-104.
[57]Robinson, 83.
[58]Robinson, 82.
[59]Robinson, 82-83.

promises are won. The promise comes as conflict precisely because of the human situation of bondage to Satan's powers.

THE NATURE AND DEVELOPMENT OF THE CONFLICT

Consideration of the nature and substance of the controversies between Jesus and his opponents bears this observation out. The conflict turns on a stark either/or that Mark characterizes as "thinking the things of God" vs. "thinking the things of human beings"—human beings captive to Satan.[60] Though the narrative makes clear the necessity of aligning oneself with God's redemptive purposes and identifies one's response to Jesus as the key to doing so, as Malbon puts it, "responding *appropriately* to Jesus, being a follower, is not a simple matter. . . . The complexity of Marcan characterization reflects the complexity of Marcan religious and theological affirmations."[61]

Mark obviously does not simply engage in "negative campaigning," but presents through the conflict between Jesus and his opponents the positive alternative to "thinking the things of human beings." Just as the struggles take place within history, so too the issues around which the debates turn are genuine historical issues. By this I do not mean that their primary reference is to actual conflict in Mark's historical community, or that the conflicts should be read in order to reconstruct historically the genesis of Mark's Gospel; rather, the rhetorical shape of the conflict creates an implied audience which experiences God's promises in sharp conflict with the wills and powers which exercise control in the world as they experience it. Conflict is thus an unavoidable and constitutive component of the good news in a world oriented in opposition to God. By tracing the development of the conflict in the plot and examining what is at issue in the alternatives presented by Jesus on the one hand and the authorities on the other, I will attempt in what follows to illuminate the way in which Mark utilizes the conflict rhetorically to form an

---

[60]Robinson's schematic representation of the different narrative levels in Mark reveals that human opposition to God is synonymous with Satan's opposition.

[61]Malbon, "The Jewish Leaders in the Gospel of Mark," 280-81.

implied audience which experiences in itself the sense of conflict, urgency, and crisis the story relates.

The narrative develops the conflict between Jesus and the religious authorities with the same swiftness and urgency with which it presents Jesus' ministry as a whole. From the very opening of Jesus' public ministry, Mark makes clear that what the prologue foreshadowed will indeed be the case: that Jesus' authoritative, liberating, and life-giving ministry is inextricably intertwined with a life and death struggle. We have already seen that Mark presents the unfolding conflict between Jesus and the authorities in the light of the cosmic battle between God and Satan. As the development of the conflict in the plot reveals, the same urgency which attends the cosmic conflict is reflected in Jesus' battles with the authorities. Mark understands the world which God has set out to redeem as one held captive by forces opposed to God, comprised of human beings whose hearts have been hardened to God's redemptive intentions.[62] But as we shall see, the "way" of God, the manner in which God works out these intentions, precludes utilizing the type of brute force which exercises control over the human disposition—that is Satan's *modus operandi*. Thus Jesus' mission is characterized not by the exercise of power over those he has been sent to redeem, but by the elimination of Satan's hold on them, so that being grasped by God's redemption becomes a genuine possibility.

This is especially discernible in the exorcisms and healings; before Jesus' intervention, the "victims" of possession and disease (the same thing in Mark) were captive to their infirmity and its consequences. After the exorcism or healing, it becomes clear that Jesus cannot, or chooses not, to exercise control over their response; cf. 1:40-45; 5:14-20; 10:52. Such a strategy limits one's options in a struggle, of course; it represents a kind of unilateral disarmament. And it helps explain Jesus' varied "success" among those whom he

---

[62]See Dan Via, *The Ethics of Mark's Gospel*, 45-46. Rhoads and Michie highlight the parable of the vineyard as the key to the larger story: "The story implies that human authorities have been ruling for themselves rather than God and that Satan has been the strong man in charge of the house. It is at this point in the story world that the narrative opens, with the lord of the vineyard beginning something new by sending his son to the vineyard" (*Mark as Story*, 74).

encounters. Those who suffer infirmity of some kind understand in a way others cannot the death-dealing influence of Satan, and have typically exhausted any hope of being liberated through human means (cf., e.g., 5:1-20; 21-43; 9:24). Jesus is least success-ful—indeed, on one level, unsuccessful—with those who actually have something to lose in terms of their power and influence in the world by acknowledging and responding appropriately to Jesus.[63] They are no less under the sway of Satan than the demoniacs, as we saw above in Mark's characterization of them; the difference here, however, seems to be that Satan has tapped into a fundamental feature of the human character: the willingness to allow their hearts to be hardened to God when the "pay-off" for such a stance involves the consolidation of power over others. This state of affairs deter-mines for Mark that the battle will revolve around the question of authority; and since his principal opponents present themselves as the "tenants" and preservers of the authority of God, the conflict can be more precisely characterized as one over the shape and nature of divine authority and the criteria for determining who exercises it. It also leads to a situation in which the very act of exercising the divine understanding of power in a world still under Satan's sway leads to conflict and death.[64]

The narrative moves to establish and sustain this association between Jesus' mission, his authority, and his death through the pervasiveness, intensity and swiftness of the development of the conflict. As noted above, Jesus' initial public activity is presented in such a way that it expresses *in nuce* the issue around which conflict will develop: the crowd recognizes the unmistakable, astonishing, and new authority with which Jesus teaches and acts, and contrasts it with the teaching of the scribes (1:21-28).[65] From this ominous

---

[63]See Rhoads and Michie, *Mark as Story*, 79-80.

[64]As I will point out below, this also determines that the resolution of the conflict will be ironic; as God did countless times in Israel's history, God will utilize precisely this hardness of heart to accomplish God's designs, so that, e.g., as Joseph tells his brothers, "Even though you intended to do harm, God intended it for good" (Gen 50:20).

[65]See von der Osten-Sacken, 378; Tannehill, "The Gospel of Mark as Narrative Christology," 66.

note, a conflict develops which will pit the authority of the Son of God against the authority of the religious leaders.

My discussion of the development and nature of the conflict between Jesus and the religious authorities will focus on the two controversy cycles in Mark's narrative, one of which comes in the Galilean portion of the Gospel (2:1-3:6), the other in the Jerusalem portion (11:27-12:44). These units serve to provide the narrative tension that drives the story forward and endangers the promise, to elucidate the substance of the conflict, and develop the inseparable connection between the exercise and acknowledgment of divine authority and its violent consequences, both for the characters and the audience.

Shattering Boundaries: 1:16-3:6

The first movement of the first major rhetorical division in Mark's Gospel encompasses Jesus' initial public actions and the responses they generate. From 1:16 to 3:6 the narrative unfolds at a breathless pace; it presents Jesus as moving swiftly from place to place teaching, preaching, healing, and choosing disciples, pursued both by crowds attracted to these activities and religious authorities suspicious of them.[66] The summary of this activity contained in 3:7-12 provides the bridge to the first scene in which Jesus is actually able to escape his pursuers and tend to some "administrative" matters his mission requires—i.e., choosing twelve followers as an inner circle (3:13-19). By this point in the narrative, Mark has established the principal characters and character groups and their roles or commissions in the story.[67] Jesus has received his commission from

---

[66]This brief opening section contains no fewer than eleven different "scene changes": 1:16, 21, 29, 35, 39; 2:1, 13, 15, 23; 3:1, 7.

[67]Robert Tannehill sees Mark's plot as the working out of various commissions communicated to each character or group; he finds in this evidence that Mark is a "unified narrative" ("The Gospel of Mark as Narrative Christology," 60-61). His analysis is very helpful, though I disagree with it with respect to the roles he accords the "supplicants and demons." He suggests that they do represent "commissioned" characters in the story, but do not contribute to the principal narrative lines which develop through Jesus' relationship with his disciples and the authorities (67). As noted above, I see both groups as a crucial aspect of Jesus' commission—the liberation

God at his baptism (1:9-11), which involves the proclamation of the nearness of the reign of God in his word and work; the disciples receive theirs from Jesus (1:16-20; 2:13-14; spelled out more explicitly in 3:13-19); and the authorities receive theirs (from Satan?) in direct response to Jesus' (3:6).[68] As Tannehill puts it, the development of the plot can be seen as revolving around the fulfillment or nonfulfillment of these commissions.[69]

1:16-3:6 plays a central role in the first rhetorical division, and indeed in the development of the narrative as a whole, because it expresses both the essential elements of Jesus' commission (some explicitly, some, through foreshadowing, in an anticipatory way), as well as the fact and the basis of the authorities' opposing commission. And most important, it establishes the connection between these two narrative elements, revealing from the beginning how and why Jesus' commission comes to involve the cross.[70]

The initial activity of Jesus as described in this opening movement sets the tone for the narrative's understanding of the nature and shape of the reign of God Jesus has been commissioned to establish. As I suggested in the previous chapter, the prologue, which immediately precedes this section, has "prepared the way" for an understanding of the good news of Jesus the Messiah which both accords with and radically challenges traditional expectations regarding God's eschatological redemption. The most powerful expression of this, as we saw, is the scene of Jesus' baptism, in which a jarring juxtaposition of images aims at preparing the audience for a surprising, scandalous confirmation of God's promises. Especially

---

of creation from Satan's grasp. The supplicants, moreover, provide an important contrasting role to the disciples' failure to carry out their commission, as well as to the authorities' commission.

[68]Tannehill, 61; Tannehill understands the authorities as providing their own source for their commission; but the overlap between the authorities' goals and Satan's suggest that the Jewish leaders commission comes from Satan; though, as noted above, Mark is careful to preserve their essentially historical character (as well as that of Jesus!).

[69]Tannehill, 61.

[70]As von der Osten-Sacken notes, "Die neuen Lehre führt in den Tod, und zwar durch die, von deren Lehre sie sich als neue abhebt und die als neue Lehre die alte in Frage stellt" (380).

potent is the imagery of the tearing of the heavens (1:10), which suggests a breach of the boundary separating—or protecting!—human beings from God. As Juel has suggested, this imagery also provides a potent rubric under which to place the whole of Jesus' ministry in Mark: That Jesus' ministry of transgressing boundaries represents a working out of the cosmic breach effected at Jesus' baptism for the sake of a creation in bondage.[71] When viewed from this perspective, both Jesus' ministry and the opposition to it on the part of those who see themselves as preservers of those same boundaries emerge in sharp relief, as our examination of Mark's opening section will show.

The narrative presents Jesus as the bearer of the message of God's eschatological breach in the heavens; Jesus works, in effect, as the very presence of a God "on the loose"[72] from God's heavenly dwelling. In his opening barrage of miracles and teaching, Jesus shatters boundaries at every level of human experience:[73] cosmological boundaries continue to be breached in his exorcisms (paradigmatically in 1:23-27; cf. 1:34, 39; 3:11), and, as the scribes recognize, in his exercise of authority belonging to God alone (e.g., 2:5-11); he breaches social boundaries in his traffic with "tax collectors and sinners" (1:15-17); and he shatters boundaries of individual bodies within the culture by reaching out to those whose infirmities involve bodily fluids being "out of place"[74] (e.g., 1:40-45; cf. 5:24-34; 7:14-23).[75] It is in this sense, then, that Jesus' teaching is both "new" and "with authority" (1:27): As the crowds and the

---

[71]Juel, *Master of Surprise*, 38-41.

[72]The phrase is Juel's (e.g., *Master of Surprise*, 62).

[73]I have borrowed this three-fold categorization of boundaries from Mary Douglas, *Natural Symbols: Explorations in Cosmology* (New York: Pantheon, 1982), 62-104. For a helpful summary of her work, and an exploration of its potential for illuminating the issue of boundary-crossing in Mark's Gospel, see David Rhoads, "Social Criticism: Crossing Boundaries," in *Mark and Method: New Approaches in Biblical Studies* (ed. Janice Capel Anderson and Stephen D. Moore; (Minneapolis: Fortress Press, 1992), 135-161, esp. 150-159.

[74]On this, see Mary Douglas, *Purity and Danger: An Analysis of the Concepts of Pollution and Taboo* (London: Routledge & Kegan Paul, 1966).

[75]The section 5:1-43 also centers on Jesus' crossing of boundaries—to the realm of the dead, to a women ostracized due to a flow of blood, and the "final boundary," death itself.

recognize, Mark's Jesus presents a claim to a radically new manifestation of God's presence on earth and God's intentions with respect
to creation, one where boundaries which have functioned to draw a
line around God, to box God in to a comfortable, safe, predictable
mode of operation, are torn asunder.

The reactions to Jesus' ministry serve to underscore its radical
newness. Those who, by virtue of illness or demon possession (or
ethnicity?), have been excluded from God's presence by such
boundaries, have been deemed, in fact, a threat to God's holiness,
flock to Jesus, at times literally begging for the healing touch that
will restore them to wholeness (1:40). On the other hand, those who
have something at stake in the present order of things recognize just
as readily the threat Jesus poses to their own understanding of God,
and hence their own authority and station. And it is the clash between
these two conceptions of God and God's way in the world that the
narrative seeks to develop in such a way that the audience of the
Gospel recognizes and experiences it.

It is for this reason that the narrative focuses on the issue of
Jesus' authority (ἐξουσία, 1:22[76]), and seeks to substantiate Jesus'
divine authority in contrast to the authority exercised by the religious
authorities ("and not as the scribes," 1:22).[77] The boundary-crossing
activity of Jesus does disrupt fundamentally the present order of
things, and Mark is essentially working to shape an audience in light
of the new world order presented by Jesus. In this section, Mark
weds Jesus' authoritative teaching to his authoritative action; the
crowd in the synagogue responds to Jesus' exorcism with the words,
"What is this? A new *teaching* with authority!"[78] As the narrative

---

[76]The term is used especially frequently in Mark at the beginning of each major
rhetorical division: At the beginning of division 1 (1:22, 27; 2:10), and then again at
the beginning of division 2 (11:28, 29, 33); each time, of course, in the context of
conflict with the religious leaders.

[77]Cf. Kingsbury, *Conflict in Mark*, 65-67; he correctly notes that "Mark
presents Jesus' conflict with the religious authorities as one of authority: Does Jesus
or does he not discharge his ministry as one authorized by God?" (67).

[78]The syntax here also allows for the translation "A new teaching! With
authority he commands even the unclean spirits. . . " (NRSV). I would say the
ambiguity is either intentional, or at least results in more closely connecting Jesus'
words and actions.

continues, it becomes clear that this is a major feature of Mark's characterization of Jesus: that he speaks and acts with authority, and that the speaking and acting reinforce each other.[79] Mark develops this connection in the ensuing scenes. He shows Jesus alternating between healing (1:29-34, 40-45) and teaching (1:38), reminding the audience of the connection between the two (1:39). The healing of the paralytic drives the point home especially clearly. Jesus' authority to grant the man forgiveness of sins is grounded in his authority to grant him the ability to walk (2:1-12), which story also functions to introduce the first overt conflict between Jesus and the religious leaders.[80]

2:1-3:6 as a Rhetorical Unit. The close connection between this first series of controversy stories, 2:1-3:6, and the introduction of Jesus' ministry in Chapter 1 thus emerges clearly.[81] Jesus' authority, the working out of his divine commission, becomes established with lightening speed through his word and deed and through the response of the crowds (1:32, 37, 45). As Robinson puts it, "When [Jesus] speaks, God acts."[82] The narrative now moves to elucidate the contrast between this divinely-sanctioned authority of Jesus and the supposed authority of the religious leaders, the contrast hinted at already in 1:22. Here Jesus' exercise of authority itself engenders conflict, because it stands opposed to an existing power structure. The conflict between Jesus and the religious leaders comes about as each party acts concretely out of its respective understanding of divine power and authority. And out of this conflict, the clear either-or which faces the audience of Mark's Gospel emerges in sharp relief.

---

[79]Cf. Robinson, 97-98.

[80]As I will point out below, the cycle of controversy stories serves further to confirm this association of word and work: the outer two stories in the cycle contain miracles, deeds of authority, which serve to substantiate the words of Jesus in these and the middle stories.

[81]Cf. von der Osten Sacken, *Parabel und Streitgespräch*, 377; Tannehill, "The Gospel of Mark," 66; Juel, *Master of Surprise*, 40.

[82]Robinson, 98.

As noted above, 2:1-3:6 forms a literary sub-unit within the Gospel;[83] for much of the history of Markan scholarship, the debate has concerned the question whether the historical author has used a pre-Markan collection in either written or oral form. My interest here reflects more recent scholarship which has focused on the rhetorical patterning of this cycle of stories and its possible function(s) in the final narrative. The work of Joanna Dewey is especially helpful in this regard. In *Markan Public Debate*, Dewey examines in detail how the rhetorical form of this section serves to underscore the nature and shape of the conflict between Jesus and the religious leaders.[84] She shows that the five stories evince a "tight and well-worked-out concentric and chiastic structure,"[85] which she represents as follows:

A **2:1-12** *The healing of the paralytic*
  B **2:13-17** *The call of Levi/eating with sinners*
    C **2:18-22** *The sayings on fasting and on the old and the new*
  B' **2:23-27** *Plucking grain on the Sabbath*
A' **3:1-6** *The healing on the sabbath*

Dewey observes the following structural markers:

(1) The section is framed with references to Jesus' withdrawal due to the relentless pressure from the crowds (1:45; 3:7-8), inviting the audience to view the stories as an interconnected whole.[86]

(2) The first and last stories, A and A' (2:1-12; 3:1-6), both involve the unusual mixture of healing and controversy. A restorative healing is broken up with controversy over Jesus' actions, and concludes with the completion of the healing and a reaction by those present. They are introduced with an identical phrase: καὶ εἰσ-

---

[83]See, e.g., K. L. Schmidt, *Der Rahmen der Geschichte Jesu* (Berlin: Trowitzch & Sohn, 1919), 104; Albertz, 5-16; Martin Dibelius, *From Tradition to Gospel* (tr. E. L. Woolf; London: Ivor Nicholson & Watson, 1934), 219; Taylor, 91-92.

[84]See also the summary of her findings in "The Literary Structure of the Controversy Stories in Mark 2:1-3:6," in *The Interpretation of Mark* (ed. William Telford; Philadelphia: Fortress Press and London: SPCK, 1985), 109-118. A subsidiary concern of Dewey's in the larger work is to determine whether or not a pre-markan collection of controversy stories underlies 2:1-3:6.

[85]*Markan Public Debate*, 110.

[86]"The Literary Structure," 108-109; *Markan Public Debate*, 109.

ἦλθον πάλιν εἰς (2:1; 3:1); in each, Jesus takes the initiative in the controversy (2:8; 3:4), and then turns to the person to be healed and speaks to him (λέγει τῷ); each contains a reference to the hearts of the opponents (2:6; 3:5); and each healing is restorative in nature with overtones of resurrection.[87]

(3) B and B' are related, first, to A and A' in parallel ways: A and B both have to do with sin and sinners; B' and A' with violation of the sabbath. B and B' evince a close parallelism, especially in the center section of each, which concerns eating: Jesus' eating with sinners violates Pharisaic law, as David also ate that which was not lawful. Moreover, each concludes with a logion in the form of a general proverb (2:17, 27-28).[88]

(4) Finally, C sets itself up as the center of the chiasm through its uniqueness in form and content among the stories. Unlike the others, it has just two halves, the question and answer concerning fasting (2:18-20), and the sayings on old and new (2:21-22); there is no indication of setting, and the opponents are not specified. Yet it relates to B and B' in its concern for eating, and to A and A' with its suggestion of death and resurrection.

The most important question is the rhetorical function of such a structure. Clearly, the section highlights the fact and nature of the opposition to Jesus, which serves on the story level to generate tension and move the story forward, and on the discourse or rhetorical level to underscore the sharp distinction between Jesus and his opponents.[89] As Dewey rightly suggests, viewing this series of controversies as an organic whole serves to impress on the audience that "the opponents objected to Jesus' activity as a whole, and to the messianic claim which was the basis of Jesus' actions."[90]

---

[87]*Markan Public Debate*, 111-12.

[88]*Markan Public Debate*, 112-114; Dewey notes that the story of David's eating the bread of the presence may actually have more to do with the controversy over Jesus' eating with sinners (114).

[89]Dewey expresses this in a nice analogy: "Mark 2:1-3:6 might perhaps be compared in musical terms to the statement, early in a musical work, of a major theme which then hangs ominously over the composition, but which comes to dominate the music much later in the piece" (*Markan Public Debate*, 119).

[90]*Markan Public Debate*, 119.

Within the unit, she argues that there is both a linear development of the conflict as well as symmetry which invites the seeking of connections among the various stories. In terms of the linear development, Dewey sees a heightening of the conflict from the scribes deliberating in their hearts, to confronting Jesus' disciples, then Jesus himself, and finally issuing in the plot to destroy him.[91] The final note of the Pharisees' intention to do Jesus in results from the cumulative effect of his action, and serves, again, to underscore the close connection between Jesus' activity and his ultimate death. I would suggest, however, that the opening pericope (2:1-12) paints the issue in the sharpest terms, and is not in any sense a muted or tentative encroachment on Jesus' activity.[92] Rather, it presents in uncompromising terms the very charge with which Jesus will be handed over to Pilate: his alleged blasphemy (2:7; 14:63). Of the actions of Jesus which engender opposition in this series, only this one issues in this charge; and appropriately so, because it presents Jesus as acting in God's stead, thereby defaming the Name, and perhaps even compromising God's oneness.[93] Although one may be censured by the authorities for cavorting with the wrong types and breaking the sabbath—i.e., breaking down the boundaries which provide order to the world—only blasphemy is punishable by death.

Thus the healing/forgiveness of the paralytic represents the paradigmatic statement of the issue around which opposition to Jesus

---

[91] *Markan Public Debate*, 118-19; cf. also Kingsbury, *Conflict in Mark*, who sees a linear development in the "overall trend from indirect confrontation with Jesus or the disciples to direct confrontation with Jesus . . . and the parallel trend in the controversies according to which the emphasis shifts from questions having to do with blasphemy, tradition, and Mosaic law to the question about authority itself" (67). The remarks concerning Dewey in what follows apply to Kingsbury as well.

[92] Dewey asserts that the emphasis on the miracle overshadows the controversy, which becomes more and more explicit as the section develops (*Markan Public Debate*, 118). One might distinguish here between the story and discourse levels; because the objections of the scribes are spoken among themselves here, there is a movement from private grumbling to public opposition. But the audience is made privy to the scribes' inner thoughts, so that the principal issue of their opposition—Jesus' alleged blasphemy, a crime, unlike the other actions in the section, deserving of death—is brought onto the scene from the beginning.

[93] As noted above, Mark has the scribes voice their objection with an apparent allusion to the Shema (2:7).

turns, at least on the discourse level. The linear development from here to 3:6 and beyond is best seen as a working out of the implications of Jesus' divine claims presented in 2:1-12. Jesus' other actions and sayings evoke such harsh opposition precisely because of Jesus' claim to possess the authority to speak and act for God, an authority confirmed by the efficacy of Jesus' words and actions. When Jesus shatters the boundaries of holiness and purity as understood by the religious leaders through his association with sinners, his lack of fasting, and his redefinition of the sabbath, he claims to be revealing the very intentions of God. Peter von der Osten-Sacken puts it well:

> Krasser kann die Differenz zwischen Jesus bzw. der an ihn glaubenden christolichen Gemeinde und den Schriftgelehrten kaum bezeichnet werden: Hier die Anklage der Gotteslästerung—dort das Bekenntnis seiner Vollmacht im Gegensatz zu denen, die ihn der Lästerung bezichtigen.[94]

Precisely this difference will result in the bridegroom being taken away (2:20).

If the linear movement toward overt opposition helps move the action forward toward the inevitability of Jesus' death, the concentric and chiastic structure of this section helps the audience grasp the overall vision of Jesus' ministry, and places before it as well the question of whether Jesus is a blasphemer or the royal Son of God. The reign of God which Jesus proclaims requires, as the center of the chiasm suggests, a new wine for which old wineskins are not suited (2:21-22). The controversies revolve, in parallel fashion, around alternative structures of social order and the way each reflects a particular understanding of God's way in the world—again, the relationship among cosmic, social, and individual boundaries, and their consequences for human well-being. For Judaism, and especially for the Pharisees, the issue is expressed in terms of holiness and purity. Israel understood itself as a people "set apart"—the root meaning of holiness—in a way that reflected their understanding of God. The Levitical understanding of purity underlay both the

---

[94]"Streitgespräch und Parabel," 378.

function of the law and the temple.[95] Israel was to remain holy as God is holy (cf. Lev. 19:1), and the central social structures and institutions of Judaism were set up to reflect and maintain that holiness. There existed a hierarchy, or "map" which implicitly and explicitly ordered society and its institutions by degrees of holiness or purity.[96] Movement among these boundaries affected one's purity, and one's state of purity determined what movements one could make in society. Of itself, a state of ritual impurity or uncleanness did not necessarily constitute a sin or a defilement of God; what was to be avoided at all costs was to act in ways that were inappropriate to one's state of purity.

Such a system has a profound logic to it, of course; it existed to protect the purity of Israel, on which the presence of God in the world as a whole was thought to rest. But Mark's narrative presents through Jesus a diametrically opposite understanding of holiness, one incompatible with the understanding reflected in Jesus' opponents in Mark.[97] From the perspective of the religious leaders, Jesus' claims to be operating as God's emissary fly in the face of his actions. Association with the impure renders one impure and moves one away from God; as Jonathan Smith puts it, in a social order centered around protective boundaries, "To break out, to cross boundaries, is

---

[95]See Rhoads, "Social Criticism," 144-149; also Jerome Neyrey, "The Idea of Purity in Mark's Gospel," *Semeia* 35 (1986), 91-128; Juel, *Master of Surprise*, 40-41.

[96]Passages in the Mishnah and Tosefta map this structure out explicitly; e.g., Mishnah *Kelim* 1:6-9 charts the hierarchy of place: "The land of Israel is holier than any other land. . . . The walled cities of Israel are still more holy . . . "—moving to the Holy of Holies in the temple as the most holy site. People, too, are ranked according to purity (*t. Meg*): from High Priests at the top, to Priests, Levites, Israelites, converts, freed slaves, disqualified priests, temple slaves, bastardy, eunuchs, to others with physical deformities.

[97]It is important to point out, of course, that Jesus' understanding of holiness as presented in Mark is not a completely "new" idea; in many ways, the conflict reflects a tension within Israel's scriptures themselves; the idea that protecting and preserving human life takes precedent over concern for ritual purity is rooted in Israel's prophetic tradition (e.g., Isa 1:10-17; Amos 5:21-24); see, e.g, Gerhard von Rad, *Theologie des Alte Testaments: Band II: Die theologie der prophetischen Überliefurungen Israels* (München: Chr. Kaiser Verlag, 1960), 339-356.

to open the world to the threat of chaos, to commit transgression."[98] Thus the only logical conclusion could be that Jesus' incontrovertible power had its source in God's opposite; and indeed, in their next encounter with him, they accuse him of being in league with the prince of demons (3:22-30). In Mark's Jesus, however, we encounter a vision of holiness which works in the opposite direction; in these controversy stories, as elsewhere in the narrative, as Rhoads puts it, "Instead of using purity regulations to protect, the Markan Jesus transgresses the boundaries of purity. Through the agency of the Holy Spirit upon Jesus, God enters the arena of impurity without regard to the risk of defilement."[99]

In 2:1-3:6, these alternative visions of holiness appear in a rhythmic, flowing form which serves to bring utmost clarity to the conflict. Each of the corresponding stories, as well as the centerpiece of the chiasm, reveals the close connection between Jesus' life-giving activity and the deathward momentum it generates. In the outer pericopes, Jesus is shown spreading holiness through restoring human beings to wholeness. Once again, the divine authority of his vision manifests itself and is confirmed by the result of his work. For Mark's Jesus, the intention of God to bring life where there is brokenness supplants the system of holiness which would limit God's capacity to act in response to human need.

The consequences of acting out God's intentions, however, are also made clear; each of these healing stories frames an intense opposition, borne of the recognition that such boundary-shattering activity spells the death of the present order. Likewise, the inner corresponding stories (B and B') represent a similar reversal of priorities: rather than rendering Jesus impure, Jesus' presence among the tax collectors and sinners cleanses them; their need (χρείαν, 2:17) takes priority over any concern about ritual impurity. And the disciples' need (χρείαν, 2:25) for nourishment outstrips the concern for the sanctity of the sabbath; indeed, the Sabbath is sanctified precisely through the fulfillment of want.

---

[98]Jonathan Z. Smith, "Animals and Plants," *Encyclopedia Britannica*, 15th ed., 1:911-18; quoted in Rhoads, "Social Criticism," 152.

[99]Rhoads, "Social Criticism," 149; cf. Juel, *Master of Surprise*, 41.

The centerpiece interprets the whole of the cycle, underscoring the interconnection between Jesus' vision of holiness and its consequences, and relating more explicitly the consequences of being grasped by Jesus' vision to the audience. It relates the central paradox of Mark's depiction of Jesus: his life-giving presence brings about his death, and yet the bringing of life out of death which character-ized his ministry will in fact result in the discarding of old wineskins for new. The presence of Jesus, the messianic bridegroom who satisfies human need, makes fasting inappropriate. But precisely because of the threat his presence poses to those now in power, the bridegroom will be taken away, and those who are left, those who have been molded by Jesus' understanding of divine power, will suffer as he did until the old gives way to the new.[100]

The Rhetorical Effects. Thus in this opening movement of the first major rhetorical division in the narrative, Mark has forcefully set forth the principal dynamic of his narrative. The newness and radicality of Jesus' message of the boundary-shattering reign of God runs head-long into fierce opposition from those who perceive it—rightly—as a threat to the present order. The narrative makes a shift from the cosmic language of the prologue into the immanent, historical language of Jesus' concrete encounters with human beings, the abruptness of which underscores the sense that the disturbance in the cosmos means something concrete for human existence—God let loose in the world. Hence it is important for Mark that the narrative roles that unfold in relation to each character group's commission have a firm foothold in concrete human experience. The narrative shows the audience the world as it experiences it, as a clash between wills which motivate human action. Both Jesus and the authorities act in ways that correspond to their respective views of God and reality. To the extent that the audience is aware of its own concrete historical existence—i.e., the extent to which it avoids a flight from history in light of the impending eschatological age—it cannot evade the reality of the conflict between its embrace of eschatological salvation in

---

[100]It might be possible to detect an allusion to Jesus' death in the bursting of the old wineskins: In effect, that is precisely what happens in Mark's story; Jesus, the new wine, is placed in a world structured out of old wineskins, which cannot contain him. Until such time that the new wineskins are in place, such will be the fate of the gospel.

Jesus and conflict with powerful forces in history which stand opposed to it. In embracing Jesus—or being embraced by God through him—the audience participates in the boundary-shattering character of Jesus' own ministry, and must expect that the consequences may be the same.

By this point in the narrative, the audience ought to have a clear picture of the nature and shape of the conflict, and, with the intensity and swiftness with which it is presented, begin to feel the inevitability of the coincidence of Jesus' vision and conflict.[101] Far from being able to distance itself from the conflict, an ideal audience will become entangled in it; even as it experiences the life-giving power of Jesus, it, too, feels the ineluctable clash between God's reign and the present structures which oppose it. This first movement contains the seeds both of Jesus' messianic authority and his death, and compels the audience to view the two together. Thus it continues the tension from the prologue, in which the gap between traditional messianic expectations and the shape of Jesus' fulfillment of them was first displayed. In its opening movement, the narrative suggests that it has no intention of resolving the apparent contradiction or filling the gap, but rather continues to emphasize the authority and the opposition, the promise and its endangerment, in the same measure. As the narrative lets the dark cloud of the threat against Jesus settle over the action which follows this section, it makes clear that God's reign poses a threat to those it embraces as well, as we will see in the next chapter.

The Development of the Conflict from 3:7-10:45

Before turning to the conflict in the second major rhetorical division (11:1-16:8), a few remarks about the development of the conflict from 3:7-10:45 are in order, focusing on the rhetorical effect of the controversies in this section. Having established the basic

---

[101]In a very real sense, this cycle as a whole gives profound expression to the unexpected nature of Jesus' Messiahship for Mark, for it shows Jesus living out the apparent contradiction between his messianic status and his humiliation on the cross; because his actions lead the authorities to bring about his death, he is literally living not to be served but to serve, and to give his life a ransom for many (10:45).

nature and shape of the debate, as well as the likelihood that it will be resolved violently, the Gospel shifts its focus to Jesus' attempts to establish a community shaped by his proclamation of the reign of God.[102] Though the plot against Jesus is not repeated explicitly again until 11:18, the narrative continues to develop the connection between Jesus' ministry and conflict established in the opening movement, never letting the audience forget the overall direction in which things are moving.

In the encounters between Jesus and the religious authorities in this section, the leaders continue their assault on Jesus' authority, and there are unmistakable hints that the conflict is widening to encompass not only local Galilean opposition, but opposition from Jerusalem itself.[103] In fact, the very next encounter moves in that direction already, involving "scribes who came down from Jerusalem" (3:22).[104] Moreover, like the first controversy story in the opening section (2:1-12), the debate pointedly poses the question that is at the heart of the Gospel, the issue over which Jesus will be tried, sentenced, and executed—i.e., blasphemy. Since the scribes cannot deny that Jesus acts with some sort of authority and power, and since his actions threaten what they see as divinely-ordained structures and boundaries, they must conclude that he is in league with Satan. Thus the stark either/or encounters the audience once again: either Jesus is

---

[102]As we will see in the next chapter, this aspect of Jesus' commission also meets with opposition which has much in common with that from the religious leaders. Also, it is important to note the rhetorical pattern emerging in these movements: Discipleship (1:16-20; 3:13-19), then conflict (2:1-3:6; 3:20-35). The same structure appears in the next movement as well (6:6b-8:26): Discipleship (6:6b-13), then conflict (6:14-29). Each of these brings the followers of Jesus more closely into the conflict.

[103]I agree with Kingsbury's analysis to this extent; there is a widening of the conflict, which intensifies it. But his suggestion that the issues of the debates themselves contribute to the intensification of the conflict is not borne out by the text. He sees a movement from questions of blasphemy, to tradition and Mosaic law, to the question of authority itself ("The Religious Authorities," 54-61). I see a much more circular pattern than a linear one; as noted, the first controversy deals with the issue which will lead directly to his death on the cross.

[104]The pairing of Jesus' popularity (a recognition of his authority) with opposition which the narrative develops in 1:16-3:6 continues here: The first mention of Jerusalem after the prologue is in a report of the "great numbers" who came to him "having heard all that he was doing" (3:8).

himself a blasphemer, or the opponents themselves blaspheme in associating the work of the Holy Spirit in Jesus with the demonic (3:28-30; the same dynamic is operative in 14:62-63). Obviously, the narrative seeks to move the audience to embrace Jesus' ministry as an expression of God's redemptive activity and reject the opponents' point of view. On the other hand, as in the opening movement, it also links such an embrace with a radically new and boundary-shattering existence, for this controversy is interposed between Jesus' own family's attempts to "reign him in" (3:21; 3:31-35). Even the very structure of the family—a sacrosanct entity in most forms of Judaism[105]— is included among those boundaries that must be broken down to the extent that they conflict with God's reign. The new family which Jesus is establishing will be constituted by those who "do the will of God" —i.e., those "around him" (3:34-35; cf. 10:28-31).

The parable of the sower which immediately follows gives parabolic and allegorical expression to the fundamental link between Jesus' ministry and conflict.[106] Its strategic rhetorical placement allows the audience to understand the parable as a lens through which to view the entire narrative (see above). It gives expression to the fundamental tension between the promise and its endangerment; indeed, it suggests that the endangerment arises precisely through the

---

[105]The commandment to honor one's father and mother comes to mind, of course; as Jacob Neusner points out, Jesus' placing of response to him and his message above familial ties represents a departure from Torah which sets him at odds with the Mosaic tradition as Judaism understands it; and, for the Rabbi Neusner, this discredits his claims to be the authoritative interpreter of the tradition. See *A Rabbi Talks with Jesus: An Intermillennial, Interfaith Exchange* (New York: Doubleday, 1994), and my review of this work in *Word and World* (1996), 388-92.

[106]I will not undertake a detailed examination of this chapter here; for an insightful discussion of the way in which the parables of ch. 4, especially the sower, are closely related to the controversy stories in Mark, see von der Osten-Sacken, "Streitgespräch und Parabel," 385-390. He notes, for example, that Mark uses the term "parable" only two other times outside of chapter four, and both are in the context of conflict (3:23; 12:1). He concludes that "Streitgespräch und Parabel bringen bei Markus je auf ihre Weise den gekreuzigten und auferstandenen Jesus zur Geltung, insofern sie die Lehre explizieren, die Jesus ans Kreuz bringt und gleichzeitig Lehre des Gekreuzigten und Auferstandenen ist" (393). See also Marcus, *The Mystery of the Kingdom of God*, 223-233.

activity of the sower.[107] The opposition from quarters such as the religious authorities is foreseen and inevitable, and the doubt it casts on the success of the sowing is acknowledged as real. Like the parable of the vineyard in the Jerusalem division of the Gospel (12:1-12), the sower parable makes clear both that there are significant obstacles to the fulfillment of the promise, but also that the seed sown will yield a bountiful harvest. What is also clear, though, is that the audience's time is the time of sowing, the time when the obstacles to the word seem to have the upper hand, a point brought home by the subsequent two parables (4:26-32), and developed fully in Chapter 13.

The next direct encounter between the "sower" and the "ones on the path" continues to widen the conflict and build toward its climax in Jerusalem and further develops the juxtaposition between Jesus' boundary-shattering authority and the opposing, boundary-protecting concerns of the scribes (7:1-13). The issue here recalls the controversies from the opening section, reminding the audience of the stark contrast between Jesus' vision of holiness and that of the religious leaders. Several elements link this controversy with those in the first series. It immediately follows reports of Jesus' healing activity and popularity (6:53-56; 1:35-45); it involves the action of Jesus' disciples (cf. 2:18-20; 23-28); it makes reference to the "hearts" of the opponents (7:6; cf. 2:6; 3:5); the opponents' arguments are refuted with authoritative reference to scripture (7:6-8; cf. 2:25-26); and, most important, it continues to delineate the sharp contrast between Jesus' conception of authority and that of the religious leaders.

Here, the issue is explicitly cast in terms of God's way over against the way of human beings (7:8-9; cf. 8:33). The narrator reports that "Pharisees and some of the scribes who had come from Jerusalem *gathered around him*" (7:1), clearly suggesting their hostile intent.[108] The grounds for their attack stem from their concern for the "traditions of the elders," which Jesus' disciples seemed to

---

[107]See Juel, *Mark*, 69-70; *Master of Surprise*, 57.

[108]Possibly in an allusion to Ps 2:2: συνάγειν (Mark 7:1) is used to describe the action of the "rulers of the earth" in "gathering against the Lord and his anointed" (Ps 2:2 LXX).

disregard by eating with "defiled hands." Mark's explanatory note concerning the tradition (7:3-4) is often cited as evidence that the narrative is addressed to a gentile audience unfamiliar with Jewish practices.[109] As noted in the previous chapter, however, the narrative as a whole clearly implies an audience familiar with both Jewish scripture and tradition. I would suggest that this note serves to render explicit the way in which this particular tradition, like those dealt with in the other controversies (association with unclean, Sabbath observance, etc.), functions to maintain the boundaries between clean and unclean which Jesus has been commissioned to tear down. The washing of hands implies that contact with people and things from "across the border"—i.e., the market place, where people from various points on the holiness "map" intermingle—renders one unclean. As we saw in our discussion of 1:16-3:6, and as the narrative continues to develop,[110] Jesus' conception of holiness in Mark involves movement in the opposite direction; the market place would be seen not as source of ritual defilement from which one must separate oneself and ritually wash to be clean again. Rather, it represents a place into which holiness needs to be spread precisely through contact with the human traffic there. This concern of Jesus is underscored in the movements he makes which surround this pericope: to the "other side" of the lake—i.e., gentile territory (5:1-20)—and, immediately following this controversy, to the region of Tyre.

The role of Scripture interpretation is especially important in this controversy (as it is in 10:1-10). It functions here both to underscore Jesus' role as authoritative emissary of God and to expose the lack of authority on the part of his opponents. Jesus counters the arguments of his opponents with appeal to God's word, directing Isaiah's harsh criticisms of Israel at them. Jesus' word and work have positively established Jesus' authority to speak for God; this authority extends to the interpretation of God's word in Scripture. The story exposes the lack of authority to do the same on the part of his opponents, using the same criterion found in the other controver-

---

[109]See, e.g., Marcus, *The Way of the Lord*, 118 n. 24; Guelich, xxix-xxx.

[110]E.g., Chapter 5; cf. Jesus' forays into Gentile territory, which bracket this controversy: 5:1-20; 7:24. See Malbon, *Narrative Space and Mythic Meaning*.

sies: their understanding results in undermining God's intention for creation, bringing harm instead of life to others. God's word, as understood and taught by Israel's leaders, has been rendered void.

The reversal of the leaders' understanding of holiness finds confirmation through Jesus' statement on clean and unclean foods: there is nothing outside which can defile, but what comes out defiles (7:4-15). Humans have the capacity to spread contamination as well as holiness through what comes out of the body.

Having been silenced once again, the Pharisees return to Jesus to ask him for a sign from heaven to substantiate his authority (8:11), an encounter which, as noted above, Mark characterizes as a "testing." Jesus' response helps drive home the way in which the world as a whole, in its present structures, stands in opposition to God's intentions for it. It is this "whole generation" that will be denied a sign (8:12). The irony of the request underscores the point;[111] Jesus' authority over the forces of Satan and his ability to restore human beings to wholeness provides what should be an incontrovertible sign of his authority; his exasperation stems from the hardness of heart which characterizes not only his opponents, but, as the surrounding narrative reveals, his own followers. Indeed, this scene provides a clear glimpse of the rhetorical goals of Mark's portrayal of the conflict between Jesus and the authorities. The very next scene contains a warning to the disciples that they should "beware of the yeast of the Pharisees and the yeast of Herod" (8:15); in other words, blindness to God's work and way can afflict those on the "inside" as well (see Chapter 5).

One final encounter occurs in the Galilean section of the Gospel; some Pharisees emerge to "test" Jesus once again (10:1-10). This controversy develops the themes already established in the narrative: the authorities' testing of Jesus, which manifests their hardness of heart; Jesus' appeal to an authoritative reading of scripture which exposes their lack of authority.

Finally, a word about the passion predictions. They serve within the plot to foreshadow the climax of the controversy; they

---

[111]See Jerry Camery-Hoggatt, *Irony in Mark's Gospel: Text and Subtext* (Cambridge: Cambridge University Press, 1992), 153-54.

reveal the severity of the hardness of heart which the narrative has been developing in the controversy stories, making it clear that it will result in Jesus' death. The necessity of Jesus' death is interpreted by the controversies: Jesus' death is made necessary not to satisfy some abstract divine need for blood, but through the hardness of heart which characterizes this generation (more on this below).

The Promise Affirmed in the Midst of Endangerment: 11:27-12:44

In the first rhetorical division, Mark's narrative has achieved a momentum that will generate a tremendous sense of expectation leading into Jesus' entrance into Jerusalem. When viewed as a whole, the first division can be seen to have developed side by side, with equal rhetorical force, both the identity of Jesus as God's beloved Son, as well as the apparently inescapable destiny of that Son, the cross; both the promise and its apparent endangerment are held in unresolved tension. The promise that Jerusalem will see some sort of resolution to this tension is met with both fear and hope: hope that the resolution will confirm the promise of eschatological redemption in Jesus which the narrative has proclaimed, but fear concerning how that apparently must happen. In fact, I wish to argue in this section that the basic pattern found in the Jerusalem section of the Gospel corresponds to and confirms the tension expressed in the first section, and represents an escalation of the tension between God's ways and human ways. Like the first section, 11:1-15:47 begins with confirmation of Jesus' identity and authority through his word and deed, interlaced with indications of how that issues in human opposition (cf. 1:16-8:26 with 11:1-12:44); it then turns explicitly to the result of this clash of worlds, the cross (cf. 8:27-10:52 with 14:1-15:47). The section brings an important rhetorical goal to climactic expression: the embrace and exercise of divine authority in a world of hardened hearts must result in the death of God's Son and in the suffering of those grasped by God's redemption. In this way, the narrative seeks to address the tension between God's promises and the reality of the world as the audience experiences it. It compels the audience to a radical trust in God's capacity to bring life out of the death-dealing forces that hold creation captive, and so the narrative must both confirm the reality of this power as well as acknowledge the experience of its opposite. Hence, in the Jerusalem controversies which lead finally to Jesus' death, the narrative moves toward grounding Jesus' authority not as much in the past confirmations of it (e.g., his baptism), but in God's vindication of it in Jesus' resurrection.

The Jerusalem controversies evince a rhetorical pattern similar to that of the Galilean cycle and contain other similarities in form and function;[112] but the Jerusalem cycle also represents a marked escalation in the conflict, which emerges from several observations. First, the setting, the temple in Jerusalem—the central religious institution in first-century Judaism, and the symbol and expression of religious power—intensifies the conflict by its very nature:[113] by the way in which the narrative has prepared the audience for the impending climax of the conflict here (especially through the passion predictions); and by the role the temple plays in the final chapters of the Gospel. As noted earlier, the temple authorities—the chief priests, elders, and scribes—wield a power above and beyond that of the local Galilean authorities. Jesus' attack on the temple which opens the section carries with it far greater consequences on the story level than his attack on Pharisaic interpretation of the law. It is also important to note, however, that the difference is one of degree, not kind; Jesus' charge against the temple authorities coheres with his charge against the Pharisees and scribes. In each case, humans have usurped or eclipsed the intention of God by setting up boundaries that work contrary to God's intentions for creation.[114]

Both situations are deeply ironic. The Pharisees' system of holiness and the worship and rites practiced in the temple were designed to safeguard God's presence among Israel. They have,

---

[112]See Dewey, *Markan Public Debate*, 152-167; see also John Donahue, "A Neglected Factor in the Theology of Mark," *JBL* 101 (1982), 563-594, esp. 570-581.

[113]Kingsbury, *Conflict in Mark*, 76; Juel, *Mesiah and Temple*, 137-42; John Donahue, *Are You the Christ?*

[114]Cf. 7:13, where the Pharisees are accused of "making void the word of God through [their] tradition that you have handed on," with 11:17, which accuses the chief priests of making God's temple, set up to be "a house of prayer for all the nations," into a "den of robbers."

however, had the opposite effect: They have erected boundaries to keep God at a safe distance and to restrict access to God. The failure of the leaders to acknowledge God's beloved Son serves to highlight this state of affairs (as the vineyard parable makes clear). The temple therefore stands under God's curse, and, like the fig tree, will "whither away to its roots" (11:21).[115]

The controversies in chapters 11-12 also represent a heightening from the Galilean cycle because they emerge from the authorities' stated intention to kill Jesus in response to his temple action (11:18), rather than culminating with such a threat (cf. 3:6). With this intention and the authority to carry it out hanging over the action, every word and deed of Jesus in the temple carries with it the possibility that the authorities will find the opportunity they seek. So they confront him directly about the authority with which he acts (11:27f.), and seek to "trap him in his word" (12:13).

Further, the cycle begins in 11:27 with a question that has been hanging over the story and the discourse for the entire Gospel: "By what authority are you doing these things? Who gave you this authority to do them?" Though the immediate referent for "these things" would seem to be Jesus' action the temple, the plural allows the whole of Jesus' ministry to be in view, and the mention of authority in the context of the scribes takes the audience back to the very opening scene of Jesus' public ministry (1:22).[116] And Jesus' reply, evasive as always, serves to reiterate the framing of the question as it has been posed throughout the narrative: Jesus' authority is either from God, and thus must be acknowledged, with all that that carries with it, or it is from human beings, and thus stands in the way of God's true intentions.

The burden of the ensuing stories is to confirm what the narrative has been attempting to establish all along, that Jesus' authority is indeed from God, and that the religious leaders operate on the basis of mere human authority. Yet it must do so in a way that

---

[115]The fig tree episode provides an interpretive frame around the temple action, compelling an association between the barrenness of the fig tree and that of the temple; see, e.g., Juel, *Mark*, 154-161.

[116]The presence of the scribes provides continuity with the first part of the Gospel.

relates to the ensuing narrative, which displays Jesus' betrayal into the same "human hands" that bring about his death. On this point, the Jerusalem cycle proves to be the complement of the Galilean cycle. There, as we saw, the rhetorical structure served to emphasize the way in which Jesus' activity "führt in den Tod,"[117] i.e., that Jesus' liberating ministry issues in opposition from hearts hardened and eyes blinded to God's redemptive activity. Confirmation of Jesus' status as God's Son was everywhere to be found in the surrounding narrative, but the centerpiece of the controversy cycle (2:18-22) revealed that the bridegroom would be taken away. So whereas the first controversy cycle emphasized the way in which Jesus' death must follow as a consequence of his life, the Jerusalem controversies point toward the life that God will bring out of his death. That is, Jesus' authority is finally grounded in God's vindication of him in the resurrection.

It is crucial to Mark's rhetorical "balancing act" that this be so; apart from God's vindication, Jesus' death spells victory for the opposition to Jesus. Yet without the cross, God's promise of redemption rings hollow in a world still under Satan's grasp. The Jerusalem controversies ground the message of the cross as God's way in the world firmly in God's vindication of Jesus.

11:27-12:44 as a Rhetorical Unit. That 11:27-12:44 form a rhetorical unit is perhaps not obvious; the section contains a wide variety of material, formally and substantively, and interpreters have divided it in different ways.[118] It comes on the heels of Jesus' triumphal entry into Jerusalem and the temple action, which is framed by the fig tree incident (11:1-19). It opens with the chief priests and scribes challenging Jesus' authority to do "these things," which Jesus refuses to answer overtly (11:27-33). There follows what Mark designates a parable—the vineyard—which concludes with a citation from Psalm 118 (12:12). The chief priests and scribes then leave Jesus and send the Pharisees and Herodians to "entrap Jesus in his talk" (11:13). This begins a series of three open debates or exchanges between Jesus and various representatives of Judaism, the

---

[117]As von der Osten-Sacken put it; see above.

[118]See Dewey, *Markan Public Debate*, 56-60; also Tolbert, *Sowing the Gospel*, 231-232.

Pharisees, the Sadducees and a scribe. The first two of these debates, which deal with the question of paying tribute to Caesar (12:13-17) and the resurrection (12:18-23), are openly hostile challenges to Jesus. The last involves a "friendly" exchange between Jesus and a scribe concerning the greatest commandment (12:28-34). The result is a mutual display of affection, and the narrator reports that "after that no one dared ask him any question" (12:34). Jesus then takes the initiative; he addresses the question of the Davidic sonship of the Messiah by means of a citation from Psalm 110 (12:35-37), and concludes his public teaching in the temple with a denouncement of the scribes (12:38-40). Finally, as his last action in the temple, he points out to his disciples the widow who, by contributing to the temple treasury out of her poverty, her whole life, she contributed more than all those who contributed (12:41-44). The next chapter has Jesus exit the temple, and the apocalyptic discourse ensues.

Though it lacks the tightness in form of the Galilean cycle, the audience is invited to view this seemingly disparate material together through several rhetorical cues. First, beginning with 11:1, the pace of the narrative retards considerably, in contrast to chapters 1-10, in which precise time and even place settings are difficult to discern. Here narrative time is marked very carefully: first in days (11:12, 20; 14:1, 12), then morning and evening (14:17, 15:1), and finally slowing down to mark the hours (15:25, 33, 34). The action of 11:27-12:44 all takes place on the third day of Jesus' Jerusalem visit.[119] Moreover, all the action in this section shares the temple setting; it is framed by Jesus' entrance into and exit from the temple (11:27; 13:1). Further, as noted above, 11:27-33 raises the issue of Jesus' authority in a climactic way, and, as I will suggest below, the ensuing material can all be viewed as addressing that question.

---

[119]For a break-down of the days of the week as suggested by this section, see Dewey, *Markan Public Debate*, 56-59. She takes 11:27-12:1-12 as the rhetorical subsection here, however, suggesting that it represents an extended controversy narrative (action-objection-vindication), thus combining days 2 and 3 (155-56). In her reading, then, the question of the authorities in 11:27 refers solely to the temple action; while this may be the case on the story level, as I suggest, on the discourse level it functions to bring the question of Jesus' authority as exercised in the entire Gospel to a head.

The internal coherence of this section does emerge with some clarity, however. Dewey has suggested that 12:1-40 evinces a loosely symmetrical, chiastic pattern.[120] Two instances of public teaching form the outer boundaries: on the one end, the vineyard parable with its threat of God's judgment (vv. 1-9), and the citation from Psalm 118 with reaction from the audience (vv. 10-12); on the other end, Jesus' citation of Psalm 110 with its audience reaction (vv. 35-37), and the warning of judgment against the scribes (vv. 38-40). The middle is set off by its inclusion of three public debates, and displays the tightest rhetorical structure: the things of God are to be given to God, Jesus says, and the audience reacts (vv. 13-17). This parallels the commands to love God and neighbor as the greatest commandments, with its audience reaction (vv. 28-34). The centerpiece is formed by the affirmation of the reality of the resurrection (vv. 18-23).

I would modify Dewey's suggestion both in terms of scope and the corresponding points in the symmetry. The structure I propose is as follows:

A   11:27-33   *The source and nature of Jesus' authority questioned*
　B   12:1-9   *Parable of the wicked tenants; God's judgment*
　　C   12:10-12   *Psalm citation: Jesus' ultimate vindication proclaimed*
　　　D   12:13-17   *Debate/teaching: The things of God to be given to God*
　　　　E   12:18-27   THE REALITY OF THE RESURRECTION
　　　D'   12:28-34   *Debate/Teaching: Commands to love God and neighbor*
　　C'   12:35-37   *Psalm citation: Jesus' ultimate vindication proclaimed*
　B'   12:38-40   *Warning against scribes; God's judgment*
A'   12:41-44   *True nature of authority exemplified by poor widow*

First of all, for reasons already cited, 11:27 marks the beginning of the rhetorical unit. Further, the scope of the pattern easily expands to encompass 11:27-33 and 12:41-44 when one recognizes the correspondence between them. Jesus' initial refusal to answer the question regarding his authority is more than just an artful dodge. In responding with the counter-question about the origin of John's baptism, Jesus exposes the Jewish leaders' lack of divine authority by suggesting that their actions are motivated by popular opinion

---

[120]*Markan Public Debate*, 156-163.

(something Pilate recognizes later, cf. 15:10). 12:41-44, the widow's offering, contrasts with this scene sharply; as one who has given her whole βίος she exemplifies the understanding of authority which Jesus has represented in his entire ministry (cf. 10:45), and which will come to fullest expression in the cross. Thus Jesus' final appearance in the temple, which deals overall with his authority, is framed by the two opposing conceptions of power and authority offered in Mark's Gospel.

As for 12:1-40 itself, I concur with Dewey's structuring, but would add some further points of correspondence and contrast. The vineyard parable and the condemnation of the scribes do indeed correspond in that each contains the threat of God's judgment; but it is important to note how the parable accomplishes this. That Mark designates it formally as a parable is significant for, as the consummate "outsiders," the authorities will receive only parables (cf. 4:11-12). Their reaction ("they realized that he had told this parable against them," 12:12) reveals that they do "see"—i.e., they understand fully who Jesus is claiming to be—but do not see—i.e., they do not understand that in seeking to kill Jesus, they have taken the side of Satan against God's plan. Nor do they see the irony which the audience must begin by now to see: that precisely by killing the heir, they accomplish God's redemptive plan, and seal their own fate as well. Thus the parable sets up the fundamental irony which pervades the passion narrative: The authorities' conception of power and authority, expressed in the parable in the words, "Come, let us kill the heir, and the inheritance will be ours" (12:7), clashes head-on with Jesus' understanding, which involves doing the will of God. The parable, relating as it does God's entire eschatological plan, sets the conflict between Jesus and the authorities within that cosmic struggle. Thus, when the scribes are condemned in 12:38-40, it is because their understanding of God's authority reveals on which side of the cosmic struggle they stand.

The death of the heir is not the end of the story, however. Appended to the parable is the citation from Psalm 118: "Have you not read this scripture: 'The very stone which the builders rejected has become the head of the corner; this was the Lord's doing, and it is marvelous in our eyes'?" (12:11). Through Jesus' vindication, God vindicates as well the nature and shape of Jesus' authority over against that of the Jewish leaders. To drive this point home for his audience, I would argue, is one of the key motivations behind the rhetorical structuring of this section. Dewey recognizes that this citation from the Psalms corresponds structurally with the citation of Psalm 110 in 12:35-37, the question about David's son. But she does not entertain the likelihood, as I think one must, that that passage as well alludes to Jesus' ultimate vindication. The function of this passage in Mark's Gospel has been much debated, with many regarding it as a refutation of the importance of the Davidic aspect of Jesus' messiahship.[121] In fact, the principal concern of 12:35-37 is not with proper titles for Jesus at all. The key to understanding its function in the Gospel is the recognition, first suggested by E. Loevestam,[122] that the nature of the problem posed by Jesus involves an alleged contradiction in scripture within the Psalm between the two occurrences of "Lord" in the first verse. The first is taken to refer to God, the second to the Messiah. Since the speaker is David himself, how can the Messiah be both David's son and David's Lord? As Juel puts it, "Only if Jesus, the son of David, has been elevated to that position at God's side [cf. 14:62] does the alleged contradiction in the Scriptures disappear."[123] Thus both Psalm 118 in 12:10-11 and Psalm 110 here allude to Jesus' ultimate victory over his opponents, and again, vindicate his identity as the one who speaks and acts for God.

---

[121]See, e.g., David M. Hay, *Glory at the Right Hand: Psalm 110 in Early Christianity* (SBLMS 18; Nashville: Abingdon Press, 1973), 110-114; Marcus, *The Way of the Lord*, 139-145. Evidence to the contrary abounds in the narrative. E.g., the story of blind Bartimaeus which immediately precedes Jesus' entrance into Jerusalem, and that entrance itself, both involve explicit use of Davidic language without any suggestion that it is inappropriate. And indeed, the whole passion narrative turns on the irony of the soldiers' and authorities' mocking Jesus as the royal Messiah which, as the audience knows, he actually is.

[122]"Die Davidssohnsfrage," *Svensk Exegetisk Årsbok* 27 (1962), 72-82; cf. Juel, *Messianic Exegesis*, 143-44; Nils Dahl, "Contradictions in Scripture," in *Studies in Paul* (Minneapolis: Augsburg, 1977), 159-177; Marcus gives a helpful introduction to the genre with reference to 9:11-13 (*The Way of the Lord*, 101-105), but disagrees that it applies in the case of 12:35-37 (151-52).

[123]*Messianic Exegesis*, 144.

The point is further driven home in the pericope which emerges as the centerpiece of the unit. In it, Sadducees, "who say there is no resurrection," (12:18) come to Jesus to challenge him on just this issue, posing a hypothetical situation in which a woman, in accordance with Levitical law, marries seven different brothers (12:18-23). "In the resurrection," they ask, "whose wife will she be?" (v. 23). Jesus' response is direct and uncompromising, and again underscores the issue of authority; the authorities deceive themselves, and "know neither the scriptures nor the power of God" (v. 24). This strong condemnation in the center of Jesus' climactic confrontation with the authorities in the temple serves well as a broad condemnation of the religious authorities as a whole. Throughout the narrative, Jesus has exposed their lack of knowledge of scripture. In fact, nowhere does an opponent even explicitly cite scripture, but their appeals are rather to the human tradition and authority.

The condemnation is also so strongly stated because of the issue at stake: the reality of the resurrection. Here is the direct complement to the Galilean cycle of controversies, in which the reality of Jesus' death formed the centerpiece (2:20). The fate of the promise rests on God's identity as the "God of the living," on God's capacity ultimately to vindicate Jesus and, as Jesus promises elsewhere, to vindicate and redeem creation as a whole (9:1; 13:26-27; 14:25, 62).

The two pericopae which immediately surround this centerpiece complete the unit. As Dewey points out,[124] they exhibit both formal and material similarities. Both have a double interchange of dialogue; both contain praise of Jesus, and are linked by the phrase ἐπ' ἀληθείας (vv. 14, 32). In content, the second story completes the thought of the first, explicating just what the "things of God" are: love of God and of neighbor. As Donahue suggests, Mark presents here a kind of "catechesis" for his audience, underscoring the pervasive theme of doing God's will as expressed by Jesus (e.g., 3:31-35, etc.).

The Rhetorical Effects. If these observations about the structure of 11:27-12:44 are convincing, it would seem that Mark has

---

[124]Dewey, 159; she is followed by Donahue, "A Neglected Factor," 588-92.

punctuated the narration of the climactic dispute over Jesus' authority with prediction of and allusions to Jesus' ultimate vindication and victory over his enemies in a rhetorical symmetry; interwoven are clear hints as to the shape with which this authority must manifest itself in this age. The symmetry works to confirm the promise which is endangered by Jesus' opponents, while at the same time acknowledging the reality of the endangerment. The reality of the resurrection in general is confirmed in the center, and the reality of Jesus' vindication through his resurrection is confirmed in parallel fashion in C and C', as is the ultimate defeat of Jesus' opponents. B and B', however, confirm the actions of the religious leaders in bringing about the death of the heir, as well as their continued capacity to wreak havoc on human beings.

The emphasis on eschatological themes—resurrection and judgment—also serves to remind the audience of the cosmic consequences of these earthly debates. The antithesis between Jesus' authority and the authority of the religious leaders is no less than that between God and Satan. As noted previously, Jesus characterizes the initial challenge in words that recall Satan's testing of Jesus (12:15). Moreover, we saw that the debates have similarities in form with the exorcisms; though there are no exorcisms in the Jerusalem section the narrator uses the verb ἐκβάλλειν to describe Jesus' action in the temple (11:15), a verb used elsewhere overwhelmingly in relation to Jesus exorcizing activity.[125]

Further, as I have also been suggesting, the question of the shape divine authority must take in a world opposed to God has been at the heart of the conflict throughout the story.[126] Being embraced by God's reign puts one in opposition to the present structures of the age, and will result in conflict, as Chapter 13 clearly suggests (especially 13:3-23). The Jerusalem conflicts, seen as a prelude to the passion narrative (14:1-15:47), cloak this message of Jesus with the authority of the one who sits at the right hand of God.

This is Mark's rhetorical balancing act; though he clearly wishes to de-emphasize the resurrection as a present reality for

---

[125]Cf., e.g., 1:34, 39, 43; 3:15, 22, 23; 6:13; 7:26; 9:18, 28, 38.

[126]It is a major theme in Jesus' conflict with the disciples, as the next chapter will show.

anyone but Jesus, thereby acknowledging the present experience of conflict between God's promises and the present age, it is equally important for him to avoid presenting suffering and death as ends in and of themselves, to grant them the final word. As Jesus' ministry shows, God sent Jesus to overcome the suffering of God's creation; there is nothing good about the suffering. The placing of the Jerusalem debates as a prelude to the passion narrative, and the rhetorical shape which allows the resurrection theme to emerge with clarity, suggest that for Mark Jesus' suffering and death, and that of those in his circle, are the inevitable result of the clash between diametrically opposed systems of power, one which works for death, one for life. He thus gives the theology of the cross a grounding in God's ultimate victory over the forces of sin, death, and Satan; but precisely because he turns an unblinking eye toward the reality of this age, in which those forces still hold sway, the way of the cross paradoxically becomes the way of life.

CONCLUSIONS

Thus the conflicts between Jesus and the religious authorities have served not to resolve the tension between Jesus' messianic identity and his fate on the cross, but to highlight it for the audience. God's intention to redeem creation takes place over against tremendous forces of opposition. These forces endanger God's promise of eschatological salvation in the story, and the narrative's acknowledgment of these forces reflects the reality of the world in which Mark's audience lives. To an audience shaped by Mark's rhetoric, and by their own experience of the power of God through Jesus, the reality of conflict is as inescapable as the reality of God's redemption in Jesus. Through the narrative, a kind of crisis is instilled in the audience, resulting from the realization that allowing oneself to be embraced and shaped by the boundary-shattering reign of God is necessary for life, but that human captivity to the forces of this age render such a response all but impossible.

Nowhere is this more graphically displayed than in the preliminary resolution to the conflict in Jesus' death. The passion narrative sets forth the intense hostility of the world toward a conception of God's reign that involves the shattering of boundaries and an understanding of authority grounded in life-giving service. The only possible response on the part of a world in Satan's grasp is to put to death the bearer of this reign.[127] In the end, even Jesus himself seems to recognize the ability of these forces to block God's purposes, the effectiveness of the boundaries erected to keep God at bay. His expression of God-forsakenness on the cross (15:34) gives pathos-filled voice to the conflict between what God has promised and what the present reality delivers. Jesus himself comes to embody the human need for divine intervention so forcefully presented by those who had come to him in his ministry, hoping that God could provide what all human powers could not—the power to bring life out of death. The course of the resolution of the conflict between Jesus and the authorities, in other words, serves rhetorically to drive the audience to God in just this way. The interpretive gap created by the narrative between Jesus' identity as Son of God and his earthly fate can only be filled by divine power. Only with God's intervention, only with God's power to bring death out of life, can the promise be reaffirmed and be rendered truly "good news." The question is thus: Does God have the power to thwart human intention? Do "the things of human beings" have finality? Can God be trusted to reaffirm God's promises?

Clearly, Mark's affirmation of Jesus' resurrection by God serves to address these questions in the affirmative with respect to this story line in the Gospel. As God had done throughout Israel's history, God reaffirms the promises in the face of seemingly overwhelming opposition, ironically turning both human and cosmic opposition to God's own purposes (cf. Gen 50:20). Yet the relative reserve that characterizes the narrative's treatment of the resurrection serves to keep the audience firmly grounded in the real world, whose opposition to God's goals persists in spite of Jesus' victory and continues to cast doubt on the reliability of God's promises. Indeed, the intensity of the conflict between Jesus and his disciples in Mark, which, as we will see, parallels the conflict between Jesus and the authorities, raises the question of whether the tension between God's

---

[127]Cf. Juel, *Master of Surprise*, 41.

promises and reality is simply too great even for Jesus' would-be followers, both within the story and in the audience, to bear. And so the question becomes, can God overcome human unfaithfulness and obduracy? It is to this question we turn in the final chapter.

CHAPTER 5

THE PROMISE ENDANGERED FROM WITHIN: THE CONFLICT WITH THE DISCIPLES

> If Mark is right that the very reading or hearing of the story can catch
> the reader or hearer up in the story itself, then it will point her or him
> to the kind of open, redemptive future needed. . . .[But] it is frightening
> to be compelled out of the miserable security of life-in-death and into
> the risk of an open future in the world. The delivered one lives with a
> sense of the indeterminate future for which there is the promise of the
> victory of life over death. (Dan Via, *The Ethics of Mark's Gospel*[1])

In this study I am seeking to show that the principal lines of conflict
in Mark—between Jesus and the authorities and between Jesus and
his disciples—interrelate, interpret and illumine one another in the
narrative, and, most important, that they have a common rhetorical
goal, to address the experience of conflict in Mark's audience
between the promises of God and the reality of the seemingly
unredeemed world inhabited by the audience. Each line of conflict
threatens, in very real ways, to undermine the very promises of God
Jesus was sent to confirm. For the audience, the essential conflict lies
in embracing Mark's narrative argument that God's promises are
confirmed in Jesus in the face of forceful opposition to God's plan
from both expected and surprising quarters.

In this chapter I will show how the shape and nature of the
conflict between Jesus and the authorities might lead Mark's
audience to experience the conflict between Jesus and the disciples

---

[1]Dan O. Via, Jr., *The Ethics of Mark: In the Middle of Time* (Philadelphia:
Fortress Press, 1985), 65.

in a particular manner. As we saw in Chapter 4, the conflict between Jesus and the religious authorities does not serve simply to move the plot forward, or to lead the audience to reject the authorities' point of view on Jesus, but highlights the very real tension which exists between Jesus' proclamation of the reign of God and the values of the present aeon, a tension which the audience will experience. That is, this conflict involves the audience in the clash between God's promises and the reality of a world whose power structures run counter to, and which endanger the reliability of those promises. I suggest that the way in which the conflict between Jesus and the disciples intersects and overlaps with the conflict between Jesus and the authorities moves the audience to view the former conflict in terms of the latter; that is, the involvement in this plot-line which the narrative hopes for moves the audience to the same point of tension between God's promises and reality. Just as the resolution to the plot involving Jesus and the authorities can only be resolved in the audience through reliance on God's capacity to overcome human opposition, so, too, the resolution of the conflict between Jesus and the disciples drives the audience to same point: Either Jesus and the disciples never reconcile, and hence God's promises cannot ultimately be trusted, or God does have the final word even over human fallibility and obduracy.

Clearly, as many have recognized, Mark wishes his audience to experience essential truths about Christian existence in their narrative encounter with the first followers of Jesus, and in this sense the conflict has its own distinct shape, as I will discuss below. Nevertheless, these two conflicts bear many striking common features, as I will try to reveal in this chapter. Most important is the way in which Mark presents the conflict with the disciples in the same eschatological/cosmic perspective as the conflict with those "outside." To the degree that it can be shown that Mark leads his audience to experience the obduracy of the disciples as a manifestation of Satan's hold on them, the conflict emerges in its cosmic perspective, and the question of whether the disciples will ever "get it" becomes less a question of their own will or personal shortcomings, and more a question of which power operative in their lives will prevail: God's or Satan's. That is, I will argue in this chapter that

Jesus' conflicts with the disciples issue in essentially the same question as those with the authorities: Can God's promises be trusted? And if so, on what grounds? Once again, I will argue that Mark seeks to strike a balance between the reality of failure and the reality of God's power that will resonate with his audience's experience of the world. Through the disciples, the narrative sets before the audience in the starkest terms the question of whether God's redemptive goals can overcome human unfaithfulness, and it drives the audience to the conclusion that if there is a future for the disciples—and thus a future for themselves—it rests on trusting the character and power of God, which the narrative seeks to confirm.[2]

The chapter will unfold as follows. First, I will briefly review the context in which any discussion of the disciples in Mark must begin—the debate in current scholarship over their function in Mark's narrative—and set my own work within that context. Then I will show how the conflict with the disciples intertwines with the conflict with the authorities, with an eye toward the rhetorical effect of this intertwining. Next, I will place central scenes of the conflict in the context of the narrative's "logic" of promise and failure; this is where I will suggest Mark leads the audience to embrace both the failure and God's restoration of the disciples, and discuss the rhetorical and theological implications of this suggestion. Finally, I will conclude the chapter and this study by suggesting some ways in which the rhetorical shape of conflict in Mark links Mark's story (and the audience's) with the larger story of God's endangered and reaffirmed promises.

THE DISCIPLES IN MARK: THE PASTORAL/POLEMICAL DEBATE

Interest in the question of Mark's portrayal of the disciples has generated a voluminous bibliography in recent decades,[3] due, no

---

[2]I will argue that the obverse of this statement is true as well: If there is no future for the disciples, there is no future for the audience, either.

[3]For a concise and very helpful review of the question, see Frank Matera, *What are they saying about Mark?* (New York: Paulist Press, 1987), 38-55; also William Telford, "Introduction: The Gospel of Mark," in *The Interpretation of Mark* (ed.

doubt, to the prominence of the theme of disciples and discipleship in the Gospel, as well as to the strikingly harsh treatment the disciples receive at Mark's hand.[4] While all of the Gospels record the

---

William Telford; Issues in Religion and Theology 7; Philadelphia: Fortress Press, 1985), 23-28. Studies of the disciples include Ernest Best, "Discipleship in Mark: 8:22-10:52," *Scottish Journal of Theology* 23 (1970), 323-37; *idem*, "The Role of the Disciples in Mark," *NTS* 23 (1976-7), 377-401; *idem*, *Following Jesus. Discipleship in the Gospel of Mark* (Sheffield: JSOT Press, 1981); Eduard Schweizer, "The Portrayal of the Life of Faith in the Gospel of Mark," in *Interpreting the Gospels* (ed. James Luther Mays; Philadelphia: Fortress Press, 1981) ; J. B. Tyson, "The Blindness of the Disciples in Mark," *JBL* 80 (1961), 261-268; Theodore J. Weeden, "The Heresy that necessitated Mark's Gospel," *ZNW* 59 (1968), 145-158 (reprinted in *The Interpretation of Mark*, 64-77); *idem*, *Mark—Traditions in Conflict* (Philadelphia: Fortress Press, 1971); Karl-Georg Reploh, *Markus-Lehrer der Gemeinde: eine redaktionsgeschichtliche Studie zu den Jüngerperikopen des Markus-Evangeliums* (Stuttgarter Biblische Monographien 9; Stuttgart: Katholisches Bibelwerk, 1969); David J. Hawkin, "The Incomprehension of the disciples in the Marcan Redaction," *JBL* 91 (1972), 491-500; John R. Donahue, *The Theology and Setting of Discipleship in the Gospel of Mark* (Milwaukee: Marquette University, 1983); Werner Kelber, *Mark's Story of Jesus* (Philadelphia: Fortress Press, 1979); *idem*, "Apostolic Tradition and the Form of the Gospel," in *Discipleship in the New Testament* (ed. Fernando F. Segovia; Philadelphia: Fortress Press, 1985), 24-46; Robert Tannehill, "The Disciples in Mark: The Function of a Narrative Role," *JR* 57 (1977), 386-405, reprinted in *The Interpretation of Mark*, 134-57; Vernon Robbins, *Jesus the Teacher: A Socio-Rhetorical Interpretation of Mark* (Philadelphia: Fortress Press, 1984); Joanna Dewey, "Point of View and the Disciples in Mark," *Society of Biblical Literature 1982 Seminar Papers* (ed. K. H. Richards; Chico, CA: Scholars Press, 1982), 97-106; Elizabeth Struthers Malbon, "Fallible Followers: Women and Men in the Gospel of Mark," *Semeia* 28 (1983), 29-48; *idem*, "Disciples/Crowds/Whoever: Markan Characters and Readers," *NovT* 28 (1986), 104-30; C. Clifton Black, *The Disciples According to Mark: Markan Redaction in Current Debate* (JSNTSS 27; Sheffield: JSOT, 1989); Jack Kingsbury, *Conflict in Mark: Jesus, Authorities, Disciples* (Minneapolis: Fortress Press, 1989); Andrew T. Lincoln, "The Promise and the Failure—Mark 16:7, 8," *JBL* 108 (1989), 283-300; Donald Juel, *A Master of Surprise: Mark Interpreted* (Minneapolis: Fortress Press, 1994), 65-76.

[4]I limit my examination to the disciples in Mark's Gospel, that is, the group whom he calls to himself and teaches in private; the centerpiece of this group is the twelve, but it is not limited to it. I recognize that the question of "discipleship" in Mark goes beyond the role of the disciples; the women, the exceptional characters who respond to Jesus and then disappear, as well as some of the exceptional Jewish leaders, give the question of discipleship in Mark a much wider context (see Malbon, "Fallible Followers," 29-32; Donahue, "A Neglected Factor," 583; Schweizer, "The Portrayal of the Life of Faith," 172-73). But I am not concerned with the question of "discipleship" in general, but with the implications of particular readings of the fate

disciples' difficulties in comprehending their master's mission and their ultimate flight from Jesus' side in the face of his crucifixion, Mark stands out among the four both with respect to the severity of the disciples' lack of insight, and due to the lack of a narrated post-resurrection reconciliation with Jesus.[5] On the other hand, Mark does portray the disciples' faithful and obedient response to Jesus' initial call (e.g., 1:16-20), shows them successfully carrying out a "missionary journey" at Jesus' command (6:6-13, 30), and makes reference to an ostensible future role of the disciples in the post-resurrection church (13:9-23). We will treat each of these aspects of Mark's portrayal in more detail below; here my interest is in how recent interpretation of Mark has responded to this puzzling portrait, and what may be at stake in the debate.

---

of the disciples for understanding conflict in Mark's Gospel. Though Mark certainly views followers of Jesus to be comprised by a circle much larger than his immediate disciples, it is this smaller circle upon which the narrative line of conflict focuses. To this group Jesus grants special privileges (4:10-12), and with this group Jesus has a sustained, conflict-laden relationship. And it is the fate of this group which impinges directly on the question of the confirmation of God's promises as Mark understands them.

[5] A comparison with Matthew is especially revealing; for example, Mark 6:52 records the disciples' unbelieving response to the appearance of Jesus walking on the sea, making reference to their "hardness of heart," a trait previously ascribed to the religious authorities (3:5; cf. 10:5); Matthew, on the other hand, has Jesus chide them for being "of little faith" (14:31), but then relates that "those in the boat worshiped him, saying, 'Truly you are the Son of God'" (14:33). The obduracy of the disciples in Mark in the first half of the Gospel comes to a climax in the third scene in the boat (8:14-21), in which Jesus describes them in the same (seemingly hopeless!) terms as he had described those "outside" in 4:10-12; Matthew resolves the tension here by concluding the scene on a positive note: "Then the disciples understood that he had not told them to beware of the yeast of bread, but of the teaching of the Pharisees and Sadducees" (16:12). The inspiration for Peter's confession of Jesus at Caesarea Philippi (Matt. 16:13-20; Mark 8:27-33) is explicitly said to be divine in Matthew's account (16:17-19), and Peter is blessed as the rock of the church; in Mark, as we will see below, Peter's inspiration is highly suspect, and he is "rebuked" immediately by Jesus. A final example (my favorite): In Mark, James and John, the sons of Zebedee, request to sit at Jesus' right and left hand in his glory (10:35-40), revealing how utterly clueless they are about the nature of following Jesus; but in Matthew, it is the *mother* of James and John who requests this of Jesus for her sons (20:2-23)!

On the surface, it would appear that interpreters are divided into two opposing camps.[6] On the one hand are those who view Mark's treatment of the disciples as essentially pastoral, and who see Mark's portrayal of the failure and unfaithfulness of the first followers as a means of encouraging his audience in the face of their own failures.[7] On the other side are the interpreters who see Mark's purpose as essentially polemical, that his goal is to discredit the disciples—and especially their christological ideas—utterly, thus compelling the audience to take the way of the Markan Jesus.[8] In a sense, of course, this is a false dichotomy; both "sides" of the debate acknowledge that Mark has a rhetorical goal involving the instruction of his audience.[9] But the most interesting and important feature of this divide is the way in which the rhetorical purpose envisioned by the interpreter—the narrative's discourse—generally corresponds with a particular reading (or experience) of the *story* of the disciples.

The Polemical Reading

Those who see Mark's rhetorical purpose as polemical read the story of the disciples as one of abject and irredeemable failure. Weeden's observations are dramatically illustrative of this reading:

> I conclude that Mark is assiduously involved in a vendetta against the disciples. He is intent on totally discrediting them. He paints them as obtuse, obdurate, recalcitrant men who at first are unperceptive of Jesus' messiahship, then oppose its style and character, and finally

---

[6]Matera, *What are they saying about Mark?*, 41.

[7]E.g., Best, *Following Jesus*, "The Role of the Disciples;" Malbon, "Fallible Followers;" Tannehill, "The Disciples in Mark;" Reploh, *Markus—Lehrer der Gemeinde*; Norman Petersen, "When is the End not an End? Literary Reflections on the Ending of Mark's Gospel," *Interpretation* 34 (1980), 151-66; Lincoln, "The Promise and the Failure;" Kingsbury, *Conflict in Mark*.

[8]The classic statements of Mark's polemical thrust are Tyson, "The Blindness of the Disciples" and Weeden, *Mark: Traditions in Conflict*; they have been followed, but with some different nuances, by Kelber, *Mark's Story of Jesus*, Tolbert, *Sowing the Gospel*, and, to some extent, Fowler, *Let the Reader Understand*.

[9]See Fowler, *Let the Reader Understand*, 257.

totally reject it. As the coup de grace, Mark closes his Gospel without rehabilitating the disciples.[10]

Weeden's remarks express the two key story-level facets of this reading. First, the negative portrayal of the disciples, which is generally thought to begin with the boat scenes in Chapters 4-8,[11] and accelerates through the rest of the Gospel, overwhelms completely any positive evaluations of the disciples, either within the plotted story or beyond it. Second, and closely related, is the matter of the ending of the Gospel, which in this view is seen to preclude any possibility of reconciliation, since the women apparently did not report the young man's message to the disciples (16:7-8). The understanding of Mark's supposed purpose in so thoroughly discrediting the disciples differs in detail among those who read the disciples' story in this way.[12] They have in common, however, the

---

[10]Weeden, *Traditions in Conflict*, 50-51. Others are equally dramatic; Tolbert, in her discussion of the Gethsemane scene, in which the disciples fail to watch and pray with Jesus, and finally abandon him (14:32-50), interprets the enigmatic ἀπέχει (v. 41) to mean that the disciples' "last chance has passed. . . . Jesus, the sower, has taught, cajoled, threatened, exhorted, warned, admonished, and repeatedly explained to them what is necessary for entering the kingdom of god. Now in this climactic hour he has given them three final opportunities to watch and pray that they 'may not enter into temptation.' All has failed; their bill is paid in full; the account book on them is now closed; their fate is sealed. 'The hour has come'" (*Sowing the Gospel*, 217). Kelber concludes his analysis of Mark's story in a similar way: "By retracing the journey of Jesus and his disciples, the readers are thus gradually and methodically prepared for a final parting of the ways. In reading the gospel one hopes that eventually the disciples will repent and believe in the gospel of the Kingdom. Yet the further we read the story, the more Mark discourages our hopes. After the dismal failure of the disciples at Jesus' passion, all remaining hopes focus on the final outcome of the story. But Mark, instead of reversing the disciples' course, brings it to its logical conclusion. He has reserved the ending of the gospel to deliver the mortal blow to the fate of the disciples. At that moment, having read Mark's story from beginning to end, it must dawn on the reader that the disciples missed the way into the Kingdom" (*Mark's Story of Jesus*, 93).

[11]In 4:35-41, the disciples respond to Jesus' power over the storm with confusion over Jesus' identity (4:41); in 6:47-52, the narrator reports that their stupefied reaction to Jesus' stroll on the water was due to their hardened hearts (6:52); and in 8:14-21, the theme culminates with Jesus' harsh condemnation of their blindness, deafness, and hardened hearts (8:17-18); see Weeden, 26-32.

[12]Weeden's interest is christological and historical: the disciples must be discredited because they represent a group in Mark's community which espouses a

basic idea that Mark wishes to communicate to his audience the necessity of completely rejecting the disciples—both their "theology" and their behavior—and of embracing the Markan Jesus' way as the correct one.[13] The story of Jesus' disciples in Mark serves this goal by compelling the audience to distance itself completely from the disciples' theology and behavior. Thus the readers are to understand that the ending of Mark's narrative is the end of the story of the disciples in Mark; they never receive the message of the angel which confirms Jesus promise to them that he would meet them in Galilee (14:27; 16:6). They remain outsiders—forever.

The Pastoral Reading

The same correspondence between rhetorical purpose and interpretation of story is displayed on the pastoral side of the debate as well. Interpreters such as Best, Petersen and Tannehill acknowledge the harsh terms in which the narrative portrays the disciples, but insist that Mark, though he leaves the relationship between Jesus and the disciples unresolved at the end of his story, means his audience to project that a reconciliation between them beyond the end of the narration is at least possible.[14] These interpreters generally point to

---

"divine man" christology which Mark considers a "heresy" (cf. 51); Kelber agrees, but is more focused on the question of eschatology: Mark's portrayal results from his desire to explain the demise of the Jerusalem church in the war with Rome; the disciples represent the Jerusalem, apostolic church, who thought that the kingdom would come in Jerusalem, and that the war was a sign of its coming. Through his story, Mark discredits this idea, setting up a new time (after the war) and a new place (Galilee) for the Kingdom's arrival (*Mark's Story of Jesus*, 88-96). Tolbert's interest is narrative-rhetorical; she views the purpose of Mark's story of the disciples' ultimate failure to be to create in the reader the perfect disciple (*Sowing the Gospel*, 295-299).

[13]Tolbert's comments illustrate this view well: "Portraying the *disciples* as failing foils to Jesus manipulates the reader to respond by becoming a *better disciple*. In rejecting the views and actions of the Twelve and affirming the words and work of Jesus, the reader herself or himself becomes a faithful disciple" (*Sowing the Gospel*, 224; cf. 295-299).

[14]Tannehill, it should be noted, is the most equivocal; in his view, Mark holds out the possibility of reconciliation, but notes that "there are indications that this renewal is not a simple and automatic affair. A positive development is indicated but negative possibilities are also suggested" ("The Disciples in Mark," 152). This places Tannehill somewhat in the middle of the debate, for this ambiguity strikes the audience

two aspects of the narrative which compel such a reading. First, Jesus makes predictions concerning a post-resurrection meeting with the disciples (9:9; 14:25, 27). Mark's narrative serves in every other way to highlight the trustworthiness of Jesus' predictions[15] (indeed, as I will argue below, this is a principal rhetorical goal of the narrative). As the momentum of the promise-fulfillment scheme builds through the narrative, it propels the audience over the final verse of the Gospel, in which the women flee from the tomb and "say nothing to anyone" (16:8). As Lincoln puts it, "[T]he silence of the women was overcome by Jesus' word of promise."[16] Likewise, these interpreters point out that Jesus' Olivet discourse (Chapter 13) assumes a significant role for the disciples in the post-resurrection period (cf. 13:9-23).[17] Again, the audience is directed to fill in the gap created by the Gospel's ending in a way that projects the resolution of the conflict between Jesus and the disciples.

Once again, there are nuances among these readers with respect to the precise nature of Mark's rhetorical goal; but the essential message that, in spite of their failures, the disciples are rehabilitated offers hope and encouragement that human failure is not the last word of the Gospel.[18]

What to make of this impasse? On the one hand, of course, it illustrates well the way in which the meaning and force of a narrative emerge out of the interaction between text and audience; as I

---

not simply as pastoral comfort but as challenge: "the outcome of the story depends on decisions which the Church, including the reader, must still make" (152). More on this below.

[15]See, e.g., Juel, *Master of Surprise*, 114-15; Petersen, "When is the End," 154-55; Lincoln, "The Promise and the Failure," 291-92; Kingsbury, 113. I will explore this aspect of the disciples' story in more detail below.

[16]"The Promise and the Failure," 292.

[17]Juel, *Master of Surprise*, 115; Petersen, "When is the End," 164-66; Lincoln, "The Promise and the Failure," 292; Tannehill, "The Disciples in Mark," 150.

[18]Best argues, for example, that "the failure of the historical disciples followed by their eventual forgiveness and known success as missionaries [would be] a source of great encouragement" (*Following Jesus*, 12); Lincoln illustrates this view as well: "If, as disciples, the readers fail to stand up to the rigors of the way of the cross set out in the story, all is not necessarily lost. Christ's powerful word of promise will still prevail. . . . Mark's story allows for human failure even after the resurrection yet holds out the triumph of God's purposes despite this" ("The Promise and the Failure," 297).

discussed in Chapter 2, what a reader or hearer experiences in an encounter with the narrative will depend on what he or she brings to the text as much as on the "text itself." In this sense, one might say that it is fruitless to contend that one reading is right and the other wrong. On the other hand, on this interpretive issue there is a tremendous amount at stake. The entire thrust of the Gospel changes drastically depending on whether one comes to the end and concludes, "Well, it's up to me now; I'd better prove more faithful than those disciples or I'll be shut out for good, too," or is led to conclude that "with God, all things are possible." And with each respective reaction comes a whole conception of God's way in the world and a corresponding understanding of the shape of Christian existence.

Robert Fowler has attempted to clear the confusion generated by these opposing readings of the Gospel by suggesting that it emerges from the failure of interpreters to distinguish properly between story and discourse. Fowler points especially to the critics of the polemical view as expressed by Weeden and Kelber. Both sides agree, he says, that the disciples serve to instruct the audience in some way. However, proponents of the pastoral view, Fowler claims, "think that the story must therefore march in step with the discourse, that the characterization of the twelve in the story cannot be so harsh."[19] And so he suggests that the pastoral interpreters mitigate the severity of the disciples' treatment. For Fowler, the enigma of Mark as a whole lies in the fact that it is

> a narrative whose story and discourse are often at odds with each other. Understanding how a narrative whose story is so full of failure and stupidity could nevertheless be a narrative 'about' insight, understanding, and success has been difficult. The key is that the success of the narrative occurs, *if* it occurs, not in the story but at the level of discourse.[20]

---

[19]*Let the Reader Understand*, 257-58. As I noted above, I would say that both sides seek to achieve this unity between story and discourse.

[20]*Let the Reader Understand*, 258. Fowler attributes the desire to project a "happy ending" for the disciples to the power of the "reading grid" provided by Matthew (259). I do not think this is fair or accurate, as I will argue below.

To the extent that the projection of a reconciliation between Jesus and the disciples dissolves the tension of Mark's open-ended and disturbing final scene for the sake of an unambiguous "happy ending," Fowler is perhaps right.[21] I would argue, however, that Fowler takes this feature of Mark's narrative too far here. It is precisely at this point that story and discourse must cohere. For how can readers of the narrative separate their concern for the fate of disciples, human beings in whom both Jesus and the audience have invested so much, from the Gospel's "message"? Granted, Mark does not set forth an easily digestible picture of the disciples and their failures. But to suggest, as Fowler does, that Mark "is so eager to secure the reader's adherence to the Jesus of his story that he is willing to sacrifice the disciples of his story,"[22] surely undermines the credibility of both the narrator and Jesus—even God himself![23] Such an idea calls to mind the story of Moses imploring God not to destroy the Israelites after their apostasy with the golden calves (Exodus 32), in which Moses points out to God how capricious it makes God look to have chosen a people for his purposes, rescued them from slavery, only to "consume them from the face of the earth" (Exod 32:12). And Fowler's attempt to assure us that this is not history, but "only a story," so we need only be concerned about what it is trying to do to

---

[21]Such a flat reading is illustrated by Kingsbury, who simply states that "Mark invites the reader to think of the disciples as reconciled to Jesus following Easter. . . To be sure, Mark does not narrate a scene describing this fulfillment. Nevertheless, he obligates the reader to project it. As the reader projects the fulfillment of Jesus' promise, the reader in effect projects the resolution of Jesus' conflict with the disciples" (*Conflict in Mark*, 113). Moreover, the reader is to project that the disciples come to understand everything Jesus had taught them about his identity and purpose, and that the essence of discipleship is servanthood (113-14). I would argue that such a reading is far too simplistic, and destroys the artful and difficult ambiguity of Mark's story *and* his discourse. As I will suggest below, Mark ends the way it does precisely because Mark recognizes that discipleship remains a difficult thing for the audience; the tension and ambiguity does not magically disappear with Jesus' resurrection.

[22]*Let the Reader Understand*, 80.

[23]As Petersen aptly puts it, if this is the case, "God made a really big mistake" ("When is the End not the End," 162); cf. also Juel, who points out how "cruel" it would be "to open the prospect of insight for insiders only to demonstrate that no way is available for the blind and deaf to heal themselves, no means by which those whose hearts have been hardened can engineer their escape" (*Master of Surprise*, 59; cf. 63).

us, hardly dispels such misgivings. The truth and persuasiveness of the Gospel rests, in some measure, at least, on the correspondence between the story and the world to which it refers.

The Tension Preserved

I would argue that the question of the fate of the disciples should be seen in the same light as the question of Jesus' fate at the hands of his enemies. That is, I, too, am attempting a way out of the impasse. It seems to me that the purely pastoral side, especially as represented by Best and Malbon, does not take seriously enough the darkness of the disciples' portrayal. Best's suggestion that the slowness of the disciples serves to give further occasions for instruction by Jesus for the sake of the audience, while it holds much truth, and is a common literary device (cf. Aristotle), cannot sufficiently account for the harshness of the portrayal—the disciples do not need to be quite so obdurate to make that point! This idea accords much more with Matthew's treatment. On the other hand, those who argue for the utter failure and eternal exclusion of the disciples do not take seriously enough the clear indications that they will be "resurrected." It is precisely in the tension between these two aspects of the portrayal that the rhetorical force lies. Both raise the question of whether the "things of human beings" will have finality, or whether the "things of God" can overcome them.[24] If the disciples have been forever shut out of the kingdom, God's promises to them become void, and, to invoke the apostle Paul, Mark's proclamation has been in vain, and the reader's faith has been in vain (1 Cor. 15:14). Far from removing the tension and ambiguity which arises out of Mark's story of the disciples, to acknowledge fully both the failure of the disciples and the trustworthiness of God in the face of such failure brings the tension into sharp relief. After all, to be reconciled to Jesus places the disciples in the same relation to a world opposed to God as Jesus was. The resurrection vindicates not only Jesus' messiahship in its unexpected nature, but the shape of the existence to which he called those who would follow him, as well.

---

[24]Cf. Petersen, "When is the End," 161.

Precisely because Mark's portrayal of the disciples is so harsh, the posited—and necessary—reconciliation between them and Jesus is all the more radical, perhaps even scandalous. And far from simply providing comfort and encouragement, the post-resurrection reconciliation of the disciples puts the audience on notice that even unfaithfulness and fear cannot keep them safe from being embraced by the boundary-shattering reign of God.

Thus, in the next two sections, I will attempt to show, first, how Mark's portrayal of the disciples serves to instill in the audience a keen awareness of the power and influence of those forces opposed to God; and second, how, through the inevitability of the reconciliation which comes at Jesus' initiative, Mark brings the audience to the recognition that God's eschatological salvation will break through any barriers erected to keep it at bay. The first involves an examination of the rhetorical force of Mark's negative portrayal of the disciples; I will focus on the way in which Mark compels the audience to see the disciples' conflict with Jesus in the light of the conflict with the authorities. The second will examine the momentum which leads the audience beyond the negative portrayal and into the disciples'—and audience's—future.

FROM LIGHT INTO DARKNESS:
THE BLINDNESS OF THE DISCIPLES

As Robert Tannehill has shown in his seminal essay, the narrative role of the disciples in Mark functions as one of the Mark's primary means of enveloping his audience in the drama of the Gospel.[25] An audience's interest in and experience of a narrative is greatly enhanced when it finds a character or group of characters with whom it can identify in some meaningful way. As I argued in Chapter 3, Mark sets up his narrative in such a way that it encompasses the audience's location in time and space, thus bringing the audience into the story world. Following the prologue, Mark moves immediately to begin the story of Jesus in relation to those whom he calls to follow him (1:16-20). This move signals the significance of

---

[25]Tannehill, "The Disciples in Mark," 139-40.

the "theme" of following Jesus for Mark's narrative;[26] but more important, it draws the audience further into the story by introducing characters with whom it presumably has much in common. As Tannehill puts it, "a reader will identify most easily and immediately with characters who seem to share the reader's situation. Assuming that the majority of the first readers of the Gospel were Christians, they would relate most easily and immediately to characters in the story who respond positively to Jesus."[27] Further, I agree with Tannehill's judgment that "the author of Mark anticipated this response by his readers. He composed his story so as to make use of this initial tendency to identify with the disciples in order to speak indirectly to the reader through the disciples' story."[28] If this is the case, then we must, as Fowler suggests, pay close attention to both the story of the disciples, and the discourse which underlies it; what will Mark's ideal audience experience and learn through its identification with the disciples' story?

As suggested above, the issue is often framed in terms of which aspect of Mark's dialectical portrait of the disciples will finally prevail in the audience's experience of the narrative: the positive side, signaled both by the disciples' initially faithful response to Jesus' call, and then adumbrated by their presumed rehabilitation beyond the narrative; or the negative side, revealed by their unperceptiveness, misconception, and final rejection of Jesus and his gospel. If the audience experiences initially the positive portrait of the disciples, the key question becomes how it will respond to the dramatic shift in the disciples' relationship to Jesus. Will the audience be forced to "reject the views and actions of the Twelve and [affirm] the words and work of Jesus," thereby "becoming faithful

---

[26]As most commentators recognize; see, e.g., Leander Keck ("The Introduction to Mark's Gospel," *NTS* 12 [1965] 352-370, 362-364), who supports his claim that the prologue encompasses 1:1-15 by noting that 1:16-20 provides an appropriate introduction to Jesus' public ministry in its principal aim: "namely the steady emphasis on the disciples' participation in the work of Jesus. What makes the story of Jesus εὐαγγέλιον for Mark is not . . . who Jesus is *in se* but who he is *pro nobis*" (364).

[27]"The Disciples in Mark," 139. I would add that the statement applies not only to the first audience of the Gospel, but to any subsequent audience—including a contemporary one—as well.

[28]"The Disciples in Mark," 140.

disciples"?[29] Or is there another possible response? It seems to me that Mark's audience would take its cue from what it comes to understand about the *nature* and *source* of the disciples' obduracy. And I would suggest that Mark invites the audience to see in it not something which a would-be follower of Jesus might him- or herself, unlike the disciples, overcome through sheer force of will; rather, Mark characterizes the conflict between Jesus and the disciples as a conflict between God and those forces opposed to God *over* the lives of would-be followers. The fate of the disciples, in other words, rests not in their own capacity to overcome their failures, but in God's capacity to break through their unbelief and rescue them from their darkness.

The narrative encourages this experience of the role of the disciples in at least two ways. First, the initial positive portrayal of the disciples does more than just encourage identification on the part of the audience; it involves an investment (or promise) on God's part concerning the relationship between the disciples and the ultimate fruitfulness of the gospel. That is, Mark makes it clear in the opening chapters that the fate of the disciples is related in an integral way to the fate of (or reliability of) the promises contained in the gospel. Second, the nature of the disciples' malady reveals the ways in which it reflects Satan's grasp on the disciples, a grasp that bears many of the marks of the authorities' opposition to Jesus. Thus the audience is led to view the opposition of the disciples to Jesus' mission as endangering the promise every bit as much as the conflict between Jesus and the authorities: it revolves around many of the same issues (e.g., authority, boundaries, etc.), and climaxes in a crisis that can only be resolved if God's promises prove reliable.

---

[29]Tolbert, *Sowing the Gospel*, 224. On this point, Tannehill's stance between the pastoral and polemical sides becomes evident; he, too, suggests that "as the inadequacies of the disciples' response to Jesus become increasingly clear, the reader must distance himself from the disciples and begin to seek another way" ("The Disciples in Mark," 142).

"To you has been given": The Investment in the Disciples

The introduction of the disciples in the narrative not only encourages identification with them, but sets up the question of their fate as an integral feature of the plot of the Gospel. Jesus' initial call of Simon and Andrew (1:16-20) establishes the two fishermen as sympathetic characters, whose obedient response to the call of Jesus brings them into the circle of those who would respond to the gospel of God (1:14-15).[30] Perhaps more important, it also indicates an unambiguous and unqualified intention toward and promise of Jesus to them (and to the audience): "I will make you (ποιήσω) become fishers of human beings" (1:17). This promise carries with it the same force as the promise of the opening verses of the Gospel, where it is said of John the Baptist that he will "make straight the paths" of the Lord (1:3). That is, the establishment of a community faithful to the gospel is the result of God's creative (and redemptive) activity.[31] In Chapter 3 I pointed out how the prologue prepares the way for the audience's experience of the endangerment of this promise in both John's and Jesus' fates (especially in the allusion to John's death in 1:14). The promise to the first disciples carries with it that same undercurrent of threat; Jesus comes "after John" (ὀπίσω μου, 1:7), that is, he follows the deathward path prepared for him by John. Likewise, the disciples come "after" Jesus (ὀπίσω μου, 1:17, 20; cf. 8:34), which suggests that they, too, will tread the same path. God will make of Simon and Andrew fishers of human beings, but it will be over against forces opposed to God's redemptive goals. Like the fates of John and Jesus, the fate of the disciples will rest in God's ability to reaffirm the promises in the face of the cosmic opposition manifested in the historical forces of a hardened world.

And Mark continues this association of discipleship with God's creative activity by using the same term to speak of Jesus' appoint-

---

[30]Cf. Schweizer, "The Portrayal of the Life of Faith," 172.

[31]In this light, perhaps Tannehill's suggestion that the disciples represent a "commissioned" group is not quite accurate ("The Gospel of Mark as Narrative Christology," *Semeia* 16 [1979], 57-95). The focus is perhaps not so much on the disciples' execution of their charge, but on God's promise to them that they will function this way.

ment of the Twelve. Mark alone among the Gospels relates, a little awkwardly, that Jesus "created" (ἐποίησεν) the Twelve.[32] This kind of investment ensures that the audience of the Gospel will not easily come to reject the Twelve, for their fate is linked to the broader question of the reliability and power behind God's promises. The ensuing scenes in the Gospel display even further God's investment in the disciples, as well the sense of the likelihood that they will encounter opposition. The key here is the way in which Mark intertwines the emerging conflict between Jesus and the authorities with the story-line of the disciples. As noted in the previous chapter, the Gospel moves to set out the fact and importance of the authorities' opposition to Jesus very early in the Gospel (1:22; 2:1-3:6). These stories serve, as we saw, to clarify the shape of Jesus' boundary-shattering ministry, and highlight the consequences of embracing it. The clearly-announced presence of the disciples in the first major controversies between Jesus and the authorities in 2:1-3:6 implicates them in the consequences of his ministry, as well.[33] They are shown engaging in behavior characteristic of Jesus' minis-try—eating with outcasts, not fasting, reinterpreting the Sabbath. Their presence with Jesus as he (and they) are attacked gives the audience initially some refuge from the threat posed by religious establishment who, we are gradually convinced, represent the cosmic opposition to God's goals displayed in the prologue. Though the challenges and reality-altering consequences of Jesus' ministry are clearly laid out, the audience will perhaps be encouraged that the group Jesus called to follow him will indeed result in the formation of a community capable of living in light of the gospel.

The narrative then renders explicit the disciples' role in God's redemptive plan, which was implied in their presence with Jesus in these controversies. It becomes clear that there is an explicit purpose behind Jesus' "creation" of them: They are to "to be with him, and to be sent out to proclaim the message, and to have authority to cast

---

[32]Cf. Matt. 10:1, where Jesus "summons" (προσκαλεσάμενος) the Twelve, and Luke 6:13, where he simply "chooses" (ἐκλεξάμενος) them. The NRSV's rendering of Mark 3:14 ("he appointed the twelve") fails to bring this connotation across.

[33]See Joanna Dewey, *Markan Public Debate* (SBLDS 48; Chico, CA: Scholars Press, 1980), 87, 126-28.

out demons" (3:14-15). That is, they are to be extensions of Jesus' ministry, performing the self-same tasks (proclaiming and casting out demons; cf. 1:14-15; 32-34; 38-39; 3:7-12) with the same authority (ἐξουσία; cf. 1:22, 27; 2:10), and, presumably, with the same goal: to signal the in-breaking of God's reign to the world. The identification of the disciples with Jesus' goals, over against the opposition of the religious authorities, is then confirmed in 3:20-35, when they are included in the circle around Jesus, part of the true family of Jesus comprised of those who "do the will of God" (3:31-35).

At this point in the audience's experience of the narrative, then, it would seem that the lines marking insiders and outsiders have been clearly drawn. Jesus has made an investment in followers who will stand with him over against the powers opposed to God. And indeed, the first part of Chapter 4, the parable discourse, seems to confirm the disciples' insider status, and expresses powerfully the nature and degree of God's investment in them. As noted in the previous chapter, the parable of the sower serves a crucial rhetorical function in the Gospel. It clarifies for the audience the nature of Jesus' activity: he is the sower of the word, whose work will yield a tremendous harvest in spite of the unfruitful soil on which much of the seed is sown;[34] and it focuses attention on the reception of the word: though much ground will prove barren, there will be good soil which brings forth grain and bears fruit "thirty and sixty and a hundred-fold" (4:20).

With respect to the audience response to the disciples, I would suggest that this chapter accomplishes two principal rhetorical goals. On the one hand, it reveals the disciples' inextricable relationship with the promise of the gospel. 4:10-12, the infamous "parable theory," makes this especially clear. These verses have received a tremendous amount of scrutiny, of course; a complete examination of the various interpretative possibilities is beyond the scope of this study.[35] As Juel notes, there have been endless attempts to get around

---

[34]As Juel notes, the parables in chapter four deal with implied objections to the nature of Jesus' messiahship: "What evidence is there that his efforts have anything to do with the glorious days to come?" (*Master of Surprise*, 56).

[35]See Juel, *Master of Surprise*, 50-54 for a helpful review of recent proposals; see also Joel Marcus, *The Mystery of the Kingdom of God* (SBLDS 90; Atlanta:

the scandal that arises out of what Jesus seems to be saying in these verses. The words are troubling on at least two counts. When asked by the disciples and "those around him"[36] about the parables, Jesus tells them, first, that this insider group has been given the "secret" (μυστήριον) of the reign of God. The scandal here, of course, is that which always attends the notion of God's free election of individuals and groups, a feature of God's activity since the election of Israel.[37] Yet the verse does create a relationship between this insider group and God's purposes; just as God's purposes for the world depended upon God's revelation to Israel and its faithful response, so, too, God's redemptive purposes as expressed eschatologically in Jesus depend upon the creation of a faithful, fruitful community. Interpreters have often tried to soften the scandalous aspect of this freedom by suggesting that the parables simply serve to reveal the separation between insiders and outsiders that has already been manifested through people's response to Jesus.[38] But the next verse precludes such a reading, for the citation from Isaiah 6 reveals the *purpose* of Jesus' teaching in parables; it is precisely *"in order that* (ἵνα)'they [the outsiders] may indeed look, but not perceive, and may indeed listen, but not understand; *so that* (μήποτε) they may not turn again and be forgiven'" (4:12). So the scandal is actually deepened; Jesus' parabolic speech is designed to prevent outsiders from becoming insiders. The gift of the mystery of the reign of God, and his explanations to the insiders in private (cf. 3:34; are these coextensive?) are meant to secure a relationship with a group of faithful insiders who will have a crucial role to play in the harvest; they will—indeed, they must—form the good soil.[39]

Scholars Press, 1986).

[36] A reference back to 3:34, where "those around him" constitute his family, those who do the will of God (3:35).

[37] E.g., his words to Moses, "I will have mercy on whom I have mercy, and I will have compassion on whom I have compassion" (Exod 33:19).

[38] Consider, e.g., Tolbert's statement that "outsiders *will not* understand, *because they are outsiders*, and insiders *will* understand *because they are insiders*. The parables . . . do not force people outside or pull people inside; they simply reveal the type of ground already present" (*Sowing the Gospel*, 160-61.

[39] Once again, I must reject the idea here that Mark's story and discourse are at odds (see above), that, in other words, this whole scene takes place for the sake of

Yet if, on the one hand, the parable chapter serves to under-score the need for good soil in order for the word to produce a harvest, and seems to identify this insider group in such a way that the disciples are included, it also contains hints that things are not quite this simple. The chapter serves as a bridge from the positive portrayal of the disciples up to this point to the negative portrayal which comes to predominate in the rest of the narrative.[40] The first hint of trouble comes immediately following the explanation of Jesus' parabolic discourse, when he turns to the very ones to whom the gift of the secret of the reign of God had been given, and chides them for *their* lack of understanding: "Do you not understand this parable? Then how will you understand all the parables?" (4:13) The juxtaposition of this revelation of their lack of insight with the pronouncement of their insider status introduces the tension that will now become the focus of the narrative. Jesus' parables have made it clear that the harvest depends on good soil, and have promised that such good soil will be found. But as the disciples begin to reveal characteristics of the other types of soil, the prospects for the eschatological harvest grow correspondingly grim. We turn our attention now to the way in which the narrative develops this tension between the necessity and apparent impossibility of creating good soil out of the disciples, and the way it brings this conflict to the point of crisis for both the story and the discourse.

The Gospel Turned Inside Out

There is little disagreement among interpreters that, from chapter 4 on, and especially after the first feeding story (6:31-44), the

---

making insiders out of the readers without respect to the fate of the disciples' status as insiders (cf. Fowler, *Let the Reader Understand*, 169-70). Granted, the strong hint in 4:13 that the disciples may prove to be outsiders is borne out in the ensuing narrative; but if the reader's insider status is purchased at the expense of keeping the disciples out forever, the reader's insider status reveals itself as a Pyrrhic victory, for it suggests that human opposition and blindness can have the final word.

[40]Cf. Tannehill, "The Disciples in Mark," 146; Tolbert, *Sowing the Gospel*, 198. Of course, one should note that the very first hint of trouble comes in the initial creation of the Twelve, in the relative clause appended to the last named disciple, "Judas Iscariot, who betrayed him" (3:19).

story of the disciples begins a downward spiral that plunges them into a complete break with Jesus. This aspect of Mark's story has been well brought out in other studies,[41] so we need only review it briefly here. My interest lies, once again, in how the narrative seems to direct the audience's response to the disciples' gradual and inevitable demise in the story—that is, the question of the rhetorical goal of this portrayal. The question, as it emerges from our review of recent interpretation, is whether the audience is led to a rejection of the disciples and a search for another, better model for discipleship—the view of most interpreters; or whether, as I will argue, the audience is drawn into the conflict between Jesus and the disciples so that, as the distance between Jesus and the disciples increases to crisis proportions, the audience's interest in and concern for the fate of the disciples grows correspondingly. I will argue that the latter is the case, precisely because, as shown above, the narrative has linked the fate of the disciples to the fate of God's promises.

The narrative presents the story of the disciples from chapter 4 on in three carefully structured stages. The first stage revolves around three boat scenes (4:35-41; 6:47-52; 8:14-21), each of which focuses on the disciples' failure to grasp significant aspects of Jesus' identity; the third scene brings this movement to a climax. The next stage (8:27-10:45) begins with Peter's acknowledgment of Jesus' identity, but then shifts the emphasis to the disciples' inability to understand Jesus' fate as Messiah, his suffering and death, as demonstrated through their failure to act in accordance with the values of God's reign as expressed through a suffering Messiah. The three passion predictions in this section give it its structure. Finally, in the passion narrative, the disciples' opposition to Jesus issues in their betrayal, denial, and flight.

The Disciples and the Authorities: In the Same Boat? As we saw in the previous chapter, after the first series of controversies

---

[41]See, e.g., Weeden, *Traditions in Conflict*, 23-51; Tannehill, "The Disciples in Mark," 144-152; Tolbert, *Sowing the Gospel*, 195-218; Rhoads and Michie, *Mark as Story: An Introduction to the Narrative of a Gospel* (Philadelphia: Fortress Press, 1982), 89-100; Kingsbury, *Conflict in Mark*, 89-118; Kelber, *Mark's Story of Jesus*; Petersen, *Literary Criticism for New Testament Critics* (Philadelphia: Fortress Press, 1978), 54-80.

between Jesus and the religious authorities (2:1-3:6), the plot against Jesus' life with which this series culminates (3:6) is left hanging over the ensuing narrative, not to be taken up again until the Jerusalem section of the Gospel (11:18). But the issues around which the conflict revolved, as well as the cloud of threat to God's promises, continue to influence the narrative.

In Chapter 4, as noted above, Mark turns the audience's attention to the relationship between Jesus and his disciples, giving the impression that clear lines have been drawn for the plot: Jesus and his disciples ("those around him") on the one hand, opposed by the authorities on the other ("those outside"). However, in 4:35-8:21, the slight hint in the parable discourse that things might not be so simple balloons into full-blown conflict between Jesus and his would-be followers. Mark guides the audience's response to the disciples in this section in two closely intertwined ways: First, the boat scenes display their lack of understanding (4:35-41; 6:47-52; 8:14-21), an obduracy which, paradoxically, increases in inverse proportion to their experiences of Jesus' power. And second, the narrative gradually blurs the neat line between insiders and outsiders established in 3:31-4:12, principally by revealing disturbing similarities between the authorities' lack of perception and that of the disciples.

Recent scholarship has pointed out and examined the structure and importance of the boat scenes in this section.[42] The boat is actually introduced in the summary of 3:7-12, in which Jesus requests his disciples to "have a boat ready for him because of the crowd, so that they would not crush him" (3:9).[43] And in the first use of the boat (4:1), that is precisely how Jesus uses it: he delivers his crucial parable discourse ("he taught them many things in parables," 4:2) from the boat because of the crowd. Thus Mark has set the stage for an ironic juxtaposition. The boat is initially introduced as a means

---

[42]The most detailed examination of this section is from Norman Petersen, "The Composition of Mark 4:1-8:26," *Harvard Theological Review* 73 (1980), 185-217; see also Robert Fowler, *Loaves and Fishes: the Function of the Feeding Stories in the Gospel of Mark* (SBLDS 54; Chico, CA: Scholars Press, 1981), especially 57-68.

[43]Here it is πλοιάριον, lit. "small boat;" in all the other occurrences (4:1, 36, 37; 5:2, 18, 21; 6:32, 45, 47, 51, 54; 8:10,14), it is πλοῖον. The frequency and concentration of the term clearly suggests its importance as a unifying theme for this section.

of escaping crowds who flock to Jesus because they recognize his authority in teaching and healing, but it becomes the stage for the revelation of the disciples' increasing incomprehension. In each scene, the disciples' lack of insight follows on the "crest" of some display of Jesus' authority in teaching, healing, or both. The first crossing (4:35-41) comes immediately after the completion of Jesus' teaching in parables (4:1-34). As they are crossing, and while Jesus is getting some much-deserved rest at the back of the boat, a storm arises which threatens to sink the little boat. The disciples wake him, and he "rebukes" the wind and the sea. Clearly, this scene taps into the association of the sea with the evil forces of chaos, and the verbs ἐπιτιμῶν and φιμῶν link up with Jesus' exorcizing and healing activity;[44] Jesus in effect exorcizes the sea.[45] Jesus then chides the disciples (again, those to whom he had just accorded "insider" status) for their fear and lack of faith. Their bewildered response is surprising in light of what the audience has come to expect from the disciples: "Who then is this, that even the wind and the sea obey him?" (4:41).

In its context, this scene serves to develop the emerging tension between Jesus and his disciples. The audience will be struck by the way in which Jesus' control over the wind and waves confirms the authority of his teaching—an important rhetorical move, for, as we saw, Chapter 4 deals with the incongruity between Jesus' strange ministry and the results it is to yield.[46] It will also emerge from this narrative, however, that something is going wrong; while the implied audience should by now be able to answer the question the disciples pose, the disciples, those to whom Jesus has entrusted the secret of

---

[44]Especially Jesus' initial exorcism in the synagogue; cf. 1:25.

[45]See, e.g., Morna Hooker, *The Gospel According to Saint Mark* (Peabody, MA: Hendrickson Publishers, 1991), 140. Cf. Genesis 1; Pss 89:9-10; 74:7-13; Job 41; Jonah 1:4-6.

[46]As we noted in the previous chapter, one of Mark's rhetorical goals in these opening chapters is to coordinate Jesus' word and work so that they mutually reinforce each other. In this regard, it should be noted that chapter 4 is framed by Jesus' displays of power over evil (3:22-30; 4:35-41), and that the next narrative block (5:1-43) manifests this power in three dramatic miracles—culminating in Jesus' power over death itself (5:35-43).

the kingdom, cannot. The conflict between these two aspects of this scene begins to beg for some resolution.

The next scene in which the disciples figure prominently[47] does move to ameliorate the tension, but only temporarily, and with ominous undertones. Jesus sends out the twelve as extensions of his ministry (6:6b-13), giving them the same authority and charge which he himself has manifested, and they carry out their mission successfully (6:12-13, 30). But as many interpreters have recognized, the intercalation of the story of John the Baptist's death between their departure and returns (6:14-29) foreshadows the danger that lies ahead.[48] With success in ministry comes the unwelcome attention of the ruling powers, with potentially deadly consequences. The question posed here for the audience is not whether "trouble and persecution will arise on account of the word," but whether, when it does, they will prove faithful or "fall away" (σκανδαλίζομαι, 4:17; cf. 14:27-29!). The scene emphasizes the importance of the disciples' relation to the promise of a harvest, for they are, the narrative suggests, to perform the work of the sower in his stead. The disciples' role in the feeding stories makes the same point; their role in distributing the food to the people links them in an integral way to the ministry of the gospel, making the problem of their incomprehension all the more threatening to the promise of a harvest.

Yet the next two boat scenes do nothing to encourage the audience to hope that the disciples will be up to the task, and indeed serve to bring the emerging conflict between them and Jesus into sharper relief. The way in which they are intertwined with Jesus' continuing conflict with the authorities makes for a complex expression of Mark's contrapuntal theme, i.e., Jesus' intense investment in this motley band, and their increasing opacity. These

---

[47]Though the story of the raising of Jairus' daughter should be noted, for Jesus takes three of his disciples—Peter, James and John—with him into the house, where they witness the raising (5:35-43), increasing the sense of their insider status, and thus increasing correspondingly the audience's bewilderment at their failure to understand.

[48]E.g., Tolbert, *Sowing the Gospel*, 196-198; she rightly notes the correlation between faithful execution of God's commission and the inevitability that tribulation and persecution will follow. This was the case for John and Jesus—the success of their mission brings the menacing attention of the ruling authorities to them, with deadly consequences.

two scenes are linked in that each follows one of the two miraculous feedings performed by Jesus (6:30-44; 8:1-10)—one on the "Jewish side" of the sea (6:30-44) and one on the "gentile" side (8:1-10). In between, Jesus enters into controversy with the Pharisees and some scribes from Jerusalem precisely over the central issue which separates the two sides (i.e., of the sea!): the boundaries erected to protect God from impurity (7:1-16). Interestingly—perhaps ironically?— it is a controversy brought about by the behavior of the disciples (7:2). As in Chapter 4, the motif of Jesus' private explanation of his public "parables" (as his words in 7:6-16 are described) emphasizes the theme of Jesus' investment in the disciples, and highlights their lack of understanding—even of their own behavior (7:18).

The two boat scenes, however, will most likely linger in the audience's mind, both because of the repetition, and because of the way in which they suggest that the disciples are in the "same boat" as the religious authorities. Following the first feeding, the disciples are again in the boat, straining against the wind, and Jesus comes to them, intending to pass them by (they are supposed to be followers, after all!). When they see him, they become "terrified," and the narrator reports that their astonishment and fear result from their failure to "understand about the loaves," a condition brought on by the hardening of their hearts (ἡ καρδία πεπωρωμένη, 6:52). At this point, the audience is likely to be astonished itself, because the disciples are said to display the same condition as that of the authorities (as in 3:5, τῇ πωρώσει τῆς καρδίας αὐτῶν), whose intent to destroy Jesus has been announced (3:6). As I suggested above, the audience's reaction to the opposition of the religious authorities moves it to embrace the goals of Jesus, a move whose difficulty (Chapter 4) has been ameliorated by the presence of followers who share both the vision and its consequences. Now the narrative begins to strip away that comforting presence;[49] thus, instead of guarding against the threat to the promise posed by the

---

[49] I do not see the "exceptional" characters as providing much help here, as some interpreters do. Their function is to highlight the disciples' failings, but because there is no sustained investment in them on the part of the narrator, they cannot function as models of faithful response.

authorities' opposition, the disciples bring an additional threat. If God overcomes the authorities' opposition, will there be a community composed of "good soil" through which the promise can yield a harvest?

The third and final boat scene brings the question to a climax and crisis, and prepares the way for the further development of the motif in the "way" section of the Gospel (8:27-10:52). The scene follows the second feeding (8:1-10) and a brief, hostile exchange between Jesus and the Pharisees (8:11-13). The scene would be comical were it not for the gravity of what is at stake (the fate of the promise). The disciples have witnessed two miraculous feedings, one of 5,000 people (not including women and children!) and one of 4,000. Yet they are concerned about having only one loaf for their trip across the sea (4:14)! This scene brings to a crisis the severity of the disciples' obduracy both by its juxtaposition with Jesus' engagement with the Pharisees, and by the harshness of Jesus' upbraiding of them.

As I pointed out in the last chapter, the brief encounter with the Pharisees carries with it biting dramatic irony. The Pharisees' request for a sign comes in the midst of a section that has prominently displayed Jesus' authority in word and deed. They are blind to the signs all around them, a blindness, as even here is implied, due to Satan's grasp on them—they come, as Satan had, to "tempt" (πειράζειν) him (8:11; cf. 1:13), and their hardness of heart has been lamented by Jesus (3:5). Jesus' reply is thus also ironic, in a verbal sense, because he has given abundant signs pointing to his identity and mission.

However, the next scene, the final boat episode, displays that the disciples share in this blindness. Here the line between Jesus' opponents and his followers, between insiders and outsiders, which has been eroding since Chapter 4, seems to disappear altogether. Jesus cautions them to "beware, watch out for the leaven of the Pharisees and the leaven of Herod" (8:15)—calling to mind, of course, the blindness and opposition of these adversaries, and their intent to bring an end to Jesus and his movement (3:6; 6:14-16). The disciples' reply is difficult to make sense of, but that is perhaps the point; they clearly have missed the boat completely. And Jesus' words to them complete the disciples' movement to the outside. In an unmistakable echo of the very scene in which Jesus revealed to them the purpose of his parable discourse, Jesus, seemingly himself dumbfounded,[50] confronts them with their lack of understanding:

> "Why are you talking about having no bread? Do you still not perceive or understand (συνίετε; cf. 4:12)? Are your hearts hardened (πεπωρωμένην ἔχετε τὴν καρδίαν ὑμῶν; cf. 3:5; 6:52)? Do you have eyes, and fail to see? Do you have ears, and fail to hear? And do you not remember?... Do you not yet understand (οὔπω συνίετε)?" (8:17-21)

Most commentators recognize the connection between these verses and 4:11-12; but there is an important difference, one which makes the denunciation even sharper. First, of course, the echo is not exact; 8:18 is actually an allusion to, almost a direct citation of, Jer 5:21, whereas the goal of the parables was described in terms of Isaiah 6. And in 4:11-12, as we saw, the outsiders are actually *prevented* from seeing, "*lest* they turn again and be forgiven;" but the disciples are supposed to *have* eyes and ears (4:10), so the goal of Jesus' actions towards them is precisely to bring them to repentance, and to form a community faithful to the gospel, to be the good soil on which the harvest depends. The narrative has brought the audience to a point where the promise of and to the disciples seems to have little hope of bearing fruit. They have become outsiders, and confidence in the promise is shaken to the core.

Another rhetorical feature that both underscores the disciples' failures, but also perhaps gives some indication of a direction in which hope may lie, is the oft-noted framing of this section with scenes depicting Jesus healing a deaf and mute man (7:31-37) and a blind man (8:22-26).[51] There is tremendous irony here, of course,

---

[50]I wonder if this is a case in which the narrator (and therefore God) actually knows more than Jesus. It is the narrator who reports in 6:52 that the disciples' hearts are hardened. Jesus' bewilderment seems genuine. Though the disciples' ultimate abandonment of Jesus is foretold by Jesus, the pathos of Jesus' own sense of forsakenness, expressed in the Garden of Gethsemane and on the cross, would be deepened if there was a sense in which his hopes and intentions for his disciples seemed thwarted by circumstances beyond his control.

[51]The second miracle serves a dual function; it serves as a bridge to the next section of the narrative (8:26-10:52), and with the healing of blind Bartimaeus in

since the miracles display Jesus' messianic capacity to "make the deaf to hear and the mute to speak," and give sight to the blind (cf. Isa 29:18; 35:5-6), yet his followers remain deaf, dumb, and blind. On the other hand, these healings suggest that God does have the capacity to heal such maladies, thus leaving open the possibility that, should the problem with the disciples prove to be analogous in some fundamental way to the problems presented by those who are healed or exorcized, there is yet hope for their blindness, a hope that lies outside human capacity.[52] As I will suggest below, this proves to be an important component in the question of the fate of the disciples.

It is at this point in the narrative—the climax of the disciples' lack of perception in 8:14-21—that many commentators, especially those of the polemical ilk, see the narrative's goal to be to "manipulate" the audience to begin to distance itself from the disciples, and search for another model.[53] As I have tried to suggest, however, I do not see the rhetoric moving in this way. The intense investment in the disciples on the part of Jesus (and God) has intertwined their fate with the fate of the promise of the gospel, making the question of their fate a matter of utmost—and existential—concern for the audience. The next section contains crucial support for this argument, in that it portrays the principal clue to the nature and cause of the disciples' obduracy.

The Disciples in Satan's Grasp (8:27-10:52). The narrative takes a dramatic and thematic shift in the scene in which Jesus takes his disciples up to the region of Caesarea Philippi, and poses to them the question that has been brewing on the story level since the beginning of Jesus' public ministry:[54] Who do people say that I am? In classical terms, it is the central recognition scene, one which brings about "a complete swing in the action" of the plot.[55] It

---

10:46-52, forms the first part of an important frame around that section, whose significance I will discuss below.

[52]Cf. Juel, *Mark*, 115f.

[53]E.g., Tannehill, "The Disciples in Mark," 145-49; Tolbert, *Sowing the Gospel*, 223-226.

[54]Cf., e.g., 1:27; 2:7; 3:22; 4:41; 6:2-3; 6:14-16.

[55]Cf. Aristotle, *Poetics* 10-11(Stephen Halliwell, *The Poetics of Aristotle: Translation and Commentary*, [Chapel Hill, NC: University of North Carolina Press, 1987], 42-43).

involves a dramatic shift in that it resolves, for a moment, and not unambiguously, the tension created by the disciples' obduracy; the focus shifts to the question of whether the disciples will understand the significance of their recognition of Jesus' identity. It is a thematic shift because Jesus introduces a new and urgent motif into his teaching: the inevitability of his own suffering and death, and the necessity that anyone who embraces his identity must also embrace his cross.

Our interest in this section is two-fold: First, how this section reflects the newly introduced frame for the disciples' blindness, which strongly implies a particular view of the cause and nature of their unwillingness—or inability—to embrace Jesus' destiny, to see it as the work of God, and second, the overall rhetorical goals of this piece of the disciples' portrait. The section brings to further and fuller expression both the degree of investment Jesus is making in the disciples, and the source and depth of their continued failure. Thus the section continues to develop the tension we have seen thus far between the necessity of the disciples' "success" and the dimming prospects they offer for it.

The structural features of this section of the narrative are, in a broad sense, remarkably clear, and function rhetorically to prepare the audience for both the divine inevitability of the events in Jerusalem, as well as the inevitability of the disciples' utter failure. First, it is marked by the three-fold recurrence of Jesus' private revelations of his impending passion to his disciples (8:31; 9:30-32; 10:32-34). Each passion prediction is the first component of a three-part unit which focuses on the disciples' complete misunderstanding of Jesus.[56] After each announcement of the passion and resurrection, the narrator relates an incident in which the disciples painfully display their misunderstanding. In the first unit, which will occupy most of our attention below, Peter is shown rebuking Jesus for his

---

[56]On this, see, e.g., Norman Perrin, *What is Redaction Criticism?* (Philadelphia: Fortress Press, 1969), 40-43.; *idem* (with Dennis C. Duling), *The New Testament: An Introduction* (2nd ed.; New York: Harcourt, Brace, Jovanovich, Inc., 1982), 248-251; Kingsbury, *Conflict in Mark*, 104-111; Fowler, *Let the Reader Understand*, 187-189; Tannehill, "The Gospel of Mark as Narrative Christology," *Semeia* 16 (1979), 57-95, 74; Petersen, *Literary Criticism*, 60-68; Tolbert, *Sowing the Gospel*, 177-179

attempt to link his messiahship with suffering (8:32-33); Jesus, in turn, rebukes Peter. The second passion prediction (9:33-34) is followed immediately by an argument among the disciples over who was the greatest. And, in the final unit, James and John ask for a share in Jesus' messianic "glory," hoping that he will grant them a place at his right and left hand (10:35-40). The third piece of each unit involves Jesus' "calling" (8:34; 9:35; 10:42) of the disciples around him to set them straight, in the most straightforward sayings about the paradoxical character of the gospel:[57] "Those who want to save their life will lose it" (8:35); "Whoever wants to be first must be last of all and servant of all" (9:35); "Whoever wishes to be first among you must be slave of all" (10:44).

This section of the narrative also develops the disciples' misunderstanding outside of these passion prediction units. The transfiguration (9:2-8) and the ensuing discussion between Jesus and the disciples who were privy to it (Peter, James, and John; 9:9-13) further confirms their confusion; Peter's response to the appearance of Moses and Elijah suggests how taken he is with such a glorious manifestation of Jesus' identity, in sharp contrast to his previous response to Jesus' talk of suffering.[58] And down in the valley, a demon in possession of a young boy is getting the best of the disciples, who apparently now lack the power over unclean spirits which they once possessed (6:13). Further, they seek to exclude a successful exorcist who was working in Jesus' name, because he was not "following" them (9:38); they apparently desire exclusive rights to Jesus' authority, and have failed to comprehend that Jesus' ministry is to have no such boundaries. Their "this-worldly," hier-archical view of authority manifests itself as well in their attempt to prevent children from coming to Jesus (10:13-16); and they are concerned about the reward they will receive for having left every-thing and followed Jesus (10:28-31). Again, in each case Jesus attempts to correct their faulty vision, but to no avail. As the

---

[57]Cf. Fowler, *Let the Reader Understand*, 187.

[58]Tolbert's observation is to the point: "In contrast to his utter rejection of Jesus the Messiah's words about the inevitability of suffering (8:31-33), this glorified Jesus in company with Elijah and Moses wins his approval ('it is well that we are here') and his esteem" (*Sowing the Gospel*, 205).

narrative moves on from this section into the passion narrative, despite all hopes to the contrary, the audience cannot be surprised when the disciples ultimately desert him and flee (14:50).

One further noteworthy rhetorical feature of this section is the frame provided by two healings of blind people: the strange and unique two-stage healing in Bethsaida (8:22-26), and the healing of Bartimaeus at Jericho, just before the entrance into Jerusalem (10:46-52). This is a generally recognized feature of Mark's structure;[59] but interpreters dispute how an audience will respond to it. Clearly, Mark wishes the audience to draw some crucial connections between the frame and the framed material. Is it, however, a tragic irony, one based on the fact that "Jesus can give sight to the physically blind who come to him in faith, but he cannot give insight to his fearful disciples"?[60] Or does it reflect a crucial parallel between the disciples' spiritual blindness and the physical blindness of those healed, suggesting, in other words, the disciples' need for an act of divine power?[61] The latter does far more justice to the rhetorical intent of this section; for the severity and seeming hopelessness of the disciples' blindness is brought out to the same degree as the narrative's investment in them as the fruitful soil on which the gospel is to bear fruit. The crisis which results from this tension can only be resolved when the audience has reason to trust that God's promise to them can overcome their spiritual malady. Clearly, as Tolbert has noted, this section of Mark's narrative drives the audience to search, with some sense of urgency, for the cause and nature of the disciples' blindness.[62] However, the narrative does not easily allow the conclusion that Mark is here simply recommending that such concerns as the disciples manifest—desire for greatness, glory, and reward, exclusive claims on Jesus' power, etc.—are to be avoided by Christians.[63]

---

[59]E.g., Best, *Following Jesus*, 134-145; Juel, *Mark*, 116-17; Tolbert, 178-79.
[60]Tolbert, *Sowing the Gospel*, 200.
[61]Cf. Juel, 115-17.
[62]Tolbert, *Sowing the Gospel*, 200.
[63]Tolbert, *Sowing the Gospel*, 200.

A careful reading of the scene of Peter's "confession" of Jesus in 8:27-33 suggests another possibility.[64] For here the conclusion seems unavoidable that the behavior the disciples manifested both in this section and in the Jerusalem section is not the root cause of their blindness to the nature of Jesus' messiahship, but is, rather, symptomatic of a much deeper problem, viz., the hardening of their hearts and their captivity to Satan's power. That is to say, they require treatment of the problem, not just relief of their symptoms.[65]

We move to Peter's confession from the narrative's revelation in the previous section that the disciples share the "hardness of heart" of those opposed to Jesus, a condition which, as we saw in the previous chapter, represents the historicizing of the cosmic opposition of Satan to God's redemptive goals. The suddenness and inexplicable nature of Peter's apparent flash of insight has often been noted; nothing in the narrative up to this point has prepared the audience for it, and in fact Jesus' harshest condemnation of the disciples' blindness and deafness immediately precedes it (8:14-21). As Matthew recognized, some inspiration for Peter's statement seems to underlie it (cf. Matt. 16:17-19); for Matthew, it comes from the "Father in heaven." In Mark, such an indication is lacking; in fact, as Juel has suggested, the inspiration Mark has in mind may derive from the opposite source.[66] The scene immediately takes on the aura of an exorcism, with "rebuking" (ἐπιτιμῶν) going on all over the place (8:30, 32, 33).[67] It climaxes with Jesus' identification of Peter with Satan himself. In light of the way the preceding section has moved the disciples closer to Jesus' enemies, who act out of their Satanic inspiration, the audience may understand Peter's confession, like those of the demon-possessed (1:24; 3:11; 5:7), as stemming from Satan.

---

[64]See Kelber's suggestion that characterizing Peter's statement as a confession is a misconstrual of the scene; he suggests it be termed Peter's "confrontation" (*Mark's Story of Jesus*, 48).

[65]Moreover, as we have suggested above, Mark views "hardness of heart" as a condition of the world in general, something from which human beings need to be rescued.

[66]Juel, *Master of Surprise*, 74.

[67]The word is used almost exclusively to refer to Jesus' exorcizing activity: 1:25; 3:12; 4:39 (the wind and the waves); 9:25.

The development of the controversy between Jesus and the disciples in the ensuing narrative bears out this suggestion. The "debates" between Jesus and his disciples in 8:27-10:45 allow the audience to view the way in which the characters' beliefs about messiahship and divine power come to be expressed in their actions. That is, both Jesus and the disciples display a unity between their theology or ideological point of view and their behavior.[68] Jesus' teachings about the nature of divine power, the necessity of suffering, and the attitude toward the "least"—all stemming from his "possession" by the Holy Spirit (1: 10)—are expressed in both the general shape and the particulars of his ministry. 10:45 is perhaps the clearest statement of this unity. Jesus' teaching that "whoever wishes to become great among you must be your servant" is grounded (γαρ) in the shape of his own messianic charge: "For the Son of Man came not to be served but to serve, and to give his life a ransom for many."[69] Likewise, the disciples' understanding of Jesus' messiahship, one which rejects or is unable to comprehend any notion of suffering (8:32; 9:32), but is based rather on the hope of messianic glory and the avoidance of suffering,[70] issues in action commensurate with this understanding: arguing over who is the greatest (9:33-34), wanting to prevent anyone outside the "power center" from performing God's work (9:38), concern for their reward (10:28), and wanting to sit at Jesus' side in his glory (10:35-37). This relationship between ideology and ethics suggests that it is not the concern for glory itself that blocks the disciples' capacity to "think the things of God,"[71] but the other way around: Satan's grasp on their minds leads to their misconstrual and failure. As Robinson puts it, Mark leads the audience to see "that the confusion of men's minds is a power over man requiring divine action to be overcome."[72] Thus the narrative

---

[68]See Robinson, *The Problem of History*, 99-100.

[69]Of course, the predictions of his passion express this view as well (8:31; 9:30-31; 10:32-34).

[70]Cf. Peter's attitude toward Jesus' words about his suffering (8:32) to his reaction to Jesus' glory as revealed in the transfiguration (9:5) (Tolbert, *Sowing the Gospel*, 205).

[71]See Tolbert, *Sowing the Gospel*, 209.

[72]*The Problem of History*, 98-100.

does not serve to portray a catalogue of vices in the. hopes that the audience will adjust its behavior accordingly, but presents God engaged through Jesus in a battle over the human condition brought about by Satan's confusion of minds and hardening of hearts. The narrative brings to painful expression the necessity of following Jesus in order to "save one's life," and the impossibility of doing so without divine action. This is especially clear at two rhetorically strategic points in this section, where human impotence with respect to Satan's grasp is poignantly voiced. The disciples' failure to cast out the demon from the epileptic boy requires Jesus' intervention, which leads to an exchange between Jesus and the father of the boy. "All things can be done for the one who believes," Jesus proclaims, whereupon the father of the boy replies—some manuscripts say "with tears"— "I believe; help my unbelief!" It is a prayer, precisely that which, according Jesus, must be employed to cast out "this kind" of demon (9:29). The location of this scene—the only exorcism in this half of the Gospel—between scenes displaying the disciples' obduracy gives the narrative a contrapuntal structure, moving the audience back and forth between human failure and divine promise.

The same rhetorical goal seems to underlie the disciples' equally urgent question in 10:26; Jesus' statements about the rich man highlight the apparent impossibility of faithful response to God on the part of humans (10:23-25). The disciples become "greatly astounded" (περισσῶς ἐξεπλήσσοντο) and ask, "Then who is able to be saved?" (10:26). Jesus' reply, like the question, goes beyond the context of the immediate discussion and addresses in a fundamental way the predicament of humans as expressed by the narrative, a predicament which drives the characters and the audience to the promise of God: "Jesus looked at them and said, 'For humans it is not possible, but not for God; for all things are possible for God'" (10:27). Once again, this promise comes in the midst of the portrayal of the disciples' confusion, fear, and ensnarement by the structures of the world. Lest this seem an easy "out" of the dilemma, the immediately ensuing discussion both confirms that God will create new community for those embraced by the promise, but it also suggests that that new reality will be characterized by conflict between it and the hardened world. That is to say, the promise of God is not a simple solution to the problem of faithful response, but in many ways creates the problem.

"JUST AS HE TOLD YOU": PROMISE AND FAILURE IN THE PASSION NARRATIVE (11:1-16:8)

It is with this sense of crisis and hope that we move toward the climax of the story in Jerusalem. Here the juxtaposition of failure and promise comes to a climax, as Mark portrays the disciples' eventual rejection of Jesus; at the same time, this section builds an unmistakable momentum of promises made and promises kept.

A few features of the final (narrated) chapter in the disciples' story require comment. What has to strike the audience at this point is the seeming incongruity between the increasing inevitability of the disciples' utter failure, which now comes as no surprise to Jesus, and which, in fact, he predicts (14:18, 27, 30), and Jesus' continued, even intensified investment in them, expressed perhaps most poignantly by his desire to spend his last hours with the very ones who would betray, deny, and "fall away" from him. It is this continued investment, I would suggest, which speaks most strongly against a polemical reading of the disciples' rhetorical role in the Gospel. The disciples' imperceptive participation in the events leading to Jesus' death expresses most powerfully the apparent impossibility that they will ever become the good soil in which the gospel will yield a harvest. Yet in the same way that Jesus' death itself brings to the surface the depth and breadth of the world's opposition to God's goals, which can only be overcome when God acts to vindicate Jesus in the resurrection, the disciples' utter failure represents the impossibility of a faithful response to God in the present age, apart from God's acting on the behalf of humans.

Over against the graphic portrayal of the disciples' failure, then, the narrative builds a momentum through the rhetoric of prediction and fulfillment.[73] As the audience experiences the confirmation of many and various predictions of Jesus in the narrative itself, it gains confidence that those predictions of Jesus that reach

---

[73]Cf. Juel, *Master of Surprise*, 114-15; Lincoln, 197-98.

beyond the plotted narrative are reliable as well. This works to ensure, first, that the audience will see the endangerment to the promise posed by Jesus' move toward the cross as something Jesus fully expects, and as an inevitable component of God's redemptive purposes. The passion predictions in 8:27-10:52 are the most obvious indications of this. Events unfold exactly as Mark's Jesus has predicted they would: Jesus is "handed over to the chief priests and scribes" (10:33; 14:42), who "condemn him to death" (10:33; 14:64), spit on him (10:34; 14:65), and mock him (10:34; 15:31). They, in turn, "hand Jesus over to the Gentiles" (10:33; 15:1), who flog him (10:34; 15:15), mock him (10:34; 15:17-20), and kill him (10:34; 15:24). This is not to say that Jesus' death is "necessary" in some abstract theological sense, but rather, as suggested in the previous chapter, that it is inevitable given the clash between "the things of God" and "the things of human beings." Jesus' death is integrally linked to the boundary-shattering ministry he exercised, which the present power structures—neither "Jewish" nor gentile—could not countenance.[74]

The same holds true for the predictions concerning the disciples' abandonment of Jesus. Their failure is not predestined in the sense that it represents God's moving them around like chess pieces, but rather it is inevitable given the reality that God's reign overlaps the present age in its Satan-induced opposition to God. The tremendous irony here is that it is precisely in the "promise" of the disciples' failure that the reliability of the promise of their resurrection lies. It is the narrative's way of displaying how God works in the world in a way that acknowledges the reality of human existence in a world opposed to God; but precisely through that acknowledgment, God's promise of life achieves credibility such that it can serve as the ground for a future for human existence.

The promises which deserve special note in terms of our concern here—the fate of the disciples—are those which extend beyond the plotted narrative, those in chapter 13 (especially 13:5-23),

---

[74]Other predictions that help build this momentum include Jesus' instructions for his entrance into Jerusalem (11:1-6) and for the preparations for the passion (14:16); in both cases, the disciples find "everything just as Jesus had told them" (14:17).

that promise the disciples a role in the post-resurrection period, and those suggesting a post-resurrection "reconciliation" between Jesus and the failed disciples (14:28, 16:7). Given the establishment of the reliability of Jesus' word, it seems inescapable that Jesus' words concerning the future of the disciples ought to carry significant weight. The question is not whether the disciples have a future; the assurance that they do marks a principal rhetorical goal of their portrayal. The question is rather, first, in what sense they do, that is, how their future is created, and, second, what Mark accomplishes rhetorically by choosing not to narrate it.

First, the rhetorical force of Mark's ending makes it a fitting conclusion to a story in which divine promise and human failure have been relentlessly juxtaposed.[75] In my view, the much-discussed question of whether the women actually kept their silence or not (16:8) is misguided. The reliability of Jesus' promise that "after I am raised up, I will go before you to Galilee" (14:28) is actually confirmed by the promise which precedes it: "You will all become deserters" (14:27). The point is precisely that God overcomes human failure through the power of God's promise. Should the women's fear and silence prove capable of thwarting God's intention to reconcile the disciples to Jesus, every other promise in the Gospel becomes suspect, as well, as does God's power and God's character.[76]

Rather, the inevitability of the disciples' own "resurrection" in the face of their utter failure (and here I would include the women at the tomb) represents the Gospel's rhetorical goal. The disciples cannot escape Jesus so easily, and neither can the audience. The reconciliation takes place because God wills it. It happens not because of any change in the disciples' point of view or behavior, but in spite of it. The Gospel does not call on readers to fill in the gap left by the rejection of the disciples by God by being more faithful disciples themselves; given the way Mark has portrayed the world in his narrative, that would hardly be good news. Mark's narrative puts

---

[75]Cf. Lincoln, 195-99.

[76]Cf. Petersen, "When is the End;" this does not, however, necessitate the conclusion that "Mark did not mean what he said" in 16:8. That resolves the tension in the other direction.

the audience on notice that no such evasionary tactics will keep them safe from God's redemptive purposes. It graphically portrays the lack of a future for the world without God's intervention, but it puts no one in a position to lay exclusive claim to it. It is God's action that creates a future for the disciples, and a future for the world. Austin Farrer has put it eloquently and poignantly:

> St. Mark offers small comfort or support to believers in natural wisdom or virtue. Nothing earthly, not even Jesus in the flesh, not the healing touch of those blessed hands, or the divine persuasions of his tongue, not the spectacle of his passion or the angelic tidings of his resurrection, nothing but the Godhead of Jesus apparent in his risen being could lift men up to take hold of the life of God. Not until Peter and the rest were apprehended by the Lord of Glory in Galilee would they be made to stand, for the Godhead itself would have come upon them, from which we can no more run than we can from the dawn.[77]

CONCLUSIONS

Thus in rhetorically significant ways, the conflict between Jesus and the disciples and that between Jesus and the authorities interweave, interpret, and illumine each other. The first has to do with issues over which the controversies come to evolve. Like the religious leaders, the disciples fail to grasp the essential nature of God's boundary-shattering reign, which expresses itself in a conception of messianic authority oriented not to power over others, but power exercised to spread holiness and life to a world locked in Satan's grasp. Both the disciples and the authorities stand to lose much in such a kingdom; both fail to grasp the paradoxical truth driven home time and again by the Markan Jesus through his teaching, healing, and suffering, that only by losing one's life to the powers of the world which stand opposed to God can one save it.

The disciples' story line is further linked to that of the authorities by the way in which the narrative presents the source of their opposition to Jesus. For both, it is their relation to a world in Satan's grasp that issues in their blindness, unfaithfulness, and

---

[77]Austin Farrer, *The Glass of Vision* (London: Dacre Press, 1958), 143.

opposition. Like the authorities, the disciples' opposition requires God's radical intervention.

Thus, most important, both conflicts lead to a crisis concerning the promises of God. When all is said and done, only the reality of God's power to bring life out of death can render meaningful the suffering that results from living in the light of God's reign in a world opposed to God meaningful. Jesus' death at the hands of those powers results, as we saw, precisely from his willingness to live in this way. It is God who vindicates Jesus' untraditional and boundary-shattering messiahship, who reaffirms the promise of redemption in the face of its endangerment by the authorities. Without a sense of confidence that God has, in fact, reaffirmed God's promises by raising Jesus, the death-dealing forces of this world have the final say, and God is proven either unwilling or unable to make good on what has been promised.

The way I have suggested Mark wishes the audience to respond to the conflict between Jesus and the disciples moves in this same direction and with this same logic. The disciples' malady goes beyond what human effort can overcome, and is due to their existence in a world in Satan's grasp. Mark portrays their obduracy in such a way that the audience cannot but recognize and experience their helplessness; and so far from rejecting them, the audience is led to exclaim with them, "Who then can be saved?" The narrative has so interwoven the fate of the disciples with the fate of the gospel that if, in the end, God is not able to create of them "fishers of human beings," as God promised, once again, human beings have the final word, and God's character and power is called radically into question. Without a future for the disciples, there is no good news, only failure and darkness; if the disciples' future is closed, there can be no future for the audience either.

The question becomes, of course, why Mark has chosen to compel the audience to make these connections; why, in other words, neither Jesus' resurrection nor reconciliation lies within the narrative as Mark has plotted it. I would note, first, that we have seen from the very opening verses of the Gospel how much Mark expects of his audience. It is, as we noted, a very audience-oriented composition, full of gaps and holes which require the audience's participation.

And further, I would return to the image of Mark's rhetorical balancing act. For Mark, the reality of God's promise, character, and capacity to bring life out of death must be proclaimed over against the reality of the world in which he and his audience exists. As Via has put it, "The kingdom overlaps a segment in the history of hardness of heart . . . . Since faith is given by the *uncompleted* eschatological salvation event, the disciple both has faith and does not."[78] The resurrection of Jesus and the rehabilitation of the disciples does not provide any ultimate closure to the story; nor would it even if it were narrated. It does not solve the problem of the conflict, but rather brings it to its clearest expression, for it makes both sides of the conflict equally undeniable. Present Christian existence is based on radical trust in God's promises, not on a false sense of victory. God's past actions reveal that God is faithful to those promises, but do not resolve the tension between them and the reality of a world as yet incompletely redeemed. They serve to create a future for those embraced by the promises, a future in which human opposition and failure do not have the last word. For Mark, Christian existence is characterized by the tension between Good Friday and Easter, between the reality of an unredeemed world and a hope in God's promises firmly grounded in that reality. It is a gap which can only be filled by radical trust in God's promises.

---

[78]Via, *The Ethics of Mark's Gospel*, 186.

CONCLUSION

THE ENDANGERED AND
REAFFIRMED PROMISES

In this study I have sought to accomplish two principal goals, one with respect to methodology, the other with respect to a particular reading of Mark's Gospel. First, I have attempted to set forth the merits of a particular reading strategy for biblical narrative. My ultimate goal in reading Mark's Gospel, and biblical narrative in general, is to place myself—and my audience—in the most advantageous position to experience and be impacted by the claims the narrative attempts to exercise through its rhetoric. In this sense, I see myself engaged in a form of theological interpretation which seeks to interpret and further the New Testament witness to the gospel of Jesus Christ. Granted, no method can guarantee fruitful results; in the end, it is the reading itself which will prove persuasive or not. That does not mean, however, that attention to method is unimportant. I have argued that an approach to biblical narrative which focuses on the effect, the rhetorical impact of the narrative is especially appropriate for theological engagement with the text, because it calls attention to what biblical narratives are attempting to *do* to those who encounter them, namely, to render the gospel's claim on them in some way irresistible. Historical and textually-centered literary work play a crucial role in this task, but the special merit of an audience-oriented approach is that it attempts to lay bear the full impact of a text in both its cognitive and affective dimensions. The goal of audience-oriented criticism, as I see it, is to prepare an audience for an encounter with the biblical narrative that will, in fact, result in the experience of God's salvation. To put it in more traditional theological terms, those of Phillip Melanchthon, "To know Christ is to know his benefits."

The second goal of this study has been to apply some of these methodological insights to a reading of conflict in Mark's Gospel. I tried to build on the observations of recent audience-oriented interpreters (e.g., Robert Fowler) who highlight the essentially rhetorical nature of Mark's Gospel. That is, I am not as interested in how the conflict between Jesus and the religious leaders and that between Jesus and his disciples reflects the historical situation of Mark's first-century community, or even how these conflicts convey certain theological ideas about Jesus, discipleship, etc. I am more concerned with the way in which an audience might be moved to respond to a narrative which sets God's promises of redemption over against quite powerful forces opposed to God. My goal has been to elucidate those features of the narrative which, when an audience is attuned to them, can be experienced as both acknowledging the reality of the audience's seemingly unredeemed world and reaffirming God's promises to bring about the redemption of that world. I suggested in Chapter 3 that the prologue to the Gospel (1:1-15) prepares the way for such an experience by setting the proclamation of the confirmation of God's promises over against narrative elements that threaten those promises. In Chapter 4 I attempted to read the story of the conflict between Jesus and the authorities in such a way that the reality of the threat posed to Jesus by the authorities emerged with the same force as the reality of God's triumph over them.

Finally, in Chapter 5, I emphasized the way in which, in Mark, an audience will be moved to experience Jesus' conflict with the disciples in a manner similar to Jesus' conflict with the authorities. Not only are the promises of God endangered by overt opposition to God's plans from outside the community of the faithful, but even by those who are enlisted by God and who experience at some significant level the power of the gospel. These two conflicts, taken together, address the audience's own experience of conflict between God's promises and opposition to them from within and without. The narrative leads readers to experience both the necessity and the apparent impossibility of being embraced by the gospel. The Gospel is punctuated with cries which express this dilemma (e.g., 9:24; 10:26; 14:72; even 15:3), and it gives grounds for trust in God's capacity to resolve it.

I have suggested at several points that a crucial component of this narrative rhetoric involves creating the sense within the audience that Mark's story of Jesus, which is characterized by this tension between promise and its endangerment, is part of a larger story, the story of Israel, whose temporal coordinates envelope the audience's time and place, and which exhibits the same tension. In my view, Mark counts on his audience's familiarity with this feature of God's previous dealings with Israel to further the rhetorical goals of his narrative. That is, in a sense, the confidence that God's promises prove reliable in the face of human opposition needs further grounding than provided in the story of Jesus itself. Mark is asking his audience to place ultimate trust in the character of a God who makes promises and fulfills them. To the degree that Mark can get his audience to see his story of Jesus, the authorities, and the disciples in this light, his rhetorical goals will be given much greater force.

One of the most important rhetorical goals of the New Testament as a whole is to connect the saving activity of God in Jesus to God's promises to and previous dealings with Israel as recorded in Israel's scriptures.[1] That the two are continuous is a

---

[1] The question of the "Old Testament in the New" has, of course, been much studied and debated; a full review of the history of this question is not possible here, but some of the basic approaches will be outlined below. Important studies of the question include C.H. Dodd, *According to the Scriptures: The Substructure of New Testament Theology* (London: Nisbet, 1952); Barnabas Lindars, *New Testament Apologetic* (London: SCM, 1961); more recently, Donald Juel, *Messianic Exegesis: Christological Interpretation of the Old Testament in Early Christianity* (Philadelphia: Fortress Press, 1988). Studies on Mark's use of the Old Testament include Ulrich Mauser, *Christ in the Wilderness: The Wilderness Theme in the Second Gospel and its Basis in the Biblical Tradition* (London: SCM, 1963); J. D. M. Derrett, *The Making of Mark: The Scriptural Bases of the Earliest Gospel* (Shipston-on-Stour: Drink water, 1985); Wolfgang Roth, *Hebrew Gospel: Cracking the code of Mark* (Oak park, Ill.: Meyer-stone Books, 1988); H.-J. Steichele, *Der leidende Sohn Gottes: eine Untersuchung einiger alttestamentlicher Motive in der Christologie des Markusevangeliums* (Biblische Untersuchungen 14; Regensburg: Pustet, 1980); Joel

presupposition of early Christianity: The God who raised Jesus from the dead is the God of Abraham, Isaac, and Jacob (e.g., Romans 4). Precisely *how* they are related presented one of the most significant theological challenges faced by those who first experienced God's salvation in Jesus (and continues to challenge Christian theology today). Paul wrestled with the problem in nearly all of his writings; recent studies of Paul's use of scripture have explored his insistence on the continuity between God's promises to Israel and the "Christ event."[2] Indeed, Leander Keck and others have suggested convincingly that the phrase "the righteousness of God," especially as found in Romans, denotes God's "covenant faithfulness." That is, in bringing salvation through a crucified Messiah, God is not changing God's *modus operandi* in some capricious way, as might (and did to many) appear at first glance, but rather is revealing the central feature of God's "character": constancy and integrity in dealing with God's people Israel.

Although Paul seeks to connect the God of Jesus Christ with the God of Israel's Scriptures through discursive argument in his letters, the Gospels do so by a different mode of argumentation: narrative. Each of the Gospels, for example, begins its story by connecting it with the larger story of God's dealings with Israel and the world: Matthew rehearses Israel's whole history through Jesus' genealogy; Mark shows how John the Baptist's appearance fulfills promises in Exodus and Isaiah; Luke patterns the births of John the Baptist and Jesus after the births of previous of Israel's great figures; and John proclaims that Jesus is the Word by and through which God brought all things into being.

Mark's narrative argument concerns us here, of course; it is precisely by showing the connection between God's past dealings with Israel and the story of Jesus that Mark addresses the tension between God's promises of salvation in Jesus and the reality of a seemingly unredeemed world. The opposition and conflict which characterized Jesus' ministry, both from external "enemies" of God

---

Marcus, *The Way of the Lord: Christological Exegesis of the Old Testament in the Gospel of Mark* (Louisville: Westminster/John Knox, 1992).

[2]E.g., Richard Hays, *Echoes of Scripture in the Letters of Paul* (New Haven: Yale University Press, 1989).

and internal failures of the community Jesus sought to establish, links up at a very basic and rhetorically powerful level with the general shape of the story of Israel's attempts to live out of God's promises to it. From the choosing of Abraham to the Latter Prophets' pronouncements of an everlasting reign of peace, and continuing into Israel's post-biblical experiences, the promises of God as played out in the life of Israel were constantly endangered in just this way. From outside Israel, its enemies threatened Israel's very existence (Egypt, the Philistines, Babylonia, the Greek and Roman empires); while from inside, Israel's unfaithfulness to God strained the covenant God made with it almost to the breaking point.[3] Moreover, as the idea of a malevolent force opposed to God developed, largely through the emergence of apocalyptic thought, Satan entered the scene and lent an extra-historical element to the conflict.

Indeed, Israel's Scriptures are infused with this theme of God's endangered promises; it is arguably their principal concern (an observation which later Christians were quick to turn to their advantage as justification for God's supposed abandonment of Israel in favor of Christians). But the endangerment of the promise is only half of the pattern: God's reaffirmation of those promises in the wake of their threatened undermining emerges every bit as clearly.[4]

Thus I have attempted to show that a fruitful way to understand how the Gospel of Mark employs the various conflicts in the story of Jesus in service of his rhetorical aim is to recognize that the Gospel makes use of a narrative pattern deeply imbedded in Israel's scriptures.[5] Mark's story of Jesus, whose driving force is the conflict

---

[3]At many points in Israel's story, of course, these two sources of endangerment are in a cause and effect relationship: The biblical authors often (but not always) attributed Israel's defeats at the hands of other nations to God's chastisement of the people for their unfaithfulness—e.g., it was God who brought the Assyrians against Israel and the Babylonians upon Judah (II Kings). The entire Deuteronomic History, and many of the prophetic writings, are infused with this perspective. But this was not always the case (see, e.g., Pss 44:9-26; 89:19-52; Job).

[4]See, e.g., Amos 9.

[5]Nils Dahl first suggested this theme in a seminal essay addressed to the question of the relation between the Hebrew Bible and the New Testament ("The Crucified Messiah and the Endangered Promises," in *Jesus the Christ: The Historical Origins of Christological Doctrine* [ed. Donald Juel; Minneapolis: Fortress Press,

between the promise of God of salvation in Jesus and opposition to that promise, emerges from, echoes, and is intertwined inextricably with the narrative pattern that characterizes much of Israel's history: the endangered and reaffirmed promises of God. For Mark, this motif provides a familiar and rhetorically powerful framework for presenting Jesus' seemingly unlikely messiahship, and for addressing the tension created by the conflicts and experienced by the reader between the hopes generated by Jesus and the realities experienced by the Gospel's audience. When an audience hears the story of Jesus as part of the larger story of Israel, as Mark certainly wishes it to, that audience stands addressed not only by Mark's text but by the larger narrative as well. The reliability of God's character and promises is consistently shown in the way in which God overcomes cosmic opposition and human faithlessness by using human intention which stems from this faithlessness to bring God's goals to fruition (cf. Gen 50:20). That is, those who think they are opposing God's plans, or who do so out of ignorance, actually turn out, ironically, to have played a role in accomplishing them.

The good news that Mark's Gospel proclaims, and that the narrative seeks to make a reality for its audience, is that there is, indeed, a future for the disciples, for creation, and for the audience, and that that future comes often in spite of, not because of, human initiative. The rhetorical effectiveness of Mark's narrative lies in its willingness to bring its audience to an experience both of the world as it really is—with all that endangers God's promise of a future—and the world as it ought to be, transformed by the affirmation of God's promise of redemption, and in its ability to transform fearful, unfaithful disciples into agents of that redemption.

1991], 65-79); he suggests that precisely this narrative pattern provides a fruitful way of understanding that relation. Dahl is well known for his assertion that the earliest reflection on the significance of Jesus took the shape of exegesis of scripture. Jesus' identity as the Christ formed the presupposition of this reflection, and interpretation provided the content of the conviction that "all God's promises find their 'yes'" in Jesus. This recognition, though, he observes, has left the modern "critical" audience in a quandary: critical scholarship has rendered it difficult, if not impossible, to allow the Old Testament to be read christologically. He proposes that the connection needs to be seen on a literary level, along the lines suggested above.

BIBLIOGRAPHY

Alter, Robert. *The Art of Biblical Narrative*. New York: Basic Books, Inc., 1981.

————. *The World of Biblical Literature*. New York: Basic Books, Inc., 1992.

Anderson, Charles. "New Criticism." In *Literary Theories in Praxis*, ed. Shirley F. Stanton, 205-33. Philadelphia: University of Pennsylvania, 1987.

Anderson, Janice Capel and Stephen D. Moore, eds. *Mark and Method: New Approaches in Biblical Studies*. Minneapolis: Fortress Press, 1992.

Auerbach, Eric. *Mimesis: The Representation of Reality in Western Literature*. Translated by W. Trask. Princeton: Princeton University Press, 1953.

Austin, J. L. *How to do Things with Words*. Oxford: Oxford University Press, 1962.

Banks, Robert. *Jesus and the Law in the Synoptic Tradition*. SNTSMS 28. Cambridge: Cambridge University Press, 1975.

Barlink, Heinrich. *Anfängliches Evangelium: Ein Beitrag zur näheren Bestimmung der theologischen Motive im Markusevangelium*. Kampen: Kok, 1977.

Barton, John. *Reading the Old Testament: Method in Biblical Study*. Philadelphia: Westminster Press, 1984.

Bassler, Jouette. "The Parable of the Loaves." *JR* 66 (1986): 157-72.

Bauer, Walter, William F. Arndt, F. Wilbur Gingrich, and Frederick W. Danker. *A Greek-English Lexicon of the New Testament and other Early Christian Literature*. Chicago: University of Chicago Press, 1979.

Beardslee, William. *Literary Criticism of the New Testament*. Philadelphia: Fortress Press, 1969.

Berg, Temma F. "Reading In/To Mark." *Semeia* 48 (1989): 187-206.

Best, Ernest. "Discipleship in Mark 8:22-10:52." *Scottish Journal of Theology* 23 (1970): 323-37.

————. *Following Jesus: Discipleship in the Gospel of Mark*. Sheffield: JSOT Press, 1981.

————. "The Role of the Disciples in Mark." *NTS* 23 (1976-7): 377-401.

Bilezekian, G. G. *The Liberated Gospel: A Comparison of the Gospel of Mark and Greek Tragedy*. Grand Rapids: Baker, 1977.

Black, C. Clifton. *The Disciples According to Mark: Markan Redaction in Current Debate*. Journal for the Study of the New Testament Supplement Series 27. Sheffield: JSOT Press, 1989.

Bloom, Harold. *The Anxiety of Influence*. New York: Oxford University Press, 1973.

Boomershine, Thomas. "Mark 16:8 and the Apostolic Commission." *JBL* 100 (1981): 225-39.

Booth, Wayne. *The Rhetoric of Fiction*. Chicago: University of Chicago Press, 1983.

Boring, M. Eugene. "The Christology of Mark: Hermeneutical Issues for Systematic Theology." *Semeia* 32 (1983): 125-153.

———. "Mark 1:1-15 and the Beginning of the Gospel." *Semeia* 52 (1991): 43-91.

———. Review of *The Christology of Mark's Gospel*, by Jack D. Kingsbury. In *JBL* 104 (1985): 732-35.

Bornkamm, Günther, Gerhard Barth, and Heinz Joachim Held. *Tradition and Interpretation in Matthew*. Philadelphia: Westminster, 1963.

Bultmann, Rudolf. *History of the Synoptic Tradition*. Translated by John Marsh. New York and San Francisco: Harper & Row, 1963.

———. *Theology of the New Testament*. Translated by Kendrick Grobel. New York: Charles Scribner's Sons, 1951.

Buttrick, G. A., ed. *The Interpreter's Dictionary of the Bible*, ed. G. A. Buttrick. 5 volumes. Nashville: Abingdon, 1962. S. v. "Biblical Theology, Contemporary," by Krister Stendahl.

Camery-Hoggatt, Jerry. *Irony in Mark's Gospel: Text and Subtext*. Cambridge: Cambridge University Press, 1992.

Charlesworth, James, ed. *The Old Testament Pseudepigrapha Volume 1: Apocalyptic Literature and Testaments*. Garden City, NY: Doubleday & Co., 1983.

Chatman, Seymour. *Story and Discourse: Narrative Structure in Fiction and Film*. Ithica, NY: Cornell University Press, 1978.

Chilton, Bruce. *A Galilean Rabbi and His Bible: Jesus' Use of the Interpreted Scripture of his Time*. Good News Studies 8. Wilmington, DE: Michael Glazier, 1984.

Conzelmann, Hans. *The Theology of St. Luke*. Translated by Geoffrey Buswell. Philadelphia: Fortress Press, 1982.

Cook, Michael *Mark's Treatment of the Jewish Leaders*. NovTSup 51. Leiden: E.J. Brill, 1978.

Crossan, John Dominic. *Who Killed Jesus? Exposing the Roots of Anti-Semitism in the Gospel Story of the Death of Jesus*. San Francisco: Harper Collins, 1995.

Culler, Jonathan. *On Deconstruction: Theory and Criticism after Structuralism*. Ithaca, NY: Cornell University Press, 1981.

———. *Structuralist Poetics: Structuralism, Linguistics, and the Study of Literature*. Ithaca, NY: Cornell University Press, 1975.

Cullmann, Oscar *The Christology of the New Testament*. Translated by Shirley Guthrie and Charles Hall. Philadelphia: Westminster Press, 1963.

Culpepper, R. Alan. *Anatomy of the Fourth Gospel: A Study in Literary Design*. Philadelphia: Fortress Press, 1983.

Cunningham, David. *Faithful Persuasion: In Aid of a Rhetoric of Christian Theology*. Notre Dame: University of Notre Dame Press, 1991.

Dahl, Nils. "Contradictions in Scripture." In *Studies in Paul*. Minneapolis: Augsburg, 1977.

———. *Jesus the Christ: The Historical Origins of Christological Doctrine*, ed. Donald Juel. Minneapolis: Fortress Press, 1991.

Danove, Paul. *The End of Mark's Story: A Methodological Study*. Leiden: E.J. Brill, 1993.

Derrett, J.D.M. *The Making of Mark: The Scriptural Bases of the Earliest Gospel*. Shipston-on-Stour: Drinkwater, 1985.

Dewey, Joanna. "The Literary Structure of the Controversy Stories in Mark 2:1-3:6," in *The Interpretation of Mark*, ed. William Telford, 109-118. Philadelphia: Fortress Press and London: SPCK, 1985.

———. *Markan Public Debate: Literary Technique, Concentric Structure, and Theology in Mark 2:1-3:6*. SBLDS 48. Chico, CA: Scholars Press, 1980.

———. "Point of View and the Disciples in Mark." *Society of Biblical Literature 1982 Seminar Papers*, ed. K. H. Richards. Chico, CA: Scholars Press, 1982.

Dibelius, Martin. *From Tradition to Gospel*. Translated by E. L. Woolf. London: Ivor Nicholson & Watson, 1934.

———. *Gospel Criticism and Christology*. London: Ivor, Nicholson & Watson, 1935.

Dodd, C.H. *According to the Scriptures: The Substructure of New Testament Theology*. London: Nisbet, 1952.

Donahue, John. *Are You the Christ? The Trial Narrative in the Gospel of Mark*. SBLDS 10. Missoula, MT: Scholars Press, 1973.

———. *The Gospel in Parable*. Philadelphia: Fortress Press, 1988.

———. "Jesus as Parable of God in the Gospel of Mark." *Interpretation* 32 (1978): 369-86.

———. "A Neglected Factor in the Theology of Mark." *JBL* 101 (1982): 563-594.

———. *The Theology and Setting of Discipleship in the Gospel of Mark*. Milwaukee: Marquette University, 1983.

Donin, Hayim. *To Be a Jew: A Guide to Jewish Observance in Contemporary Life*. New York: Basic Books, 1972.

Douglas, Mary. *Natural Symbols: Explorations in Cosmology*. New York: Pantheon, 1982.

———. *Purity and Danger: An Analysis of the Concepts of Pollution and Taboo*. London: Routledge & Kegan Paul, 1966.

Drury, John. "Mark 1:1-15: An Interpretation." In *Alternative Approaches to New Testament Study*, ed. A. E. Harvey, 25-36. London: SPCK, 1985.

———. *Parables in the Gospels: History and Allegory*. New York: Crossroad, 1985.

Eagleton, Terry. *Literary Theory: An Introduction*. Minneapolis: University of Minnesota Press, 1983.

Edwards, Richard A. *Matthew's Story of Jesus*. Philadelphia: Fortress Press, 1985.

Ellis, P. F. "Patterns and Structures of Mark's Gospel." In *Biblical Studies in Contemporary Thought*, ed. M. Ward, 54-79. Somerville, MA: Greeno, Hadden and Co., 1975.

Farrer, Austin. *The Glass of Vision*. London: Dacre Press, 1958.

Fish, Stanley. *Is There a Text in This Class? The Authority of Interpretive Communities*. Cambridge: Harvard University Press, 1980.

Fishbane, Michael. *Biblical Interpretaiton in Ancient Israel*. Oxford: Clarendon, 1985.

Foley, John Miles *Oral-Formulaic Theory and Research: An Introduction and Annotated Bibliography*. New York: Garland Press, 1985.

Fowler, Robert. *Let the Reader Understand: Reader-Response Criticism and the Gospel of Mark*. Minneapolis: Fortress Press, 1991.

———. *Loaves and Fishes: the Function of the Feeding Stories in the Gospel of Mark*. SBLDS 54. Chico, CA: Scholars Press, 1981.

Frei, Hans. *The Eclipse of Biblical Narrative: A Study in Eighteenth and Nineteenth Century Hermeneutics*. New Haven: Yale University Press, 1974.

258   *The Endangered Promises*

————. *The Identity of Jesus Christ.* Philadelphia: Fortress Press, 1975.

Funk, Robert. *Poetics of Biblical Narrative.* Sonoma: Polebridge, 1988.

Gnilka, J. *Das Evangelium nach Markus.* Evangelisch-Katholisches Kommentar zum Neuen Testament 2. Zürich: Benziger/Neukirchener, 1978.

Goppelt, Leonhard. *Theology of the New Testament, Vol. 1: The Ministry of Jesus in its Theological Significance.* Translated by John Alsup. Grand Rapids, MI: William B. Eerdmans Publishing, 1981.

Guelich, R. A. "'The Beginning of the Gospel'--Mark 1:1-15." *Biblical Research* 27 (1982): 1-14.

————. *Mark 1-8:26.* Word Biblical Commentary 34A. Dallas: Word Books, 1989.

Hahn, Ferdinand *The Titles of Jesus in New Testament Christology.* Translated by Harold Knight and George Ogg. New York: World Publishing, 1969.

Halliwell, Stephen. *The Poetics of Aristotle: Translation and Commentary.* Chapel Hill, NC: University of North Carolina Press, 1987.

Hanson, James. Review of *A Rabbi Talks with Jesus: An Intermillennial, Interfaith Exchange*, by Jacob Neusner. In *Word and World* 14 (1996): 388-92.

Hawkin, David J. "The Incomprehension of the Disciples in the Marcan Redaction." *JBL* 91 (1972): 491-500.

Hay, David M. *Glory at the Right Hand: Psalm 110 in Early Christianity.* SBLMS 18. Nashville: Abingdon Press, 1973.

Hays, Richard. *Echoes of Scripture in the Letters of Paul.* New Haven: Yale University Press, 1989.

Hernadi, Paul. "Literary Theory: A Compass for Critics." *Critical Inquiry* 3 (1976): 369-86.

Hooker, Morna D. "The Beginning of the Gospel." In *The Future of Christology: Essays in Honor of Leander Keck*, ed. Abraham Malherbe and Wayne Meeks, 18-28. Minneapolis: Fortress Press, 1993.

————. *The Gospel According to Saint Mark.* Black's New Testament Commentaries. Peabody, MA: Hendrickson Publishers, 1991.

Hultgren, Arland J. *Jesus and His Adversaries: The Form and Function of the Conflict Stories in the Synoptic Tradition.* Minneapolis: Augsburg Publishing, 1979.

Hurst, L. D. and N. T. Wright, eds. *The Glory of Christ in the New Testament: Studies in Christology in Memory of George Bradford Caire.* Oxford: Clarendon Press, 1987.

Iser, Wolfgang. *The Act of Reading: A Theory of Aesthetic Response.* Baltimore: Johns Hopkins University Press, 1978.

————. *The Implied Reader: Patterns of Communication in Prose Fiction from Bunyan to Beckett.* Baltimore: Johns Hopkins University Press, 1974.

Jeremias, Joachim. *New Testament Theology: The Proclamation of Jesus.* Translated by John Bowden. New York: Charles Scribner's Sons, 1971.

Josipovici, Gabriel. *The Book of God: A Response to the Bible.* New Haven: Yale University Press, 1988.

Juel, Donald. *Mark.* Augsburg Commentary on the New Testament. Minneapolis: Augsburg Press, 1990.

————. *A Master of Surprise: Mark Interpreted.* Minneapolis: Fortress Press, 1994.

————. *Messiah and Temple: The Trial of Jesus in the Gospel of Mark.* SBLDS 31. Missoula, MT: Scholar's Press, 1977.

———. *Messianic Exegesis: Christological Interpretation of the Old Testament in Early Christianity.* Philadelphia: Fortress Press, 1988.

Kay, James F. "Theological Table-Talk: Myth or Narrative? Bultmann's 'New Testament and Mythology' Turns Fifty." *Theology Today* 48 (1991) 326-32.

Kazmierski, Carl R. *Jesus, the Son of God: A Study of the Markan Tradition and Its Redaction by the Evangelist.* Forschung zur Bibel 33. Würzburg: Echter Verlag, 1979.

Kealy, Sean. *Mark's Gospel: A History of its Interpretation.* New York: Paulist Press, 1982.

Keck, Leander. "The Introduction to Mark's Gospel." *NTS* 12 (1965): 352-370.

———. "Jesus in New Testament Christology." *Australian Biblical Review* 28 (1980): 1-20.

———. *Paul and his Letters.* Proclamation Commentaries. Philadelphia: Fortress Press, 1988.

———. "Toward the Renewal of New Testament Christology." *NTS* 32 (1986): 362-377.

Keifert, Patrick. "Interpretive Paradigms: A Proposal Concerning New Testament Christology." *Semeia* 32 (1983): 203-216.

Kelber, Werner. "Apostolic Tradition and the Form of the Gospel." In *Discipleship in the New Testament,* ed. Fernando F. Segovia, 24-46. Philadelphia: Fortress Press, 1985.

———. "Gospel Narrative and Critical Theory." *Biblical Theology Bulletin* 18 (1988): 130-136.

———. *Mark's Story of Jesus.* Philadelphia: Fortress Press, 1979.

———. *The Oral and the Written Gospel: The Hermeneutics of Speaking and Writing in the Synoptic Tradition, Mark, Paul, and Q.* Philadelphia: Fortress Press, 1983.

Kennedy, G.A. *New Testament Interpretation Through Rhetorical Criticism.* Chapel Hill, N.C.: University of North Carolina Press, 1984.

Kermode, Frank. *The Genesis of Secrecy: On the Interpretation of Narrative.* Cambridge, MA: Harvard University Press, 1979.

———. *The Art of Telling: Essays on Fiction.* Cambridge, MA: Harvard University Press, 1983.

Kingsbury, Jack D. *The Christology of Mark's Gospel.* Philadelphia: Fortress Press, 1983.

———. *Conflict in Luke: Jesus, Authorities, Disciples.* Minneapolis: Fortress Press, 1991.

———. *Conflict in Mark: Jesus, Authorities, Disciples.* Minneapolis: Fortress Press, 1989.

———. "The Religious Authorities in the Gospel of Mark." *NTS* 36 (1990): 42-65.

Koch, D.-A. "Inhaltiche Gliederung und geographischer Aufriss im Markus-evangelium." *NTS* 29 (1983): 145-66.

Kraftchick, Steven. "A Legacy in Probate: Bultmann's Use of History." Unpublished paper, 1989.

Krieger, Murray. *A Window to Criticism.* Princeton: Princeton University Press, 1964.

Kümmel, Werner Georg. *Introduction to the New Testament.* Translated by H. C. Kee. Nashville: Abingdon, 1975.

Lentricchia, Frank. *After the New Criticism.* Chicago: University of Chicago Press, 1980.

Levenson, Jon D. *The Death and Resurrection of the Beloved Son: The Transformation of Child Sacrifice in Judaism and Christianity.* New Haven: Yale University Press, 1993.

Lightfoot, R. H. *The Gospel Message of St. Mark.* Oxford: Clarendon, 1950.

Lincoln, Andrew T. "The Promise and the Failure--Mark 16:7, 8." *JBL* 108 (1989): 283-300.

Lindars, Barnabas. *New Testament Apologetic.* London: SCM, 1961.

Lohmeyer, Ernst. *Das Evangelium des Markus.* Kritisch-exegetischer Kommentar über das Neue Testament 2. 17th ed. Göttingen: Vandenhoeck & Ruprecht, 1967.

Loevestam, E. "Die Davidssohnsfrage." *Svensk Exegetisk Årsbok* 27 (1962): 72-82.

Lührmann, Dieter. *Das Markusevangelium.* Handbuch zum Neuen Testament 3. Tübingen: J.C.B. Mohr (Paul Siebeck), 1987.

————. "Die Pharisäer und die Schriftgelehrten im Markusevangelium." *ZNW* 78 (1987): 169-85.

Luz, Ulrich. "Das Geheiminismotiv und die markinische Christologie." *ZNW* 56 (1965): 9-30.

Malbon, Elizabeth Struthers. "Disciples/Crowds/Whoever: Markan Characters and Readers." *NovT* 28 (1986): 104-30.

————. "Fallible Followers: Women and Men in the Gospel of Mark." *Semeia* 28 (1983): 29-48.

————. "The Jewish Leaders in the Gospel of Mark: A Literary Study of Marcan Characterization." *JBL* 108 (1989): 259-281.

————. *Narrative Space and Mythic Meaning in Mark.* San Francisco: Harper & Row, 1986.

Marcus, Joel. "Authority to Forgive Sins upon the Earth: The *Shema* in the Gospel of Mark." In *The Gospels and the Scriptures of Israel,* ed. C. A. Evans and W. R. Stegner, 196-211. JSNTS2 104/Studies in Scripture in Early Judaism and Christianity 3. Sheffield: Sheffield Academic Press, 1994.

————. *The Mystery of the Kingdom of God.* SBLDS 90. Atlanta: Scholars Press, 1986.

————. *The Way of the Lord: Christological Exegesis of the Old Testament in the Gospel of Mark.* Louisville: Westminster/John Knox Press, 1992.

Martyn, J. L. *History and Theology in the Fourth Gospel.* Nashville: Abingdon Press, 1979.

Marxsen, Willi. *Mark the Evangelist: Studies on the Redaction History of the Gospel.* Translated by James Boyce, Donald Juel, and William Poehlmann. Nashville: Abingdon Press, 1969.

Matera, Frank. *The Kingship of Jesus: Composition and Theology in Mark 15.* SBLDS 66. Chico, CA: Scholars Press, 1982.

————. "The Prologue as the Interpretative Key to Mark's Gospel." *JSNT* 34 (1988): 3-20.

————. *What are they saying about Mark?* New York: Paulist Press, 1987.

Mauser, Ulrich. *Christ in the Wilderness: The Wilderness Theme in the Second Gospel and its Basis in the Biblical Tradition.* London: SCM, 1963.

McConnell, Frank, ed. *The Bible and the Narrative Tradition*. New York: Oxford University Press, 1986.

McKim, Donald, ed. *A Guide to Contemporary Hermeneutics : Major Trends in Biblical Interperation*. Grand Rapids, MI : Eerdmans, 1986.

McKnight, Edgar V. *Meaning in Texts: The Historical Shaping of a Narrative*. Philadelphia: Fortress Press, 1978.

Meyers, Ched. *Binding the Strong Man: A Political Reading of Mark's Story of Jesus*. Maryknoll, NY: Orbis Books, 1988.

Moore, Stephen. *Literary Criticism and the Gospels: The Theoretical Challenge*. New Haven: Yale University Press, 1989.

————. *Mark and Luke in Poststructuralist Perspectives: Jesus Begins to Write*. New Haven: Yale University Press, 1992.

————. *Poststructuralism and the New Testament: Derrida and Foucault at the Foot of the Cross* (Minneapolis: Fortress Press, 1994).

Morgan, Robert. "The Historical Jesus and the Theology of the New Tesatment." In *The Glory of Christ in the New Testament: Studies in Christology in Memory of George Bradford Caird*, ed. L. D. Hurst and N. T. Wright, 187-206. Oxford: Clarendon Press, 1987.

———— and John Barton. *Biblical Interpretation*. The Oxford Bible Series. Oxford: Oxford University Press.

Moule, C.F.D. *The Origin of Christology*. Cambridge: Cambridge University Press, 1977.

Mulholland, Moston Robert, Jr. "The Markan Opponents of Jesus." Ph.D. diss., Harvard University, 1977).

Mudiso Mbâ Mundla, Jean-Gaspard. *Jesus und die Führer Israels: Studien zu den sog. Jerusalemer Streitgesprächen*. Münster: Aschendorff, 1984.

Neusner, Jacob. *From Politics to Piety: The Emergence of Pharisaic Judaism*. Englewood Cliffs, NJ: Prentice-Hall, 1973.

————. *Judaism in the Matrix of Christianity*. Philadelphia: Fortress Press, 1986.

————. *A Rabbi Talks with Jesus: An Intermillennial, Interfaith Exchange*. New York: Doubleday, 1994.

Neyrey, Jerome. "The Idea of Purity in Mark's Gospel." *Semeia* 35 (1986): 91-128.

Ollenburger, Ben C. "What Krister Stendahl 'Meant'—A Normative Critique of 'Descriptive Biblical Theology.'" *Horizons in Biblical Theology* 8 (1986): 61-98.

Ong, Walter. *The Gutenberg Galaxy: The Making of Typographic Man*. Toronto: University of Toronto Press, 1962.

————. "Text as Interpretation: Mark and After." *Semeia* 39 (1987): 10-35.

————. *Understanding Media: The Extensions of Man*. New York: McGraw-Hill, 1964.

Perkins, Pheme. *Resurrection*. London: Geoffrey Chapman, 1984.

Perrin, Norman. "The Christology of Mark: A Study in Methodology." In *The Interpretation of Mark*, ed. William Telford, 95-108. Philadelphia: Fortress Press, 1985.

————. *What is Redaction Criticism?* Philadelphia: Fortress Press, 1969.

———— and Dennis Duling. *The New Testament: An Introduction.* New York: Harcourt Brace Jovanovich, Inc., 1982.

Pesch, Rudolph. *Das Markusevangelium.* Herders Theologische Kommentar zum Neuen Testament 2. Freiburg/Basel/Wien: Herder, 1976.

Petersen, Norman. "The Composition of Mark 4:1-8:26." *HTR* 73 (1980): 185-217.

————. *Literary Criticism for New Testament Critics.* Philadelhpia: Fortress Press, 1978.

————. "'Point of View' in Mark's Narrative." *Semeia* 12 (1978): 97-121.

————. "When is the End not an End? Literary Reflections on the Ending of Mark's Gospel." *Interpretation* 34 (1980): 151-66.

Poland, Lynn. *Literary Criticism and Biblical Hermeneutics: A Critique of Formalist Approaches.* AARAS 48. Chico, CA: Scholars Press, 1985.

Powell, Mark Allan. *What is Narrative Criticism?* Minneapolis: Fortress Press, 1990.

Quesnell, Quentin. *The Mind of Mark: Interpretation and Method through the Exegesis of Mark 6:52.* Analecta Biblical 38. Rome: Sacra Pagina, 1969.

Rabinowitz, P. J. "Truth in Fiction: A Reexamination of Audience." *Critical Inquiry* 4 1977.

Räisänen, Heikki. *The 'Messianic Secret' in Mark's Gospel.* Translated by Christopher Tuckett. Edinburgh: T. & T. Clark, 1990.

Reploh, Karl-Georg. *Markus—Lehrer der Gemeinde: Eine redaktionsgeschichtliche Studie zu den Jüngerperikopen des Markus-Evangeliums.* Stuttgarter Biblische Monographien 9. Stuttgart: Katholisches Bibelwerk, 1969.

Resseguie, James. "Reader-Response Criticism and the Synoptic Gospels." *JAAR* 52 (1984): 307-24.

Rhoads, David. *Israel in Revolution 6-74 C.E.: A Political History Based on the Writings of Josephus.* Philadelphia: Fortress Press, 1976.

————. "Social Criticism: Crossing Boundaries." In *Mark and Method: New Approaches in Biblical Studies,* ed. Janice Capel Anderson and Stephen D. Moore, 135-161. Minneapolis: Fortress Press, 1992.

———— and Donald Michie. *Mark as Story: An Introduction to the Narrative of a Gospel.* Philadelphia: Fortress Press, 1982.

Rivkin, Ellis. *What Crucified Jesus?* Nashville: Abingdon Press, 1984.

Robbins, Vernon. *Jesus the Teacher: A Socio-Rhetorical Interpretation of Mark.* Philadelphia: Fortress Press, 1984.

Robinson, James M. *The Problem of History in Mark and Other Marcan Studies.* Philadelphia: Fortress Press, 1982.

Roth, Wolfgang. *Hebrew Gospel: Cracking the Code of Mark.* Oak Park, IL: Meyer-Stone Books, 1988.

Saldarini, Anthony J. "The Social Class of the Pharisees in Mark." In *The Social World of Formative Christianity and Judaism: Essays in Tribute to Howard Clark Kee,* ed. J. Neusner. Philadelphia: Fortress Press, 1988.

Saunders, Stanley. "'No One Dared Ask Any More Questions': Contextual Readings of the Controversy Stories in Matthew." Ph.D. diss, Princeton Theological Seminary, 1990.

Schenke, L. "Der Aufbau des Markusevangeliums--ein hermeneutischer Schlüssel?" *BN* 32 (1986): 54-82.

Schmidt, K. L. *Der Rahmen der Geschichte Jesu.* Berlin: Trowitzch, 1919.

Scholes, R. and R. Kellogg. *The Nature of Narrative*. London: Oxford University Press, 1966.

Schreiber, Johannes. "Die Christologie des Markusevangeliums." *ZTK* 58 (1961): 154-83.

————. *Theologie des Vertrauens. Eine redaktionsgeschichtliche Untersuchung des Markusevangeliums*. Hamburg: Furche-Verlag, 1967.

Schwartz, Regina. *The Book and the Text: The Bible and Literary Theory*. Cambridge, MA: Basil Blackwell, 1990.

Schweitzer, Albert. *The Quest of the Historical Jesus*. Translated by W. Montgomery. New York: Macmillan Co., 1961.

Schweizer, Eduard. "The Portrayal of the Life of Faith in the Gospel of Mark." In *Interpreting the Gospels*, ed. James Luther Mays, 168-82. Philadelphia: Fortress Press, 1981.

Scott, Bernard Brandon. *Hear Then the Parable: A Commentary on the Parables of Jesus* Minneapolis: Fortress Press, 1989.

Searle, John R. *Speech Acts: An Essay in the Philosophy of Language*. Cambridge: Cambridge University Press, 1969.

Segal, Alan. *Rebecca's Children: Judaism and Christianity in the Roman World*. Cambridge: Harvard University Press, 1985.

————. *Two Powers in Heaven: Early Rabbinic Reports about Christianity and Gnosticism*. Leiden: E. J. Brill, 1977.

Selden, Raman. *A Reader's Guide to Contemporary Literary Theory*. Lexington, KY: The University Press of Kentucky, 1989.

Senior, Donald. *The Passion of Jesus in the Gospel of Mark*. Wilmington, Delaware: Michael Glazier, Inc., 1984.

Smith, Dennis E. "Narrative Beginnings in Ancient Literature and Theory." *Semeia* 52 (1991): 1-9.

Spiegel, Shalom. *The Last Trial*. Translated by Judah Goldin. New York: Schocken Books, 1969.

Spivey, Robert and D. Moody Smith. *Anatomy of the New Testament: A Guide to Its Structure and Meaning*. 4th ed. New York: Macmillan Publishing Company, 1989.

Staley, Jeffery Lloyd. *The Print's First Kiss: A Rhetorical Investigation of the Implied Reader in the Fourth Gospel*. SBLDS 82. Atlanta: Scholars Press, 1988.

Steichele, Hans-Jorg. *Der leidende Sohn Gottes: Eine Untersuchung einiger alttestamentlicher Motive in der Christologie des Markusevangeliums*. Biblische Untersuchungen 14. Regensburg: Pustet, 1980.

Steiner, George. "'Critic'/'Reader.'" *New Literary History* 10 (1979): 423-52.

————. *Real Presences*. Chicago: University of Chicago Press, 1989.

Sternberg, Meir. *The Poetics of Biblical Narrative: Ideological Literature and the Drama of Reading*. Bloomington: Indiana University Press, 1987.

Suleiman, Susan R. and Inge Crosman, eds. *The Reader in the Text: Essays on Audience and Interpretation*. Princeton: Princeton University Press, 1980.

Tannehill, Robert. "The Disciples in Mark: The Function of a Narrative Role." *JR* 57 (1977): 386-405; reprinted in *The Interpretation of Mark*, ed. William Telford, 134-57. Philadelphia: Fortress Press, 1985.

————. "The Gospel of Mark as Narrative Christology." *Semeia* 16 (1979): 57-95.

Taylor, Vincent. *The Gospel According to St. Mark*. London: Macmillan, 1959.

Telford, William, ed. *The Interpretation of Mark*. Issues in Religion and Theology 7. Philadelphia: Fortress Press and London: SPCK.

Thiemann, Ronald. *Revelation and Theology: The Gospel as Narrated Promise*. Notre Dame: University of Notre Dame Press, 1985.

Thiselton, Anthony C. *The Two Horizons: New Testament Hermeneutics and Philosophical Description*. Grand Rapids, MI: Eerdmans, 1980.

Tolbert, Mary Ann. *Sowing the Gospel: Mark's World in Literary-Historical Perspective*. Minneapolis: Fortress Press, 1989.

Tomkins, J. P. "The Reader in History: The Changing Shape of Literary Response." In *Reader-Response Criticism: From Formalism to Post-structuralism*, ed. J. P. Tomkins, 200-14. Baltimore: Johns Hopkins University Press, 1980.

Trocmé, Etienne. *The Formation of the Gospel According to Mark*. Translated by Pamela Gaughan. Philadelphia: Westminster Press, 1973.

Tyson, J. B. "The Blindness of the Disciples in Mark." *JBL* 80 (1961): 261-268.

Via, Dan O. Jr. *The Ethics of Mark's Gospel: In the Middle of Time*. Philadelphia: Fortress Press, 1985.

————. *Kerygma and Comedy in the New Testament: A Structuralist Approach to Hermeneutic*. Philadelphia: Fortress Press, 1975.

Vielhauer, Philipp. "Erwägungen zur Christologie des Markusevangeliums." In *Aufsätze zum Neuen Testament*, 199-214. Tübingen: J. C. B. Mohr (Paul Siebeck), 1965.

von der Osten-Sacken, Peter. "Streitgespräch und Parabel als Formen markinischer Christologie." In *Jesus Christus in Historie und Theologie: Neutestamentliche Festschrift für Hans Conzelmann zum 60. Geburtstag*, ed. Georg Strecker, 375-94. Tübingen: J. C. B. Mohr (Paul Siebeck), 1975.

von Rad, Gerhard. *Theologie des Alten Testaments. Band II: Die Theologie der prophetischen Überliefurungen Israels*. München: Chr. Kaiser Verlag, 1960.

Walhout, Clarence and Leland Ryken, eds. *Contemporary Literary Theory: A Christian Appraisal*. Grand Rapids, MI: Eerdmans, 1991.

Weeden, Theodore. *Mark: Traditions in Conflict* (Philadelphia: Fortress Press, 1971).

————. "The Heresy that Necessitated Mark's Gospel." In *The Interpretation of Mark*, ed. William Telford, 64-77. Philadelphia: Fortress Press and London: SPCK, 1985.

Weiß, Wolfgang. *Eine neue Lehre in Vollmacht: die Streit- und Schulgespräche des Markus-Evangeliums*. Berlin: Walter de Gruyter, 1989.

Wolff, H. W. "Das Thema 'Umkehr' in der Alttestamentlichen Theologie." *ZTK* 48 (1951): 129-48.

INDEX OF SCRIPTURE CITATIONS

265

Index of Modern Authors